LEARNING TARGETS

Geography

Key Stage 1   Scotland P1–P3

Sue Thomas

Stanley Thornes (Publishers) Ltd

Stanley Thornes for TEACHERS:
BLUEPRINTS • PRIMARY COLOURS • LEARNING TARGETS

Stanley Thornes for Teachers publishes practical teacher's ideas books and photocopiable resources for use in primary schools. Our three key series, **Blueprints**, **Primary Colours** and **Learning Targets** together provide busy teachers with unbeatable curriculum coverage, inspiration and value for money. We mail teachers and schools about our books regularly. To join the mailing list simply photocopy and complete the form below and return using the **FREEPOST** address to receive regular updates on our new and existing titles. You may also like to add the name of a friend who would be interested in being on the mailing list. Books can be bought by credit card over the telephone and information obtained on (01242) 267280.

Please add my name to the *Stanley Thornes for* TEACHERS mailing list.

Mr/Mrs/Miss/Ms _____

Address _____

_____ postcode _____

School address _____

_____ postcode _____

Please also send information about *Stanley Thornes for* TEACHERS to:

Mr/Mrs/Miss/Ms _____

Address _____

_____ postcode _____

To: Marketing Services Dept., Stanley Thornes Ltd, FREEPOST (GR 782), Cheltenham, GL50 1BR

Text © Sue Thomas, 1999.

The right of Sue Thomas to be identified as author of this work has been asserted by her in accordance with the Copyright, Designs and Patents Act 1988.

The copyright holders authorise ONLY users of *Learning Targets*: *Geography Key Stage* 1 to make photocopies or stencil duplicates of the copymasters for their own or their classes' immediate use within the teaching context. No other rights are granted without permission in writing from the Copyright Licensing Agency Limited of Tottenham Court Road, London W1P 0LP.

First published in 1999 by
Stanley Thornes Publishers Ltd
Ellenborough House
Wellington Street
Cheltenham GL50 1YW

99 00 01 02 03 / 10 9 8 7 6 5 4 3 2 1

A catalogue record for this book is available from the British Library.

ISBN 0-7487-3588-7

Typeset by Tech-set, Gateshead, Tyne & Wear

Edited by Angela Wigmore, Cheltenham, Gloucestershire

Teacher's Notes illustrations by John Crawford Fraser, Copymasters by Susan Hutchinson and maps by Steve Ballinger.

Printed and Bound in Great Britain by Redwood Books, Trowbridge, Wiltshire.

CONTENTS

Welcome to
LEARNING TARGETS

Learning Targets is a series of practical teacher's resource books written to help you to plan and deliver well-structured, professional lessons in line with all the relevant curriculum documents.

Each Learning Target book provides exceptionally clear lesson plans that cover the whole of its stated curriculum plus a large bank of carefully structured copymasters. Links to the key curriculum documents are provided throughout to enable you to plan effectively.

The Learning Targets series has been written in response to the challenge confronting teachers not just to come up with teaching ideas which cover the curriculum but to ensure that they deliver high quality lessons every lesson with the emphasis on raising standards of pupil achievement.

The recent thinking from OFSTED, and the National Literacy and Numeracy Strategies on the key factors in effective teaching has been built into the structure of Learning Targets. These might briefly be summarised as follows:

➤➤ that effective teaching is active teaching directed to very clear objectives

➤➤ that good lessons are delivered with pace, rigour and purpose

➤➤ that good teaching requires a range of strategies - including interactive whole class sessions

➤➤ that ongoing formative assessment is essential to plan children's learning

➤➤ that differentiation is necessary but that it must be realistic.

The emphasis in Learning Targets is on absolute clarity. We have written and designed the books to enable you to access and deliver effective lessons as easily as possible, with the following aims:

➤➤ to plan and deliver rigorous, well-structured lessons

➤➤ to set explicit targets for achievement in every lesson that you teach

➤➤ to make the children aware of what they are going to learn

➤➤ to put the emphasis on direct, active teaching every time

➤➤ to make effective use of time and resources

➤➤ to employ the full range of recommended strategies: whole-class, group and individual work

➤➤ to differentiate for ability groups realistically

➤➤ to use ongoing formative assessment to plan your next step

➤➤ to have ready access to usable pupil copymasters to support your teaching.

The page opposite provides an at-a-glance guide to the key features of the Learning Targets lessons and explains how they will enable you deliver effective lessons. The key to symbols on the lesson plans is set out here. ➤➤

How to deliver structured lessons with pace, rigour and purpose

Explicit targets for achievement in every lesson

The concise subject knowledge you need

Crystal clear lesson plan layouts

The full range of teaching strategies

Rigorous and practical activities

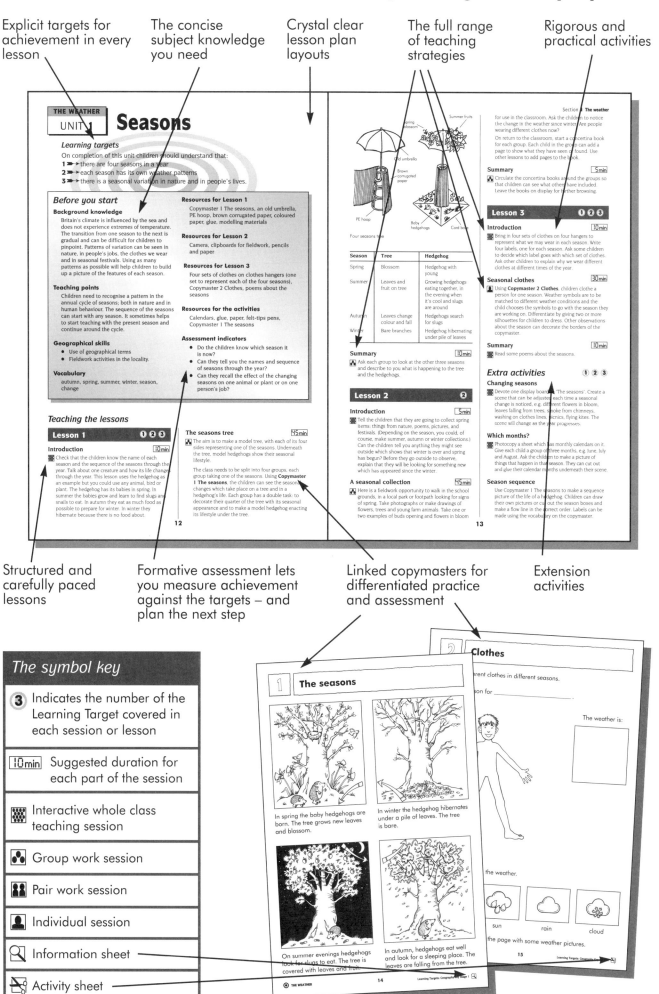

Structured and carefully paced lessons

Formative assessment lets you measure achievement against the targets – and plan the next step

Linked copymasters for differentiated practice and assessment

Extension activities

The symbol key

③	Indicates the number of the Learning Target covered in each session or lesson
10min	Suggested duration for each part of the session
▦	Interactive whole class teaching session
◕	Group work session
◪	Pair work session
◪	Individual session
◳	Information sheet
◳	Activity sheet

5

INTRODUCTION

Geography is concerned with the study of people and places. It introduces the world, with all its variety and contrasts, as part of a broad and balanced curriculum. *Learning Targets: Geography Key Stage* 1 provides lessons and activities, with educational targets in all the main geographical topics normally covered by this age group. It covers: using enquiry skills to research topics and themes; use of maps and globes and other resources; fieldwork techniques and methods; features of localities, in the UK and overseas; making observations about people and places; forming views and opinions about the environment.

The lessons and activities include map making and map reading, modelling, fieldwork, drama, research, use of stories and artwork. Links across the curriculum are evident in all sections.

How this book is organised

Sections

There are 11 sections covering geographical themes and topics, place studies and mapping skills. UK and global awareness feature in their own sections and in appropriate lessons. Each section has an introduction containing a list of resources needed, source material ideas, a brainstorm web and a teaching plan that can be used as a medium term plan or scheme of work.

The units

There are three to five units in each section, depending on the theme covered. The introduction to each unit explains its educational context, giving the three learning targets that the unit addresses. They are identified numerically against each lesson and activity.

'Background knowledge' provides information for the teacher which may not necessarily be used in the lessons but sets the scene for the topic and sometimes helps answer those questions children often ask. 'Teaching points' suggests a method of approach and reminds the teacher of things which are often taken for granted but that are outside of many children's experience. It sometimes pinpoints an important concept or gives cautionary advice. 'Geographical skills' outlines the skills children will use and learn during the unit and can include mapping, enquiry, research and fieldwork methods. 'Vocabulary' is a short list of geographical words that children should be introduced to during the unit. (*See* 'Geography words' below.) 'Assessment indicators' show the things children can achieve. They may include naming, sorting, describing, comparing, and knowing. Each unit contains three full lesson plans, a pupil activity and information sheet and some further activities to develop the unit.

The lessons

Three structured lessons cover one aspect of each unit. The lessons may:

- be steps in a progressive learning process
- approach an idea in three different ways to reinforce a concept
- teach three separate but linked ideas on a theme.

The lessons can be taught either in sequence or individually to fit with other work in cross-curricular topics.

The lessons are structured in three parts as listed below. Each part provides estimated timings, which will vary with age and ability of the class, and a suggestion for individual, group or whole class involvement.

1 An introduction where the teacher sets the scene and begins to motivate the class through enquiry questions, a discussion with artefacts, or by telling a story and then moves on to explain the task.

2 The task may use the copymasters or another resource. Within the task, activity suggestions are differentiated to help the teacher plan for children of varying abilities.

3 The summary rounds off each lesson with one of a variety of short teacher–pupil interactions to consolidate what the children have learned during the lesson.

'Extra activities' provide related activities for the teacher who wishes to extend the topic or provide work for those children who are progressing quickly. These extension activities are written to suit a range of ages and abilities.

Geography words

The introduction of new words is a part of everyday learning for young children. Geography has its own particular vocabulary for describing position, features, and for describing and evaluating and expressing opinions. Many of the terms used will already be in the children's vocabulary, but may not be refined, e.g. the varying degrees of size between 'pond', 'lake', 'sea' and 'ocean', or the varying degrees of wind from 'breeze' to 'hurricane'.

Each unit lists the vocabulary the teacher needs to focus on during the lessons. They can be used in discussions, form titles for work, be used on labels of children's pictures or used in a geography word book alongside pictures. More able children can put them into phrases or use a dictionary to find definitions. The geography word book provides a spelling aid and reference book for children, linked to the work in hand.

Integrating geography with ICT

IT requirement	Pupil activity	Where to find it
Opportunities to use a variety of equipment Explore use of computer systems in everyday life	• CD-Rom for research • programmable toys • grid references • mail sorting	Personal geography Unit 3 (page 108) Journeys Unit 3 (page 80) Our world Unit 1 (page 180) Jobs Unit 2 (page 48)
Communicate and handle information	Use a word processor for: • notices • labels • handouts • invitations • letters • graphs.	Environment Unit 2 (page 118) Places overseas Unit 1 (page 158) Environment Unit 1 (page 114) Journeys Unit 2 (page 76) School grounds Unit 3 (page 94) Jobs Unit 3 (page 52)
Controlling and modelling	• robot journeys • programmable toys • simulate TV news • use of videos • use of cassette recorders	Journeys Unit 3 (page 80) Journeys Unit 3 (page 80) Our World Unit 2 (page 184)

The table shows how information technology, including television, video and cassette recorders can be developed and applied in geography work for research, recording and communication.

Software

Adventure games with geography learning, routes and journeys:

'Granny's Garden'; 'Lost Frog'; 'Mapventure'; 'Find Spot'; 'Albert's House'; 'Maths with a story'.

CD–Roms for older, good readers:

'Local Studies'; 'My First World Explorer' (Dorling Kindersley); 'Satellite images'

Meteorological offices use satellite images transmitted to Earth every 30 minutes. These addresses may help you obtain photos for classroom use:

Remote Imaging Group, 14 Nevis Close, Leighton Buzzard, Beds LU7 7XD

MJP Geopacks, St Just, Penzance TR19 7JS. Tel. 01736 787808

National Remote Sensing Centre, 32 Barwell Street, Leicester

Integrating geography with mathematics

Maths requirement	Pupil activity	Where to find it
Using and applying maths Use and apply maths in practical tasks	surveys sorting letters	Environment Unit 1 (page 114) Around the UK Unit 3 (page 144) Homes Unit 1 (page 30) Jobs Unit 2 (page 44)
Use of a variety of forms of mathematical presentation	Venn diagrams sets bar charts	Around the UK Units 2, 5 (pages 140, 152) Places overseas Unit 1 (page 158) Homes Unit 2 (page 34) Places overseas Unit 4 (page 170) Homes Units 1, 2 (pages 30, 34) School grounds Unit 2 (page 90)

Number		
Develop an understanding of place value	odds and evens	Homes Unit 1 (page 30) Jobs Unit 2 (page 48)
	sequencing	Homes Unit 1 (page 30) Food and farms Unit 1 (page 60)
Understanding relationships between numbers	repeating patterns	The weather Unit 3 (page 20)
Shape, space and measure		
Opportunities to use IT devices	robot journeys programmable toys	Journeys Unit 3 (page 80) Journeys Unit 3 (page 80)
Understanding and using using patterns and properties of shape	grid references making 3D models and boxes	Places overseas Unit 5 (page 174) Our world Unit 1 (page 180) Homes Unit 1 (page 30) Places overseas Unit 5 (page 174)
Understanding and using properties of position and movement	directional vocabulary pattern of sun	School grounds Unit 1 (page 86) Weather Unit 3 (page 20)
Understanding and using measures	oven temperatures and weighing time	Places Overseas Unit 1 (page 180) Jobs Unit 3 (page 52) Weather Unit 3 (page 20) Jobs Unit 1 (page 44)

As part of a broad and balanced curriculum, geographical activities can be used to reinforce and practise maths concepts in all the sections of the maths programmes of study for Key Stage 1.

Integrating geography with science

Science requirement	Pupil activity	Where to find it
Systematic enquiry	rehydrate fruit	Place overseas Unit 1 (page 158)
Science in everyday life	cooking	Jobs Unit 3 (page 52) Places Overseas Unit 1 (page 158)
	making clay tiles care of environment	Jobs Unit 3 (page 52) Environment Units 1–5 (pages 112–33)
Nature of scientific ideas	cycles and patterns	Environment Unit 1 (page 114) Weather Unit 3 (page 20)
Communication	scientific words	Weather Units 1–4 (pages 12–24)
Health and safety	sun protection washing hands	Weather Unit 3 (page 20) Journeys Unit 1 (page 72)
Experimental and investigative		
Obtaining evidence	shadow sticks	Weather Unit 3 (page 20)
Life processes and living things		
Life processes	food origins	Food and farms Unit 1 (page 57)
Green plants as organisms	plants in pots plant cycles	School grounds Unit 3 (page 94) Environment Unit 1 (page 114)
Living things in the environment	bird table/snails hedgerows	Journeys Unit 1 (page 72) Environment Unit 2 (page 118)
Materials		
Properties and uses	house materials made from wood	Homes Unit 1 (page 30) Jobs Unit 3 (page 52)
Changing materials	clay bricks, bread	Jobs Units 3 (page 52)
Physical processes		
Light and dark	sun's daily pattern	Weather Unit 3 (page 20)

Both science and geography investigate the world we live in. Although they look at the world from different angles, their methods of study overlap and complement each other. Geography looks at the people and places behind the scientific processes, so there are many instances where pupil activities will combine science and geography work.

Integrating geography with English

English requirement	Pupil activity	Where to find it
Speaking and listening		
Imaginative play and drama	role play situations	Environment Unit 1 (page 114) Around the UK Unit 4 (page 148)
Reading and listening to rhymes and poetry	learning poems and rhymes about topics	Homes Unit 3 (page 38) Journeys Unit 2 (page 76) Jobs Unit 2 (page 48)
Predicting outcomes and discussing possibilities	Answering enquiries – What if and Why?	Around the UK Unit 5 (page 152) Weather Unit 4 (page 24)
Describe events, opinions and observations	Planning an assembly or presentation	School grounds Unit 3 (page 94) Journeys Unit 2 (page 76)
Listen and respond in discussions	use of enquiry questions	Environment Unit 1 (page 114) Food and farms Unit 3 (page 66)
Extend vocabulary – meanings of words	Dictionary work Dictionary Vocabulary	Around the UK Unit 2 (page 140) School grounds Unit 1 (page 86)
Reading	*Story references*	
Extensive experience of children's literature which covers poems and stories with familiar settings, books by significant authors, fairy stories, stories from a range of cultures and poems with a patterned language, learning poems, acting out stories, using reference material for different purposes.	*Wilberforce goes on a picnic* by Margaret Gorden (page 118) *Katie Morag Delivers the Mail* by Mairi Hedderwick (pages 49, 152) *Rosie's Walk* by Pat Hutchins (page 66) *The Sleeping Beauty* (page 166) *We're Going on a Bear Hunt* (page 76) *Pillarbox Red* (page 48) *St Columba* (page 148) Information sheets as a resource in each unit.	
Writing Range of writing		
Remembering	write up fieldwork	Homes Unit 2 (page 34) Jobs Unit 2 (page 48)
Communicating	letter writing	Homes Unit 3 (page 38) Environment Unit 3 (page 122)
Organising and developing ideas and information	endangered species tourist poster	Environment Unit 3 (page 122) Around the UK Unit 5 (page 152)
Range of forms • narratives • poem • notes • records • messages	caretaker's diary acrostics recording materials observations invitation	Jobs Unit 1 (page 44) Environment Unit 4 (page 126) Homes Unit 2 (page 34) School grounds Unit 3 (page 94) Journeys Unit 2 (page 76)
Spelling		
Use of dictionary and word books	geographical vocabulary using word banks	Around the UK Unit 2 (page 140) Wordbooks (Introduction) (page 6) All sections

As well as promoting children's understanding of geography, geography lessons can help develop the literacy skills of speaking and listening, reading, writing and spelling. Stories from other cultures, information books with particular themes, reporting and account writing, observation and description all have a dual role in promoting literacy and building geographical knowledge and skills.

THE WEATHER

Focus

This section provides an approach to studying the weather which can be linked either to studies of the local area or to studies of contrasting localities. The lessons concentrate on the effects of weather and how people and wildlife adapt and live in changing weather conditions. It does not include much work on recording weather as it assumes that children will already be familiar with these skills. It tries to answer the geographical enquiry question 'What effect does the weather have on people and places?'

Content

Unit 1: Seasons
Unit 2: Wind and rain
Unit 3: Sun
Unit 4: Snow

Source material

Stories to read where weather is a contributing factor:

Gordon, Margaret *Wilberforce Goes on a Picnic*, Puffin, 1984

Rutherford, Meg *Bluff and Bran and the Snowdrift*, Andre Deutsch, 1987

A non-fiction title dealing with the weather, wind and seasons:

Thomas, Susan *Clothes for Every Season*, Factfinder Series, OUP

Brainstorm

This brainstorm covers the lessons in Section 1 and can be added to for a cross-curricular topic.

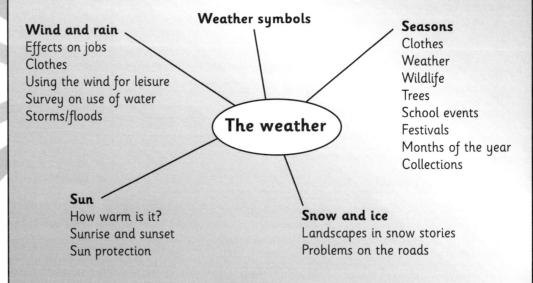

Wind and rain
Effects on jobs
Clothes
Using the wind for leisure
Survey on use of water
Storms/floods

Weather symbols

Seasons
Clothes
Weather
Wildlife
Trees
School events
Festivals
Months of the year
Collections

The weather

Sun
How warm is it?
Sunrise and sunset
Sun protection

Snow and ice
Landscapes in snow stories
Problems on the roads

Teaching plan

The table below provides a medium-term plan outlining a scheme of work for a topic on the weather. It can either be split up and used at appropriate times of the year or lessons can be taken out to link with locality studies.

Enquiry questions	Learning targets	Pupil activities
1 What seasonal patterns occur through the year?	There are four seasons, and each has its own distinctive weather patterns and features.	Seasonal investigations and collections: Unit 1 All lessons.
2 What is the weather like?	Knowledge of the different sorts of weather in the UK.	Seasons work: Unit 1 All lessons; rain survey: Unit 2 Lessons 2, 3: the sun's 24-hour pattern: Unit 3 Lesson 2.
3 What effect does the weather have on our daily lives?	The weather affects the clothes we wear and the way we cope with and use different weather.	Choice of clothes: Unit 1 Lesson 3, Unit 3 Lesson 3; Using the weather to help us: Unit 2 Lesson 2; dangerous weather: Unit 3 Lesson 3, Unit 4 Lesson 2.
4 What effect does the weather have on the jobs people do?	There is a pattern in the way jobs change through the course of the year due to changes in the weather.	Jobs in bad weather: Unit 2 Lesson 3, Unit 4 Lesson 1, 3.

National Curriculum coverage

Unit 1 Seasons

National Curriculum links
- Effects of weather on people and their surroundings.
- Undertake fieldwork activities in the locality of the school

Unit 2 Wind and rain

National Curriculum links
- Use secondary sources to obtain geographical information
- Know about the effects of weather on their surroundings.

Unit 3 Sun

National Curriculum links
- Effects of weather on people in the local area.
- Investigate physical surroundings through fieldwork.

Unit 4 Snow

National Curriculum links
- Effects of weather on people in local area.
- Make a map of imaginary place.

Scotland Environment Studies coverage

The units cover the following contexts and content for Understanding People and Places:
- Different kinds of weather and simple weather recording.
- Our responses to weather variations, from day to day and season to season.

Seasons

Learning targets

On completion of this unit children should understand that:

1 ➤➤ there are four seasons in a year
2 ➤➤ each season has its own weather patterns
3 ➤➤ there is a seasonal variation in nature and in people's lives.

Before you start

Background knowledge

Britain's climate is influenced by the sea and does not experience extremes of temperature. The transition from one season to the next is gradual and can be difficult for children to pinpoint. Patterns of variation can be seen in nature, in people's jobs, the clothes we wear and in seasonal festivals. Using as many patterns as possible will help children to build up a picture of the features of each season.

Teaching points

Children need to recognise a pattern in the annual cycle of seasons; both in nature and in human behaviour. The sequence of the seasons can start with any season. It sometimes helps to start teaching with the present season and continue around the cycle.

Geographical skills

- Use of geographical terms
- Fieldwork activities in the locality.

Vocabulary

autumn, spring, summer, winter, season, change

Resources for Lesson 1

Copymaster 1 The seasons, an old umbrella, PE hoop, brown corrugated paper, coloured paper, glue, modelling materials

Resources for Lesson 2

Camera, clipboards for fieldwork, pencils and paper

Resources for Lesson 3

Four sets of clothes on clothes hangers (one set to represent each of the four seasons), Copymaster 2 Clothes, poems about the seasons

Resources for the activities

Calendars, glue, paper, felt-tips pens, Copymaster 1 The seasons

Assessment indicators

- Do the children know which season it is now?
- Can they tell you the names and sequence of seasons through the year?
- Can they recall the effect of the changing seasons on one animal or plant or on one person's job?

Teaching the lessons

Lesson 1 ① ② ③

Introduction 10min

Check that the children know the name of each season and the sequence of the seasons through the year. Talk about one creature and how its life changes through the year. This lesson uses the hedgehog as an example but you could use any animal, bird or plant. The hedgehog has its babies in spring. In summer the babies grow and learn to find slugs and snails to eat. In autumn they eat as much food as possible to prepare for winter. In winter they hibernate because there is no food about.

The seasons tree 45min

The aim is to make a model tree, with each of its four sides representing one of the seasons. Underneath the tree, model hedgehogs show their seasonal lifestyle.

The class needs to be split into four groups, each group taking one of the seasons. Using **Copymaster 1 The seasons**, the children can see the seasonal changes which take place on a tree and in a hedgehog's life. Each group has a double task: to decorate their quarter of the tree with its seasonal appearance and to make a model hedgehog enacting its lifestyle under the tree.

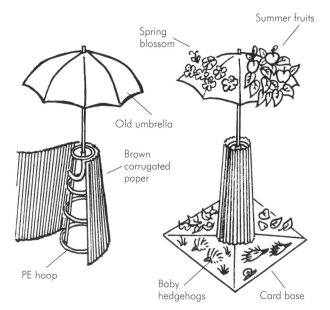

Spring blossom · Summer fruits · Old umbrella · Brown corrugated paper · PE hoop · Baby hedgehogs · Card base

Four seasons tree

Season	Tree	Hedgehog
Spring	Blossom	Hedgehog with young
Summer	Leaves and fruit on tree	Growing hedgehogs eating together, in the evening when it's cool and slugs are around
Autumn	Leaves change colour and fall	Hedgehogs search for slugs
Winter	Bare branches	Hedgehog hibernating under pile of leaves

Summary
[10 min]

Ask each group to look at the other three seasons and describe to you what is happening to the tree and the hedgehogs.

Lesson 2 ②

Introduction
[5 min]

Tell the children that they are going to collect spring items: things from nature, poems, pictures, and festivals. (Depending on the season, you could, of course, make summer, autumn or winter collections.) Can the children tell you anything they might see outside which shows that winter is over and spring has begun? Before they go outside to observe, explain that they will be looking for something new which has appeared since the winter.

A seasonal collection
[45 min]

Here is a fieldwork opportunity to walk in the school grounds, in a local park or footpath looking for signs of spring. Take photographs or make drawings of flowers, trees and young farm animals. Take one or two examples of buds opening and flowers in bloom

for use in the classroom. Ask the children to notice the change in the weather since winter. Are people wearing different clothes now?

On return to the classroom, start a concertina book for each group. Each child in the group can add a page to show what they have seen or found. Use other lessons to add pages to the book.

Summary
[5 min]

Circulate the concertina books around the groups so that children can see what others have included. Leave the books on display for further browsing.

Lesson 3 ①②③

Introduction
[10 min]

Bring in four sets of clothes on four hangers to represent what we may wear in each season. Write four labels, one for each season. Ask some children to decide which label goes with which set of clothes. Ask other children to explain why we wear different clothes at different times of the year.

Seasonal clothes
[30 min]

Using **Copymaster 2 Clothes**, children clothe a person for one season. Weather symbols are to be matched to different weather conditions and the child chooses the symbols to go with the season they are working on. Differentiate by giving two or more silhouettes for children to dress. Other observations about the season can decorate the borders of the copymaster.

Summary
[10 min]

Read some poems about the seasons.

Extra activities ①②③

Changing seasons

Devote one display board to 'The seasons'. Create a scene that can be adjusted each time a seasonal change is noticed, e.g. different flowers in bloom, leaves falling from trees, smoke from chimneys, washing on clothes lines, picnics, flying kites. The scene will change as the year progresses.

Which months?

Photocopy a sheet which has monthly calendars on it. Give each child a group of three months, e.g. June, July and August. Ask the children to make a picture of things that happen in that season. They can cut out and glue their calendar months underneath their scene.

Season sequence

Use Copymaster 1 The seasons to make a sequence picture of the life of a hedgehog. Children can draw their own pictures or cut out the season boxes and make a flow line in the correct order. Labels can be made using the vocabulary on the copymaster.

In spring the baby hedgehogs are born. The tree grows new leaves and blossom.

In winter the hedgehog hibernates under a pile of leaves. The tree is bare.

On summer evenings hedgehogs look for slugs to eat. The tree is covered with leaves and fruit.

In autumn, hedgehogs eat well and look for a sleeping place. The leaves are falling from the tree.

Clothes

We wear different clothes in different seasons.

Dress this person for _____ .

The weather is:

Match the pictures to the weather.

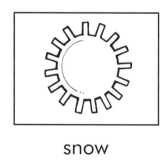

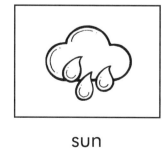

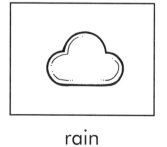

snow   sun   rain   cloud

Decorate the border of the page with some weather pictures.

Wind and rain

Learning targets

On completion of this unit children should understand that:

1 ➡➡ people use the wind to help them at work and play
2 ➡➡ rain is essential for life
3 ➡➡ too much wind and rain cause problems.

Before you start

Background knowledge

The prevailing winds in the UK are south westerlies; the warm ocean current across the Atlantic heats up the air but also brings rain to western shores. Cold east winds from Northern Europe are often responsible for very cold winter weather. Water is a familiar part of life and is essential to all living things. The 'rain' process, involving evaporation, condensation and precipitation forms the water cycle. The action of water shapes the landscape as rocks are worn away and particles are deposited elsewhere.

Teaching points

Wind and rain are essential. Some people rely on different types of weather for their jobs.

Geographical skills

- Use of secondary sources to obtain geographical information
- Observation of local effects of weather

Vocabulary

wind, rain, direction, flood, hurricane, storm

Resources for Lesson 1

Resource books on wind, PE posts, cane, string, paper, card, Copymaster 3 Who uses the wind?

Resources for Lesson 2

Paper, felt-tip pens

Resources for Lesson 3

Copymaster 4 A storm, wall map of the UK, felt-tip pens

Resources for the activities

Coloured paper, two pot plants, red ink, celery, Copymaster 2 Clothes, glue, felt-tip pens

Assessment indicators

- Can the children explain how the weather affects our lives?
- Can they name essential uses of rain?

Teaching the lessons

Lesson 1 ①

Introduction |10 min|

Working as a class, brainstorm all the ways we use the wind. A set of pictures would stimulate some ideas. Encourage suggestions which show how the wind can be used:

- for work — e.g. windmills, wind generators, sailing ships and drying washing
- for leisure — e.g. sailing, windsurfing and kite flying
- in nature — e.g. plants use the wind for seed dispersal; birds and butterflies use the wind to help with migration.

Using the wind |45 min|

Children can make a simple wind recorder that can be fixed outside, e.g. between two trees, on a pole or wire fixed to a fence, or between PE posts.

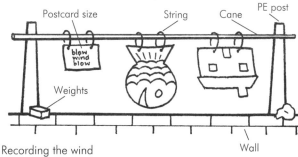

Recording the wind

Give each child a copy of **Copymaster 3 Who uses the wind?** Answering the enquiry questions may require some research so provide the children with resource books containing information on sailing boats, windmills, kites and wind dispersal of seeds. Each enquiry gives an example so that the children know what to find out.

Differentiate by giving the copymaster to a group of children to complete between them, or by spreading the research over several lessons. Link with history to investigate the use of wind power before electricity and engines were invented.

Summary ⏱5min

 Observe the effect of the wind on home made wind recorders. Repeat the exercise when the wind varies. After several observations the children should notice the effect of different wind strengths. Discuss the amount the cards move in relation to the strength of the wind.

Lesson 2

Introduction ⏱10min

 Talk about collecting rainwater and how water comes from the rain in the sky, through rivers, reservoirs and water pipes to our taps. Ask the children for ideas on who uses water and for what purposes. Start them off with a suggestion, e.g. a cook uses water to wash vegetables, firefighters use water to put out fires.

Raindrops ⏱30min

👤 Draw a large raindrop and colour it with blue splashes. Ask each child to make a raindrop like yours and draw or write on it one way that people can use water. They can take a second raindrop home for someone to write on it one way that they use water, creating, in effect, a simple survey. Display the children's and the survey raindrops around a tap of water.

Summary ⏱10min

 Use the raindrop display to discuss the way water is used most often.

Lesson 3 ③

Introduction ⏱10min

 Explain to the children that sometimes the weather is too fierce and, instead of being useful, it becomes a problem. A storm can damage things with wind and rain. Ask for words which describe stormy weather and list them. Help by adding some ideas. You could include 'gusts', 'hurricane', 'gale', 'torrential', 'flood', 'pouring rain', 'thunder'.

Storm damage ⏱40min

Copymaster 4 A storm traces the storms of January 1998 in the south of England and shows how damage occurred in different places. Working in groups, children should choose or be given one of the events to work on.

Differentiate by setting one of the following tasks depending on the ability of the group.

1 Draw or paint before and after pictures of the scene of the storm.

2 For each example, write about one person affected by the storm and one person who helped to solve the problem.

3 Make a role play of a television news programme featuring interviews with a victim of the storm.

Summary ⏱5min

Show children a wall map of the UK and point out where the places on the copymaster are. Show the route of the storm across the Atlantic and across the south of England. Point out that winds from the south west are common and often bring small storms to this area.

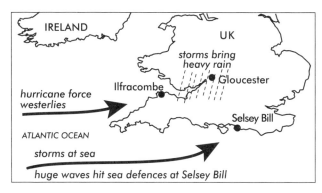

The south westerly direction of the storm of 1998

Extra activities ① ② ③

Windy words

Make a large colourful kite with a group of children. Give each child a bow for the kite's tail and ask them to write a windy word or phrase on it, e.g. 'blowing a gale' or 'breeze'. The coloured bows can be attached to the kite's long tail and hung up in the classroom.

Not enough rain

Show the importance of rain by conducting a controlled experiment. Provide the class with two similar plants in pots. Place one outside, in an unsheltered place. Keep the other inside on a window sill but do not water it. Keep a daily record of the two plants' progress. Show that a plant does take in water by standing a stick of celery in water coloured red with ink, and watch the red water move up the stem.

Rain for food

Give each child the outline figure cut out from Copymaster 2 Clothes to dress for rainy weather. Pretend the figures are farmers who have to go into the fields to pick crops for market. On a separate sheet children can draw and cut out the farmer's produce to glue onto his hand. Each farmer will have a vegetable or fruit to bring in from the fields. Display the cut out farmers as mobiles hanging from an umbrella shape, with the title 'We need rain to grow food'.

3 | Who uses the wind?

This is a dandelion. It uses the wind.

Draw what happens to its seeds.

This man is using the wind in his boat. Draw an arrow to show which way he is going.

Draw another hobby that uses the wind.

This machine uses electricity. It is called a wind generator.

Draw another way to use the wind.

A storm

Ilfracombe
A hurricane blew the roof off the hotel.

Gloucestershire
Some villages were cut off by floods.

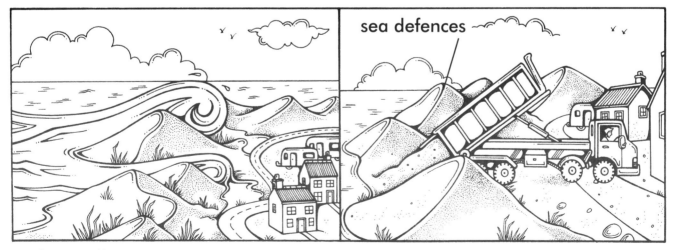

Selsey Bill
Rough seas washed away the sea defences.

Sun

Learning targets

On completion of this unit children should understand:

1 ➤➤ that the sun affects lives
2 ➤➤ the pattern of night and day
3 ➤➤ the need for sun protection.

Before you start

Background knowledge

The UK has a maritime climate. The land heats up and cools down faster than the sea. In summer the sea lowers the land air temperatures and in winter the sea has a warming effect on the land which means that there are no extremes of temperature. In summer the average daily temperature decreases as you travel north from the south of England to Scotland because the sun's rays which heat the land are more concentrated in the south. Temperature also decreases with altitude. The sun is necessary for life. Plants need it for growth, and plants are the basis of all food chains.

Teaching points

Children learn how the sun affects daily life, patterns of daylight and how people protect themselves from sunlight. Children should be warned not to look directly at the sun.

Geographical skills

- Observation skills

Vocabulary

sun, warm, sunset, sunrise, day, night, protection

Resources for Lesson 1

Copymaster 5 The sun is out, felt-tip pens

Resources for Lesson 2

Copymaster 6 Day and night, felt-tip pens, stories and poems concerning day and night, e.g. Foster, John *Night Poems*, OUP, 1993

Resources for Lesson 3

Sun hats, sunglasses, sun cream, T-shirts, parasol or umbrella, photos, drawing materials

Resources for the activities

Rounders post

Assessment indicators

- Do the children know whether it is getting warmer or cooler?
- Do they how to protect themselves from the sun?

Teaching the lessons

Lesson 1 ①

Introduction 10 min

Bring sunny weather to the attention of the class and get them to notice how warm it is when the sun comes out. Use a sunny day to show the children how to observe things not only by looking but by touching. In the classroom, give them some cold things to touch – an egg, something metallic, the window (not in full sunshine) – and some warmer things – wool, gloves warm from being worn, and ask the children to put their hand under their own arm.

The sun is warm 20 min

 Take the children outside when the sun is shining. Sit them down with their backs to the sun. After warning them not to look at the sun, ask them to

look and tell you how they know the sun is shining. Probe for shadows, blue sky and things shining.

Ask them how they could 'feel' if the sun is shining. Probe for feeling warm, hair or backs warm to the touch. Ask the children to move around the playground touching different surfaces to see whether the sun has made them warm. Before returning to the classroom, find a shady spot where the sun has not warmed anything. Let the children feel the difference.

In the classroom, children can complete **Copymaster 5 The sun is out** with their own observations and make a 'ray' for a sun to decorate the room.

Summary 10 min

Ask the children to read out their descriptions of the sun. Give them some strips of yellow paper to mount their words and phrases on and attach them to some display 'suns'.

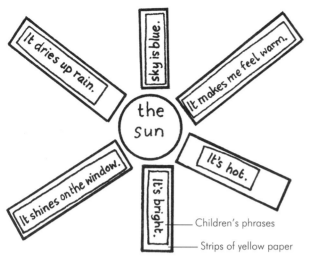

The sun's rays

Children's phrases
Strips of yellow paper

Lesson 2 ① ②

Introduction   10 min

Hold a question and answer session about day and night. 'What is a day?' 'When does it start?' 'When does it end?' 'What do you do at the beginning/in the middle/at the end of a day?' 'What is a night?' 'When does it start/end?' 'What do you do at night?' 'What do other people and animals do?'

Day and night   30 min

The daily patterns in **Copymaster 6 Day and night** can be used in different ways.

1 Cut out the boxes and match sunrise, midday and sunset to the builder's daily pattern, adding clocks to show the times of day.

2 Cut out the boxes showing the sun's daily pattern and match with pictures of the child's own daily pattern, adding meals taken at different times of the day.

3 Use the night worker's pattern to add more night worker boxes. Try using newspaper printers, airport staff, factory production workers, and night watchmen.

Differentiate by adding extra activities in between the three pictures shown on the copymaster. Match times of day to weekend activities and compare with a school day.

Extend by making patterns for animals. You could include nocturnal animals such as pet hamsters.

Summary   10 min

Read aloud poems or a story concerning the passage of time through the day or night and day to reinforce this concept. *Night Poems* by John Foster, offers eight poems to choose from.

Lesson 3 ① ③

Introduction   10 min

Make a display of sun protection aids on bright, yellow paper. Use sun hats, sunglasses, sun cream, T-shirts, parasol or umbrella, photos of shaded areas or tables under trees. As a class, discuss the items on display. Talk about the hottest part of the day when they are out at play during school time. How can they stop the sun from burning them?

Sun protection   30 min

Children can design and draw a sun hat they would like to wear. What materials would they use? Which colours? Does it have a brim to keep the sun from their face? The children can cut around their sun hat design to make a display of sun hats in the classroom. Display the sun hats on cut outs of hat stands.

Summary   5 min

Pick out the hats with brims or peaks and stress the importance of shielding eyes and face from the strong sun.

Extra activities ① ②
The wind and the sun

Tell the story of the wind and the sun, who argue about which of them can make the man take off his coat. The wind blows and the sun shines alternately. The wind blows and buffets him, but he pulls his coat in tighter. The sun shines, making him hot, and eventually he takes off his coat. Use the story for sequence drawings or for role plays.

Shadow sticks

Use a stick standing in the playground (a rounders post works well) to trace the movement of the sun through the day. At hourly intervals, mark in chalk on the playground where the shadow lies. It will move round as the sun moves from east to west during the day. It will get shorter as the sun rises higher in the sky at midday.

A sunny spot

Use a sunny day to investigate the sunny and shady parts of the school grounds. Are some places sunny all the time or are they in the shade for part of the day? Ask the children to choose a place for a bench to sit on.

Night

Brainstorm with your class all the things that happen at night while they are asleep. Include animals and birds that come out at night, people who work at night, e.g. in hospitals, for the postal service, in factories and airports. Write poems about what is happening while they are asleep in bed, or draw pictures to stick around a moon and stars on a black background.

The sun is out

Finish the pattern.

1   cloud

2   cloud and
     some sun

3   _____

     _____

The sun makes these things warm.

Cut out the ray.
Write a sunny idea on it.

ray

 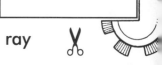

Day and night

The sun is shining all the time.
Sometimes we cannot see it.

The pictures show the sun's pattern.

sunrise   midday   sunset

Most people have a pattern in their life.
The pictures show someone's day.

Here is the pattern of someone who works at night.

Snow

Learning targets

On completion of this unit children should understand that:

1 ➤➤ snow and ice are features of winter
2 ➤➤ snow and ice affect roads and travel
3 ➤➤ snow and ice affect people's lives.

Before you start

Background knowledge

Some parts of the UK receive little or no snow for several years in succession. Take any opportunity to observe, play and work with snow even if it falls outside the topic being undertaken.

Ice is more common and can be made in freezer trays to simulate slippery roads and surfaces. Frost is formed when water vapour in the air condenses on cold surfaces such as plants, cars and paths. Temperatures below freezing point, 0°C, freeze the water vapour. Hoar frost, with its fern like structure is formed when dew freezes after it has settled.

Teaching points

Snow and ice affect daily life. Snow is fun but freezing conditions can be dangerous.

Geographical skills

- Observation skills
- Tracing routes on a map
- Making an imaginary map

Vocabulary

snow, ice, drift, freeze, danger

Assessment indicators

- Can children find and follow a route in the snow or from a map?
- Can they recognize dangers during freezing conditions?

Resources for Lesson 1

Rutherford, Meg B*luff and Bran and the Snowdrift*, Andre Deutsch, Copymaster 7 Tracks in the snow, felt-tip pens

Resources for Lesson 2

Tray of water frozen into sheet of ice, cubes of ice, plastic blocks, toy cars, sand, shiny paper, clear plastic

Resources for Lesson 3

Copymaster 8 What if it snows?, pencils, felt-tip pens

Resources for the activities

Paper, cotton wool, Christmas cards, skis, pipe-cleaners, lollipop sticks, balsa wood

Teaching the lessons

Lesson 1 ① ③

Introduction 10 min

▦ Read B*luff and Bran and the Snowdrift* by Meg Rutherford or make up a short story about the snow covering everything and an animal walking around leaving tracks, falling into a snowdrift and finding its way back. **Copymaster 7, Tracks in the snow** can be used for the background to the story.

Tracks in the snow 30 min

👤 Copymaster 7 Tracks in the snow shows a snow covered landscape with the tracks of a person going from the house to the fields, having dropped some pieces of hay.

Some information is provided about the scene and questions are asked about it. Some animal and vehicle tracks are shown for identification.

Differentiate by setting one of the following tasks.

1 Ask the children to answer the questions on the copymaster.

2 Suggest that the children add the tracks of another animal and record which animal made them and what it was doing.

3 Ask the children to make a map showing the journey made by the tracks on the picture.

Summary 5 min

▦ When snow falls in the playground, look for tracks. Discuss reasons why animals venture out in the snow. Ask the children to suggest why it is difficult for them to find food.

Lesson 2

Introduction `10 min`

Talk about how slippery icy roads and pavements can be. Show a tray of ice made in a freezer and see how pieces of ice slip and slide on it. Try it with plastic blocks and toy cars. Sprinkle it with sand to show how to prevent sliding. If it's topical, show children photos from the newspapers of icy roads causing accidents.

Icy roads `30 min`

Each member of the group is to make a car from shiny paper. Either the bonnet or the boot of the car can be concertined to make it a crash victim. The cars can be arranged on a background painted to look like a road junction, as though they have skidded together to make a crash scene. Pieces of clear plastic can simulate broken glass on the road. Words connected with the crash and the weather conditions can be written on labels and used to border each collage.

Shiny paper

Summary `5 min`

Discuss with the class a jingle or slogan which can be used as a title for the pictures and to warn drivers when roads are icy. Offer words such as 'icy', 'driving', 'danger'.

Lesson 3

Introduction `10 min`

Ask a child to think of someone's job. What if it snows? Does the job change? Ask for another job. Repeat the question 'What if it snows?' Continue until you find a job that alters when it snows. If you need to make suggestions, use some jobs which change and some which do not, e.g. a baker's jobs stays the same but a farmer has to feed his animals and keep them safe from snowdrifts.

Jobs in the snow `30 min`

Copymaster 8 What if it snows? looks at jobs associated with snow and ice. Children who have not experienced snow and ice may need help with the work on gritting lorries.

Ask the caretaker to talk to the children about the extra job of cleaning paths, or go out and observe the work that has been done.

Power supplies are often disrupted when storms bring heavy snow. Electricty is essential for heat and light so the electrician's job is very important in these weather conditions. The children may like to imagine having no light, no heat and no dinner. Children draw a picture of a caretaker clearing the snow in the empty box on the copymaster.

Summary `5 min`

Talk about the fun in the snow, mention building snowmen, snowballs, sledging and skiing.

Extra activities

Warm mittens

Remind children about the need to keep warm. Link with work on left and right and make cut outs of a left and right hand in coloured paper. Decorate the mittens and display each pair holding a snowball made from a white circle of paper with cotton wool or pieces of wool glued onto it.

The North wind doth blow

The North wind doth blow
And we shall have snow
What will the robin do then, poor thing...

Children can write a short story or poem to say what the robin will do about food and shelter.

Christmas card scenes

Collect Christmas cards with snowy landscape scenes. Many of these will depict people or animals. Give each child a card to glue on their paper. Ask them to write a few sentences to describe that scene and explain what the people or animals are doing and how they feel about the snow. You may want to talk about some of the words that the children include in their work. Ask less able children for words and phrases to be written around the card.

Skis

Let children examine and measure a pair of skis. Video winter ski competitions.

Model skiers can be made using the cut out person from **Copymaster 2 Clothes** dressed in padded warm clothes. Attach the paper skier to a pipecleaner frame. Skis can be made from lollipop sticks or balsa wood, and the skiers' pipecleaner-feet taped to the skis. Display a row of skiers on a long strip of white card.

Tracks in the snow

Last night it snowed. Only the farmer has been out. He went out to his field.

The farmer took a spade.
I wonder why?
I wonder if he took anything else?

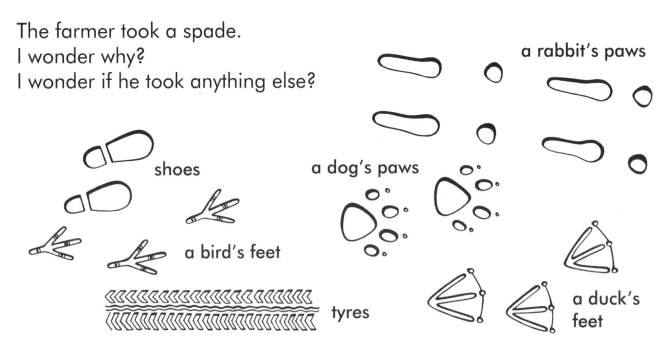

shoes

a bird's feet

tyres

a rabbit's paws

a dog's paws

a duck's feet

Here are some tracks to look for when it snows.

8 | What if it snows?

Join the labels to the picture.

flashing light   moon

COUNTY COUNCIL

icy roads   snow

grit

What is happening?

_____

_____

Why?

_____

Two jobs in the snow

1   I am an electrician

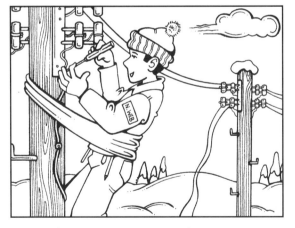

My job is important because

_____

_____

2   I clear snow at school

My job is important because

_____

_____

HOMES

Focus

Homes and houses make up the largest number of buildings in settlements. Other buildings service and provide work for the people who live there. The variety of homes is a reflection of individual tastes and requirements. This section aims to look at that variety so that children learn to observe, understand and form views on the need for housing. Homes is a familiar topic in the Key Stage 1 classroom. This section concentrates on the geographical aspect of the subject although there are plenty of cross-curricular links to language, maths, art and design within the lessons.

Content

Unit 1:   Houses
Unit 2:   In the street
Unit 3:   Who lives there?

Source material

The best resource is a collection of photographs of houses in your area. It may be worthwhile for the school to organise a series of photos of houses, streets, buildings and other geographical features for the whole school to use during local area work. Children in your class could be asked to bring in a photo of their house for work on this topic.

Large scale maps are available from your local council. The Planning Office or the Transport and Environment Office can provide, under licence, a large scale map for educational purposes. Ask for a 1:500 scale, giving them the Ordnance Survey grid reference of the street, or a map with the street highlighted.

Brainstorm

This brainstorm covers the lessons in Section 2 and can be added to for a cross-curricular topic.

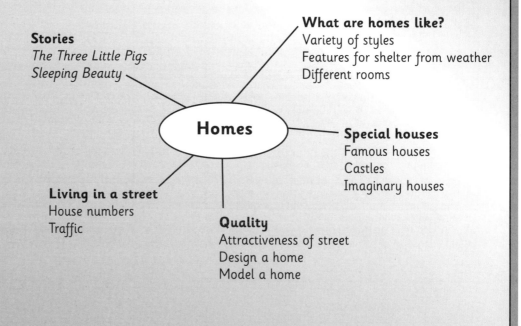

Stories
The Three Little Pigs
Sleeping Beauty

What are homes like?
Variety of styles
Features for shelter from weather
Different rooms

Homes

Special houses
Famous houses
Castles
Imaginary houses

Living in a street
House numbers
Traffic

Quality
Attractiveness of street
Design a home
Model a home

Teaching plan

This can be used as a medium-term plan and provides a scheme of work for a topic on homes.

Enquiry questions	Learning targets	Pupil activities
1 What are homes like?	There is a variety of house styles which can provide homes.	Observing features and styles of houses: Unit 1 Lessons 1 and 2; surveys and charts: Unit 1 Lesson 2, Unit 3, Lessons 1 and 2.
2 What do we need near our homes?	We need shops, transport and services near our homes.	Fieldwork observation: Unit 2 Lesson 1; using photographs: Unit 2 Lessons 2 and 3, Unit 3 Lesson 1; making maps: Unit 2 Lesson 3, Unit 3 Lesson 2.
3 What sort of home do you like?	Children can express views on features they like about homes.	Room models: Unit 1 Lesson 3; design a house Unit 3 Lesson 3.

National Curriculum coverage

Unit 1 Houses

National Curriculum links
- Study of the local area.
- Effects of weather on house styles.
- Fieldwork in the local area.

Unit 2 In the street

National Curriculum links
- Use of large scale maps.
- Fieldwork in the local area.

Unit 3 Who lives there?

National Curriculum links
- Mapmaking skills.
- UK awareness.

Scotland Environment Studies coverage

The units cover the following contexts and content for Understanding People and Places:

- Major physical and natural features in the locality.
- The uses of buildings and land in the local area.

UNIT 1 | Houses

Learning targets

On completion of this unit children should understand that:

1 ➡ houses have features for comfortable living
2 ➡ there are different sizes and styles of houses
3 ➡ houses have rooms for different purposes.

Before you start

Background knowledge

Houses fulfil the need for shelter, and develop into individual homes to suit the occupants. The climate determines certain factors, e.g. materials, weatherproofing and features concerned with heating. Other features are determined by the need for security, available space and personal taste.

Investigating children's own houses is studied further in Section 7 Personal geography.

Teaching points

Children will focus on the styles of houses and the requirements of the people who live in them. Use enquiry questions to encourage the children to work out the reason for particular features on houses.

Geographical skills

- Observation in the local area
- Fieldwork opportunities

Vocabulary

detached, semi-detached, terrace, cottage, flat, bungalow, shelter

Resources for Lesson 1

Copymaster 9 What is it for?, pencils, felt-tip pens

Resources for Lesson 2

Clipboards, tick sheets, pencils, Copymaster 10 All sorts of houses

Resources for Lesson 3

Cardboard, junk boxes, Plasticine®, fabric, etc. for modelling

Resources for the activities

Cards numbered 1–25, The Three Little Pigs

Assessment indicators

- Do the children know the reasons for the features of a house?
- Do they know the range of house types common in their area?
- Do they know the purpose of the different rooms in a house?

Teaching the lessons

Lesson 1 ①

Introduction ☐10min☐

▦ Show the children a large picture of a house. Point to each feature and ask for its name and its purpose. Roof and walls give shelter from the weather, windows let in light and air, chimneys or vents let out smoke and fumes, doors and paths allow movement in and out, gardens are for leisure, aerials are for leisure, locks are for security.

Parts of a house ☐30min☐

▣ Distribute photocopies of **Copymaster 9 What is it for?** Arrows point to the features on the house. The children can write the name of the feature and state its purpose in the boxes provided.

Differentiate by making one large house picture for a group of children who each fill in one of the boxes. Ask more able children to add other things that they find on houses which make them personal to the people who live there, e.g. a number, plants, lights.

Summary ☐10min☐

▚ Ask a group of children to play a game. One child reads the purpose of a feature on a house, e.g. 'I can look out of it'. The next child guesses 'window' and so on around the group.

Lesson 2 ②

Introduction ☐20min☐

▦ Give the children a tick sheet to count the types of houses that can be seen when you take a short walk along a street near your school. Try to choose a street with a mixture of different styles of houses. If you cannot do this, ask a local estate agent for old house details showing pictures of different housing styles in your area.

TICK AND COUNT		
HOUSE	✓when seen	𝍸 III
	detached	
	semi-detached	
	bungalow	
	terrace	
	flat	
other ?		

Housing survey

Types of houses

30min

Copymaster 10 All sorts of houses depicts houses of different styles and gives their names. The sheet can be used in various ways.

1. Children can cut out the houses and make a 'street' of the types of houses seen on the fieldtrip.
2. Children can copy the outlines of the houses and add features to personalise them, e.g. numbers, dustbins, coloured front doors.
3. Pairs or small groups can each make a poster for different house styles, with drawings and descriptions to make a display of 'Houses in our town'.
4. Children can match the house types on the sheet to photos of houses from an estate agent or property magazine.

Summary

5min

Make flashcards from Copymaster 10 and assess whether the children know the difference between the various house styles in your area.

Lesson 3

1 3

Introduction

10min

Choose one room of a house. Ask children to tell you all the things it is used for and what furniture and decorations you would find in that room, e.g. the lounge is for resting, reading, watching TV, eating and playing games. It has chairs, small table, lights, TV, bookcase, fireplace and pictures.

Rooms

40min

Children are to make a model of the room, using a corner display on a card base. They can use whatever modelling materials are available (junk boxes, fabric, Plasticine®, etc.) and decide how to show the purpose of the room. Differentiate by:

1. asking different groups to make models of different rooms
2. asking children to make four rooms, over several sessions,and fixing them together to make one floor of a house
3. making one large room that a group of children can furnish and decorate.

Summary

5min

Display the rooms with a small pile of labels for children to match to the rooms. The labels will depend on the rooms made and the way they are furnished, e.g. 'for resting', 'to watch TV', 'to cook dinner'.

Modelling a room

Extra activities

1 2

Where we live

Children draw a picture of their own house and glue it to a class bar chart that shows how many houses of different styles are represented in your class. Use the finished chart to answer questions such as, 'Where do most children live?' 'Are there any types of houses not in our chart?' 'How many of each type of house is there?'

House numbers

Discuss the reason for house names and numbers. Who needs to know? Give all but one of the children in the class a number between 1 and 25. Arrange the children in a line as if they were the house numbers in a street. The extra child is a postman. Give the postman numbered cards to deliver to each house.

Ask the children to arrange themselves into a street with odds on one side and evens on the opposite side. Can the postman organise his letters for easy delivery? Change the postman and house numbers for good maths number work.

The three pigs

Read the story of *The Three Little Pigs*. Ask the children to make pictures of the three houses. Which house would they choose to live in? They can draw themselves beside the house of their choice. Ask them to tell you or to write down a reason for their choice.

What is it for?

Write the name of the part of the house in each box.
Draw or write what it is for.

All sorts of houses

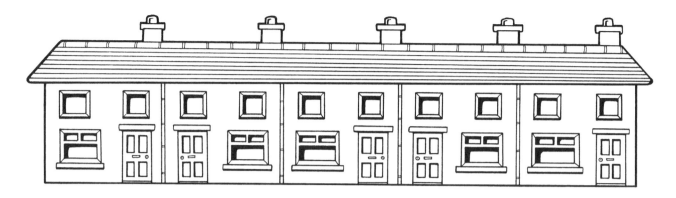

a terrace of houses

semi-detached houses

a detached house

a bungalow

a cottage

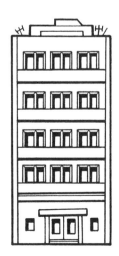

a block of flats

a flat

In the street

Learning targets

On completion of this unit children should understand that:

1 ➡➡ each street has its own buildings and features

2 ➡➡ people come to the street for different reasons

3 ➡➡ features in the street have different purposes.

Before you start

Background knowledge

Local knowledge is required to discover interesting aspects of each street. If you use the street where the school is situated it should be easy to prepare a bank of knowledge, photographs and local historical information. A large scale map of the street showing each building will be useful. Acquire knowledge of street signs and notices, building materials, change of use of buildings, species of plants and trees, range of house types, workplaces and interesting features.

Teaching points

The unit answers the questions 'What is a street like?' and 'Why do people come to this street?' Teach ways to observe and notice details. Encourage children to be inquisitive.

Geographical skills

- Observation
- Fieldwork in the local area
- Using a large scale map
- Taking and using photographs

Vocabulary

building, homes, shop, office, traffic, signs

Resources for Lesson 1

Camera, clipboards, pencils.

Resources for Lesson 2

Copymaster 11 It's in the street, felt-tip pens.

Resources for Lesson 3

Copymaster 12 All sorts of buildings, card, felt-tip pens, large scale map of the local area.

Resources for the activities

Large scale map of local area, paper, pencils, felt-tip pens.

Assessment indicators

- Can the children recognise different uses of buildings?
- Do they know that streets are different in character?
- Can they express a view on the attractiveness of a street?

Teaching the lessons

Lesson 1 ①

Introduction ⏱10min⏱

▨ Talk about the work to be carried out during a visit to the street outside the school. Explain that the task is to observe and collect information on the types of buildings, signs, useful items and services in order to get a picture of all the things that are permanently in the street. If you can take a school camera for the children to use, explain how you will share the use of it so that you create a set of photos of the different buildings and things in the street.

School road ⏱30min⏱

⚅ Choose a particular feature for each group to observe in the street and to record, e.g. the street

name on its board. Each group can record it on their leader's paper. Ask children to look for things they pass on the way and report them to their adult leader, who can make a note of it. This means children can walk and observe without carrying clipboards and pencils. Leaders can also record photographs taken. At the end of the walk along the street, each group should have one picture and a list of other features observed.

Summary ⏱15min⏱

⚅ Each member of the fieldwork group should produce a picture of something they saw in the street. A composite picture for each group will record their main feature and things they noticed on the way. A set of these pictures will reveal the most interesting features of the street.

34

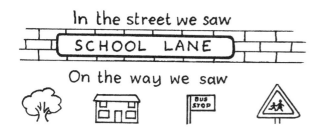

In the street we saw
SCHOOL LANE
On the way we saw

Lesson 2 ② ③

Introduction 10 min

Use the set of photographs taken on the walk in the street or a set you have taken previously. Make four labels: Enjoyment, Work, Homes and Travel. Attach the four labels to a board, leaving space to add photos underneath. Hold up one photograph at a time and ask which group it belongs to and then fix it to the board under the right heading. Some photographs belong in more than one group.

Street features 30 min

Leave the photos on the board as a resource for the children to refer to. Distribute photocopies of **Copymaster 11 It's in the street** and ask children to recall the features they saw in the street and classify them under the same headings. Children can draw a feature in each category.

Differentiate by asking more able children to list several features in each box, or allowing slower workers to fill in one sheet with a partner. The features illustrated on the copymaster are reminders and suggestions for them to use.

Summary 5 min

Talk about homes. Are most of the buildings homes or are they something else? What sorts of houses are there? Are they old or new?

Lesson 3 ① ② ③

Introduction 10 min

Display photographs of the different buildings in the street, or remind the children of some that you saw on the walk. Pick out a building and ask the children to tell you who uses it. Is it used to live in? Does someone work there? Do people visit the building for something? Ask questions about a range of buildings including homes, shops, offices, churches and the school.

Use of buildings 30 min

The task is to make a 3D map of the buildings in the street with their uses. Try to find sufficient buildings so that children can work on one each or at least in pairs. Using the information on **Copymaster 12 All sorts of buildings** as a resource, children can make a stand up card about their building. The front of

their card should show a picture of the building and inside the card children can record what the building is used for. The back of the card could show what is behind the building, inside the building or depict the people who use it.

Summary 10 min

Using a large scale map of the street for reference, children stand their cards in the correct sequence along a road painted on a strip of card.

Children are free to pick up and read the information on other buildings in the street.

Buildings in the street

Extra activities ① ② ③

Traffic

Conduct a traffic survey of vehicles passing the school over a five-minute period. Count cars, lorries, buses, delivery vehicles and bikes. Use the results to make a bar chart. Use the bar chart to assess how busy the street is and what sorts of people travel through it for their work.

Building use map

Use a large scale map of the street to colour code buildings according to their use. If these types of buildings are present in your street, include the following categories: schools, empty premises, homes, places for leisure, shops, places of worship, cafés, other workplaces. Each group colours one category of building and adds the colour and category to the key.

Street attractiveness

Use a set of photos to remind the children of the features observed in the street. Which part of the street do they like and which part is not attractive or interesting to them? Record the work as contrasting pictures, mounted with the photos in sets. Language work, such as producing contrasting poems with a range of vocabulary to express opposite feelings, could be added to the display. This lesson could be linked with work on improving and sustaining environments, by discussing how changes could be made to improve the unattractive areas.

It's in the street

Tick the pictures you saw in your street.

homes	work
travel	**enjoyment**

houses
places to live

church
a place of worship

shops
places to sell and buy things

office
a place to work

factory
a place to make things

workshop
a place to mend things

places for fun

Who lives there?

Learning targets

On completion of this unit children should:

1 ➤➤ know that houses are homes where people live
2 ➤➤ be able to make a map showing the features around houses
3 ➤➤ know the requirements of a home.

Before you start

Background knowledge

Famous houses are lived in by political, historical and royal families. In your locality there may be a famous house which could extend the work in this unit. The National Trust and English Heritage own or manage some famous houses and castles and provide pictures and brochures for educational use. There may be one near enough for a class visit.

The home of the Prime Minister at 10 Downing Street links with work on London as the capital city of the UK and there is a map with its location on page 139.

Signpost maps, rather like brainstorm webs, show all the features and services around a place rather than a being an accurate road map. These help young children to get a sense of location.

Teaching points

People choose homes for different reasons. A home is often located near a job while its size often depends on number of people living in it. Children improve their knowledge of the requirements of a home by using mapping, planning and imaginary work.

Geographical skills

- Making maps
- Using research skills.

Vocabulary

palace, castle, famous, special

Resources needed for Lesson 1

Copymaster 13 A famous house, photographs of the prime minister and places in London from newspapers and magazines, paper, pencils

Resources needed for Lesson 2

Sleeping Beauty, books on castles, Copymaster 14 Home in a castle, pencils, pens

Resources needed for Lesson 3

Painting materials

Resources needed for the activities

A selection of poems to provide stimulus for house design, paper, felt-tip pens

Assessment indicators

- Can the children make a simple map?
- Do they know the requirements of a home?

Teaching the lessons

Lesson 1 ① ②

Introduction |10min|

A class discussion on a general knowledge theme about the prime minister leads to making a signpost map. Ask 'Who is the prime minister?' 'What job does the prime minister do?' and 'Where does he live?' These questions can lead to establishing his address as 10 Downing Street. Ask why the house is there and why it has a police guard. What places and people does the prime minister need to be near?

A famous house |30min|

 Copymaster 13 A famous house shows 10 Downing Street and places in the area that the prime minister may use or need to be near. The children can make a large black door with the number 10 on it. It can be fixed along its left side only, so that it opens. Fix it to the centre of a piece of paper. Inside the door children can draw or glue a picture of the prime minister. Each child can make their own signpost map, using the pictures on the copymaster, photographs of London from newspapers and magazines, as well as drawing their own pictures.

Differentiate by asking more able children to add labels to their pictures to explain why the prime minister needs to live near these places.

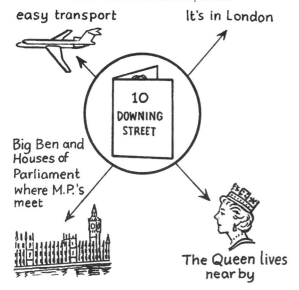

A signpost map

Summary 10 min

Suggest that you write to your MP as a class, and find out more about their jobs and working in the centre of London. What questions would they like to ask? Follow this up in a language lesson.

Lesson 2 ①

Introduction 10 min

Read a story that is set in a castle, e.g. *Sleeping Beauty*. With the class, discuss what it would be like in a castle, talk about the staircases, dungeons, battlements and moat. Picture reference books would be a useful resource for this lesson.

Living in a castle 30 min

Copymaster 14 Home in a castle has space for three activities. The first activity asks children to draw their own castle. The list of castle features can serve either as an *aide memoire* or as labels for the castle.

Homes have names or numbers, but castles have flags. In the second activity children can design a flag for the family who live in the castle. It may be a simple stripy flag or one which reflects the interests of the castle owners.

The third activity asks children to consider the inside of the castle and to imagine life in one room. Can they recreate the room including its furnishings, windows/arrow slits, staircases, etc.?

Summary 5 min

Ask members of a group to match castle feature labels to a castle picture you have drawn or found. Ask the group how and why a castle is different from their home.

Lesson 3 ③

Introduction 10 min

Talk about the basic requirements people have of a house. Mention the need for shelter, somewhere to cook and eat, and somewhere to sleep. What extras would the children like in a house?

Design a house 40 min

During this activity, make a painting area available so that the children can spend some of the time painting a picture of the outside of their imaginary house.

Remind them that each house will need a place for people to eat and sleep as well as whatever other ideas they may have. They can design the inside of a house within a frame that you supply.

Differentiate by choosing how many rooms to give each child and the size of paper for the design. Able writers could write a house description as if the house were for sale at an estate agents.

Summary 5 min

Talk with each group about their houses. Ask them to point out the eating and sleeping areas. Ask questions about any interesting features.

Extra activities ① ③

Visit a house

Visit a nearby mansion, castle, or interesting house, e.g. converted barn, oasthouse, houseboat or barge just to observe and draw the interesting features. If the owner can be persuaded to talk to you or let the children wander more closely around the outside, that would make an exciting visit.

Poems and rhymes

Use a selection of verse to provide the stimulus for house design, e.g. 'There was an old woman who lived in a shoe' and 'The House that Jack built'.

Designing rooms for houses, and labelling features will help children to recognise the basic requirements people have of their homes.

House names

Collect house names in your area. What do the names tell you about the house or the people who own it? Ask the children to choose a name and to make and decorate a house plaque. Some commonly used names include Mill House, The Pines, Windy Ridge, Sea/Bay/Beach/Field View, Belle Vue and names of places where people used to live or spend their holidays, e.g.Clovelly House.

Buckingham Palace – the Queen lives here

capital city

airports

railway stations

Houses of Parliament – where the government meets

busy city centre – places to eat, shop and meet people

Draw your castle here.

Parts of a castle

tower

battlements

keep

moat

drawbridge

Draw a flag to show who lives in the castle.

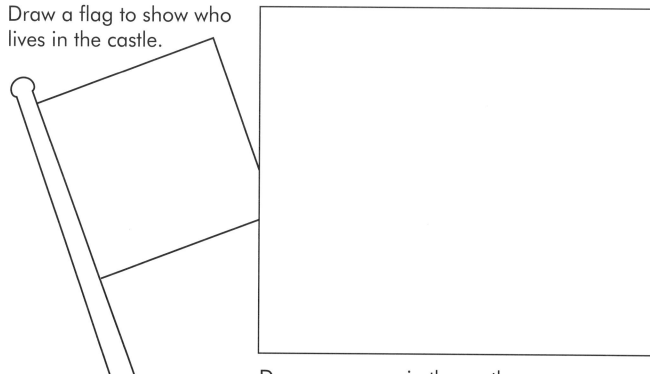

Draw one room in the castle

JOBS

Focus

Occupations can be grouped into three main categories: manufacturing, sales and service industries. This can be translated for children as 'making', 'selling' and 'helping'. The service industry includes people who help us, e.g. the police force as well as people who help to run things, e.g. secretaries. Wherever possible, try to use examples of local jobs that the children may be familiar with. Inviting people in to talk about their jobs will add a real dimension to the work and encourage community and parental involvement in the school.

Content

Unit 1:   Local jobs
Unit 2:   The Royal Mail
Unit 3:   Making things

Source material

The Royal Mail produce educational material for primary schools. Write to Royal Mail Education, PO Box 105, Rochester, Kent ME2 4BE, or telephone 01795 426465.

Scoffham, Stephen and Thomas, Sue *Primary Colours Series*: A *World of Ideas*, Stanley Thornes Publishers, 1997. This teaching resource contains ideas for displays and models about jobs, especially in the service industries.

See Section 9 pages 144–47 and Section 10 pages 162–65 of this book for lessons on bakers.

Brainstorm

This brainstorm covers the lessons in Section 3 and can be added to for a cross-curricular topic.

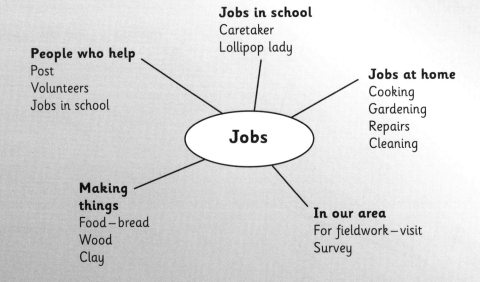

Jobs in school
Caretaker
Lollipop lady

People who help
Post
Volunteers
Jobs in school

Jobs at home
Cooking
Gardening
Repairs
Cleaning

Jobs

Making things
Food – bread
Wood
Clay

In our area
For fieldwork – visit
Survey

Teaching plan

This can be used as a medium-term plan and provides a scheme of work for a topic on jobs.

Enquiry questions	Learning targets	Pupil activities
1 Which jobs help us?	Some people have jobs that help us or help to run places.	Observation and questioning: Unit 1 Lesson 1, Unit 2 All lessons.
2 How are things made?	Most things are made in stages, one step at a time.	Observation and wood rubbings: Unit 3 Lesson 1; making bread and tiles: Unit 3 Lessons 2 and 3
3 What is it like to do some jobs?	I can try some jobs or ask questions to find out what they are like.	Visit and survey: Unit 1 Lesson 2; research: Unit 1 Lesson 3; using a story: Unit 2 Lesson 3; practical making activities: Unit 3 Lessons 2 and 3.

National Curriculum coverage

Unit 1 Local jobs

National Curriculum links
- Fieldwork in the local area.
- Use of enquiry skills.

Unit 2 The Royal Mail

National Curriculum links
- Fieldwork opportunities in the local area.
- Can investigate enquiry questions.

Unit 3 Making things

National Curriculum links
- Background knowledge for work on settlements.
- Human features in a locality.

Scotland Environment Studies coverage

The units cover the following contexts and content for Understanding People and Places:

- Major physical and natural features in the locality.
- The uses of buildings and land in the local area.
- Places used in the provision of services.

UNIT 1 | Local jobs

Learning targets

On completion of this unit children should:

1 ➡ understand that different people have different jobs
2 ➡ have knowledge of the important features of some jobs
3 ➡ be able to ask enquiry questions to gain knowledge.

Before you start

Background knowledge

Some jobs can be done in almost any location around the country, e.g. school caretaker or shopkeeper but other jobs are only found in certain places, e.g. coastguards are by the sea, farmers are in the countryside. Each locality will have jobs that can only be done in certain places. The locations of these jobs will depend on various factors: types of farm will depend on the weather and soil, conditions, air controllers and pilots will live near airports, and brickworks need a supply of clay. When choosing jobs for Lesson 2 a mix of common and specific area jobs could be included.

Teaching points

Some jobs are in manufacturing, some are in sales and others are in serving or helping people. The focus is on the everyday features and work of the jobs children can observe locally.

Geographical skills

- Using enquiry questions to gather information
- Making a simple plan
- Using secondary resources

Vocabulary

caretaker, local, workplace, tools, employ, uniform

Resources for Lesson 1

Copymaster 15 The caretaker, felt-tip pens

Resources for Lesson 2

Copymaster 16 People at work, camera, clipboards, pens

Resources for Lesson 3

Reference books on jobs, paper, felt-tip pens

Resources for the activities

Paper, felt-tip pens, pictures of people at work

Assessment indicators

- Can the children sequence a daily routine in a job?
- Can they ask a question and record the answer?
- Do they have knowledge of a local job?

Teaching the lessons

Lesson 1 ① ②

Introduction   [10 min]

Talk about your school caretaker. Do the children know his or her name? What jobs have they seen the caretaker doing around the school? What do they think the caretaker does when they are not at school? You may be able to ask the caretaker to come and talk to the class and answer some questions about the job.

The school caretaker   [30 min]

Copymaster 15 The caretaker shows the tools of the caretaker's job and a picture of one caretaker

doing part of his job. Using Copymaster 15, choose from the differentiated activities below.

1 Encourage the children to think of questions to ask the caretaker about his job.

2 Write a diary about the caretaker's job using clocks to show the passage of time through the course of the day.

3 Draw a sequence of pictures showing the caretaker using the tools and equipment illustrated on the copymaster.

Summary   [5 min]

Talk about all the jobs in school. Where does the caretaker fit in? Does he make something, sell something, or does he help to run the school?

44

Where do the other jobs belong? Conclude that most of the jobs in the school are there to help or serve people.

Lesson 2

Introduction | 10min |

Having chosen a local workplace to study, and arranged to visit it, tell the children about the proposed visit. Show them **Copymaster 16 People at work** and choose which children will ask the questions on the sheet. It may be possible to find out all the answers without talking to real employees but it would be more interesting for the children to have contact with people outside school.

A local job | 20min |

On a previsit to the site, look for a safe place for the children to stand and observe. Explain to the interviewee how many questions there are and what you would like the children to see. Check any safety requirements.

Before setting out on the field trip, rehearse the questions. Give children photocopies of Copymaster 16 and clipboards. Bring a camera on the trip to photograph the things the children are going to draw. It will help to refresh their memories, if you make a display resource and also allow the children to finish incomplete work back at school.

Differentiate by writing answers for slow writers, asking a helper to scribe answers or letting a pair of children share a sheet.

Summary | 20min |

Children will need time at school to complete their sheet, copy rough work onto a new sheet, or to make a picture of a person at work along with the tools of their trade.

Lesson 3

Introduction | 10min |

Talk about the two jobs the class have already found out about. Ask a parent or someone who works in the school to visit the class and tell the children about their job – what they do, what they like and dislike about it. You could do this yourself and tell them about the job of a teacher.

I'd like to be | 30min |

Ask the children to think of a job they would like to do. If they need stimulation for ideas, you could ask the class to think of a job for each letter of the alphabet from A to Z. Ask them to prepare a picture of themselves doing the job and a short presentation to explain to the rest of the class what they do. Research skills using reference books would be a help in this activity. Choose children to present their jobs to the class during the rest of the topic.

Summary | 5min |

With the children's help, sort their pictures of imagined jobs into three groups: manufacturing, sales and service. The pictures could be displayed with titles such as 'I make things', 'I sell things' and 'I help people'. The job titles can be displayed in sets.

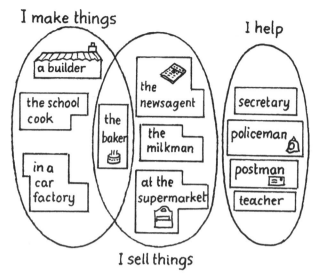

Manufacturing, sales and services jobs displayed in sets

Extra activities ① ② ③

Uniforms

Investigate some of the jobs that require uniforms. Start with the school crossing patrol. Why wear a white coat? What are reflective stripes for? Why would the person need to be easily noticed? Collect paintings of people in uniform doing their jobs.

A to Z of jobs

Make an alphabet book of jobs. Let children add a job to any letter of the alphabet. Ask for particular information, e.g. 'Where is this job done?' 'What do people need to do this job?' 'Do they wear a uniform?' Each page of the book could contain a picture and the answers to the questions. Each job could be titled with a fictitious name, e.g. Mr *Pipe the Plumber*, etc.

Volunteers

The children may know people who do voluntary work. Parents may come to school to help in the classroom, volunteers may deliver meals on wheels, run youth clubs and scouting groups, and man lifeboats. Your class may be able to suggest some work they could do to help others in the community.

Job charades

Give a child a picture of someone doing a job. Ask them to act out part of the job. Working in groups, the children can each ask one question about the job. Then they can try to guess what the job is.

45

The caretaker

The caretaker cleans the school.

He uses these.

There are different jobs to do at different times.

He has a bunch of keys.

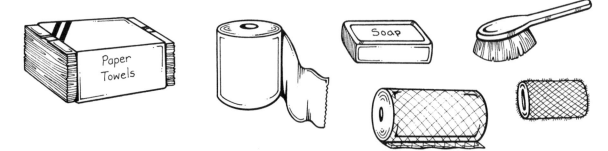

The caretaker keeps a stock of things the school needs.

People at work

The name of the place of work is _____.

How many people work here? _____

What jobs do the people do?

_____

_____

What type of workplace is it? _____

Draw one of the people at work. Show what they do.

The Royal Mail

Learning targets

On completion of this unit children should understand that:

1 ➤➤ some jobs provide a service which helps us
2 ➤➤ our address enables people to find us
3 ➤➤ a network of people are involved in the postal service.

Before you start

Background knowledge

The Royal Mail is responsible for the collection, sorting and delivery of letters and packets throughout the UK as well as abroad. Every day, mail is collected from over 120,000 points and delivered to 24.5 million addresses. Machines have been introduced to turn envelopes to face the same way, cancel stamps and sort first from second class mail. Machines also add the postcode in machine readable form. With the continuing emphasis on machine sorting, use of the 120 postcode areas is essential for a fast service. Other work relating to addresses, postboxes and street deliveries can be found in Section 2 unit 1 (*see* page 31), Section 7 unit 1 (*see* page 101) and Section 9 unit 5 (*see* page 153).

Teaching points

A network of jobs can provide a service in the community. The postman and the postbox represent only the public face of a huge organisation.

Geographical skills

- Fieldwork observation
- Making a map

Vocabulary

collection, sorting, delivery, mail, postcode, frank

Resources for Lesson 1

Letters to post, Copymaster 17 The postbox, fieldwork paper, camera

Resources for Lesson 2

Used envelopes, equal size boxes, e.g. shoe boxes, Copymaster 18 The sorting office, glue

Resources for Lesson 3

Stories about delivering post, e.g. Hedderwick, Mairi *Katie Morag Delivers the Mail*, Red Fox, 1994; Ahlberg, Janet and Alan *The Jolly Postman*, Heinemann, 1986; Cunliffe, John *Postman Pat* Hodder and Stoughton, 1998; satchel, envelopes.

Resources for the activities

Stamps, self-adhesive film, card, reference material from Royal Mail Education telephone 01795 426465, luggage labels

Assessment indicators

- Do the children know the sequence of events or stages in the postal service?
- Can they address a letter?
- Can they read information on a postbox?

Teaching the lessons

Lesson 1

Introduction
10min

 Start with a poem.

The sky is blue
The grass is green
Elephants are grey
But have you seen
A pillar box, all round and fat?
My favourite colour's the same as that
It's RED.

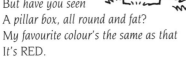

Find out who knows what a pillar box is. Where is the nearest one? Who uses it?

The postbox
30min

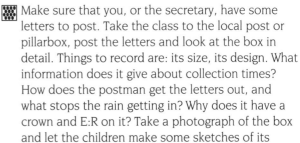 Make sure that you, or the secretary, have some letters to post. Take the class to the local post or pillarbox, post the letters and look at the box in detail. Things to record are: its size, its design. What information does it give about collection times? How does the postman get the letters out, and what stops the rain getting in? Why does it have a crown and E:R on it? Take a photograph of the box and let the children make some sketches of its design. You can use **Copymaster 17 The postbox** either on the visit or in a follow up lesson once the children have collected the information on rough fieldwork paper.

Summary
 `10min`

Give the children an opportunity to tidy up and finish their fieldwork sheets while the information is still fresh in their minds. Early finishers can learn and repeat the poem or illustrate the poem with a grey elephant posting a letter.

Lesson 2

Introduction
`10min`

Bring in a large bag of used envelopes (the school secretary will collect plenty over a few weeks). Put a number from 1 to 12 on about twenty of them. Take out one at a time and read aloud an imaginary address. Keep bringing them out giving a different number in the same street, and then some numbers which are the same. Act the part of a confused postman who cannot cope with the jumble of houses. Ask the children for suggestions on how to sort the letters so the postman can deliver them. Try out one of their ideas to see if it works.

Sorting the mail
`40min`

 Supply each group with a set of equal size boxes. Use boxes such as shoe boxes or tea bag boxes. Give each group **Copymaster 18 The sorting office** to use as a resource to help them make one section of a sorting office rack. The boxes will need to be stuck together and each partition labelled with a range of house numbers, e.g. 1–5. The top or side of the sorting rack should be labelled with the name of the road.

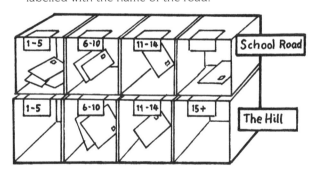

Sorting racks

Children can take it in turns to sort the bag of used envelopes that have now been numbered into the sorting rack. Once sorted, the bunch of envelopes can be removed and ordered into numerical sequence.

Summary
`10min`

Arrange the children into a 'street' and ask someone to become the postman and deliver the sorted mail. The sorting racks can be used to reinforce maths work: labelling them for odds and evens, times tables and number matching activities.

Lesson 3

Introduction
`15min`

Read a story about delivering the mail. Three which would be suitable are *Katie Morag Delivers the Mail* by

Mairi Hedderwick, any Postman Pat story, and *The Jolly Postman* by Janet and Alan Ahlberg. Talk about all the types of mail that a postman delivers. Mention letters, bills, bank statements, invitations, birthday cards, photographs and adverts.

Delivering the mail
`45min`

Ask each child to produce an item that the postman can deliver – a letter, a greetings card, an advert or a bill, etc. Each child puts their mail in an envelope and addresses it to their home address.

Provide a mailbag (an old satchel or shoulder bag) to keep the 'mail' in. The full bag can be hung in the classroom and children can read any of the letters during free reading time.

Alternatively, the contents of the envelopes can be swapped and a child can deliver the letters around the class. Other delivery activities based on number sequencing can be found in Section 2 Unit 1 (*see* page 31).

Summary
`5min`

Ask one or two children to read out the address from the envelope or the letter it contains.

Extra activities

Send a postcard

Design and make a postcard to send home. Post the mail and record how long each card took to arrive.

Stamps

Mount collections of 4–6 stamps from one country on card and cover with self-adhesive film. Make sure each group has one collection to work on. Ask the group to mark the country on a world map. Make a set of enquiry questions to suit the stamps, e.g. 'Which country?' 'What currency?' 'What do the stamps tell you about the country?' Look for answers which include mention of wildlife, buildings, sports, famous people, etc.

Flow diagram

Ask the children to make a sequence picture of what happens to a letter from posting to delivery.

Address reinforcement

Keep returning to activities which involve children in writing their address.

1 Ask them to draw a poster about a missing dog and put their address on the poster.

2 Children can write their address on a label and attach it to a balloon. The label also needs a note requesting the finder to return the label and say where the balloon was found. Let the balloons go. Does anyone get their label back?

3 Children can design and make a label for their school bag.

49

Here is one sort of postbox. If you see a different type, draw it on the other side of this paper.

Fill in the postbox with the things you can see.

Write two of the collection times on the clocks below.

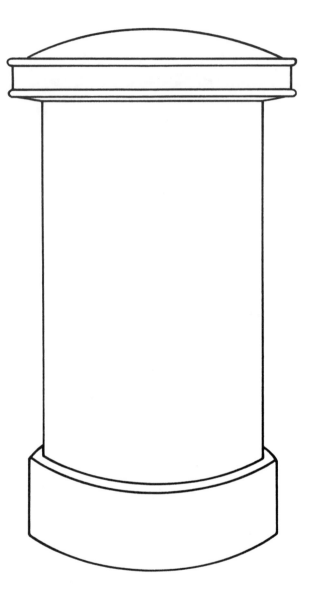

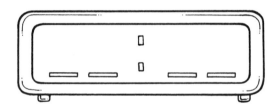

Draw the Queen's crown here.

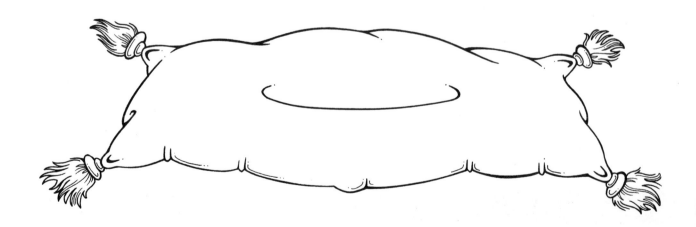

The sorting office

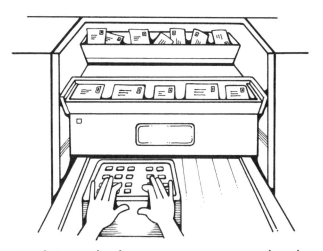

Machines help postmen sort the letters.

Letters travel by:

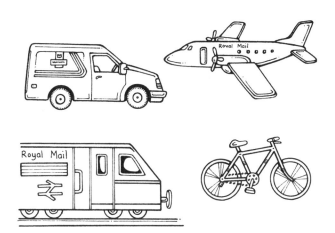

Your postman sorts his round into streets and numbers.

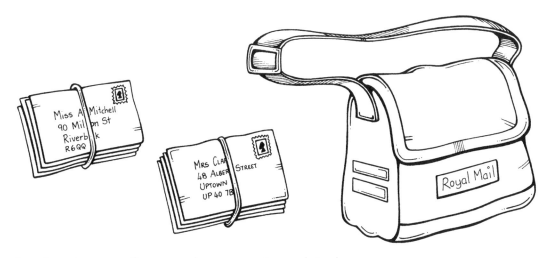

He packs the letters for each street into his bag.

Making things

Learning targets

On completion of this unit children should understand that:

1 ➤➤ different jobs need different skills
2 ➤➤ we change things in the making process
3 ➤➤ they can make things.

Before you start

Background knowledge

Out of the vast number of things which are manufactured, this unit deals with a basic food (bread) and two products (tiles and furniture) which are made from natural origins, wood and clay. Pages 59–61 in Section 4 on Food and farms explore the process of jam making and other recipes appear in Section 10 on pages 160 and 177.

Bread is a basic food made from wheat. The sequence of processes are: threshing to separate stalks and chaff, milling and baking. The simple recipe shows the change from flour to bread as a result of mixing and cooking. This particular bread should be eaten on the day it is made as it does not keep well.

Tiles are made from clay which is dug from the ground in particular areas. The tiles are cut and fired in a kiln. Then they are glazed and fired again. Hand painted tiles are finished in studios.

Wood is felled, sawn and seasoned. Furniture makers turn, join and wax their products.

Associated trades are miller, baker, carpenter, cabinet maker, potter and artist.

Teaching points

Children will make and discover for themselves the processes involved in some jobs.

Geographical skills

• Answering geographical questions

Vocabulary

miller, baker, carpenter, potter, wheat, clay

Resources for Lesson 1

Lightweight white paper, brown wax crayons, wooden fence panel, Copymaster 19 Made from wood, display items

Resources for Lesson 2

Copymaster 20 A loaf of bread, butter, self-raising flour, salt, water, mixing bowl, measuring spoons, wooden spoon, measuring jug, board, knife, baking tray, rack

Resources for Lesson 3

Wet clay, fired tile or terracotta pot, newspaper or board, pottery items for display

Resources for the activities

Pictures of manufactured products from magazines, baker's shop outline

Assessment indicators

• Can children recognise the materials which are used to make things?
• Can they explain a simple manufacturing process?
• Can they sequence the stages in making something?

Teaching the lessons

Lesson 1 ②

Introduction [10min]

Use a small section from a fence panel to show children how to make a wood rubbing. These panels usually have knots and are rough enough to get a good grain pattern. Use thick brown wax crayons and lightweight white paper. Ask each group where they have seen patterns like this and which items they know about that are made from wood.

Made of wood [30min]

Children can make their own rubbings using the fence panel section to create a page of patterned wood grain. The rubbing can be cut up to create a class collage of a pine dresser.

A display of wooden items showing grain and knots, or logs showing annual rings and pictures of wooden furniture will help in this lesson. By circling things that can be wooden on **Copymaster 19 Made from wood,** the children will notice some of the characteristics of wood.

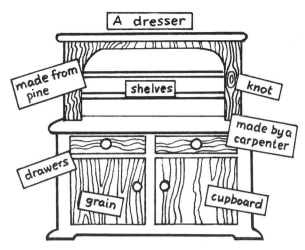

Pine dresser collage

Summary `5 min`

 Give children labels (e.g. grain, knots, shelves, made from pine, drawers, doors, made by a carpenter) to place around the finished dresser.

Lesson 2 ① ② ③

Introduction `10 min`

 The simple bread recipe on **Copymaster 20 A loaf of bread** is used an example of changing raw materials in a manufacturing process. Organise hand washing and divide the tasks on the copymaster between the groups of children.

A loaf of bread `40 min`

While the children or pairs are not involved in the breadmaking process, they can use the copymaster to make their own process or flow diagram to show each stage of the breadmaking. When they reach their job they should circle it in red. They should create a space at the end of their work entitled 'It tastes...' to fill in when the bread has cooled and been cut up for tasting.

Summary `15 min`

Some time later when the bread is baked and cooled, children can taste it and record their verdict at the end of their piece of work.

Lesson 3 ① ② ③

Introduction `10 min`

Show the children some clay (either straight from the ground or potter's clay from an art supplier) and a clay roof tile or terracotta pot. Ask them to 'Spot the difference'. Children can touch them, smell them, hold them. Look for answers which include: soft and hard, wet and dry, heavy and light.

Made of clay `30 min`

 Give each group a lump of wet clay. Ask them to roll it out on a board or on newspaper and cut it to make

a tile. Can they suggest ways of making it dry and hard like the other one? Different groups could try putting their tiles in different places to dry them – in the sun, on a radiator, or ask someone with a kiln to fire it (e.g. a larger school in the area). Can they say what the tile needs in order to be dry and hard? Make a 'Spot the Difference' sheet for the children to fill in. Differentiate by adding a process line with the missing heat source picture for them to fill in, and a 'What happened?' and 'Why?' section to record the results of their investigation.

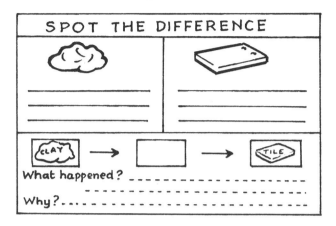

Spot the difference

Summary `10 min`

Several days later, make a display of wet clay and items made from clay. Make two labels: 'The potter uses clay', and 'The potter makes these'. Look at the clay tiles the children made. Ask where the water went and what has speeded up the drying process.

Extra activities ① ② ③

Matching games

Cut out pictures from magazines of products such as bread, furniture, a house, painting. Make job labels to match the items: baker, carpenter, builder, artist, etc. Ask the children to match the job to the manufactured item.

The baker's shop

Make an outline picture of a baker's shop (*see* pages 107 and 163). Include features with different materials: clay tiles and bricks, wooden door, glass windows, plastic gutters and so on. Ask the children to draw the baker in the doorway with a sack of flour. Give them a list of labels for the materials.

Jobs survey

Ask each child to bring in up to three jobs and type of industry of members of their family, friends and neighbours. This should produce a good range across the three categories of manufacturing, selling and service industries. Chart the results.

19 | Made from wood

Wood comes from_____.

Count the rings in a knot of wood to tell how old the branch was.

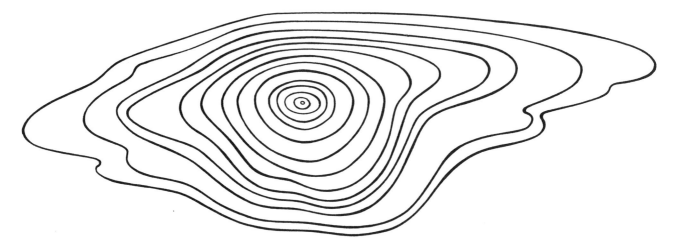

Circle the wooden things.

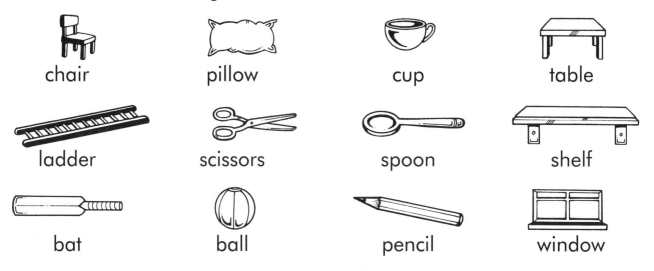

chair   pillow   cup   table

ladder   scissors   spoon   shelf

bat   ball   pencil   window

Think about the things that are made from wood.

Write down three things that describe what wood is like.

_____

_____

_____

A loaf of bread

You will need:

- 500 gms self-raising flour
- 1½ level teaspoonfuls salt
- ½ pint and 2 tablespoons water
- a baking tray
- butter.

1 Set the oven at 210°C.

2 Grease the tray.

3 Mix flour and salt.

4 Make a well in the flour. Add water and mix.

5 Knead lightly on a board with some flour

6 Shape into a round.

7 Place on a tray. Make cuts on the top.

8 Bake for 30 minutes.

9 Cool.

10 Cut and taste.

FOOD AND FARMS

Focus

Using some simple ideas to introduce this geographical theme to young children, this section looks at food products, land use and farming diversity. The work on food would link well with science or food technology. The farm study is a real farm and begins to introduce farming as a business and a place of work. As stories, rhymes and songs are a good medium for helping young children to understand the world outside their own experience, some have been incorporated in this section, linking geography with language and music.

Content

Unit 1:   Food we eat
Unit 2:   A farm study
Unit 3:   A farm story

Source material

To find Manor Farm on a map, try OS Pathfinder Series, sheet TQ 84/94 Headcorn and Charing.

Hutchins, Pat *Rosie's Walk*, Bodley Head, 1970

A local craft shop or Adult Education Centre can often put you in touch with a weaver who may start your class off on some wool spinning and weaving activities.

If you live near a sheepfarming area, fences and hedges often provide pulled pieces of fleece for children to examine in it's natural state.

The National Farmer's Union will put you in touch with source material on a variety of farming subjects.

Brainstorm

This brainstorm covers the lessons in Section 4 and can be added to for a cross-curricular topic.

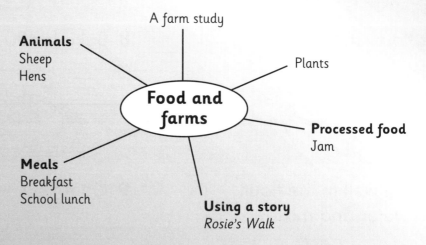

Animals
Sheep
Hens

A farm study

Plants

Food and farms

Processed food
Jam

Meals
Breakfast
School lunch

Using a story
Rosie's Walk

Teaching plan

This can be used as a medium-term plan and provides a scheme of work for a topic on food and farms.

Enquiry questions	Learning targets	Pupil activities
1 Where does our food come from?	Our food comes from plants and animals and can be factory processed.	Matching food to its origins: Unit 1 Lessons 1 and 2.
2 What's in a meal?	Meals are a balance of different foods taken together.	Making meals: Unit 1 Lessons 1 and 3.
3 What are farms like?	Farms are large areas of land, with buildings and fields used for a variety of crops and animals.	Farm maps: Unit 2 Lesson 1, Unit 3 Lesson 1.
4 What work goes on in a farm?	Farmers work to grow crops, care for animals, using their land to earn a living.	Seasonal mobile: Unit 2 Lesson 2, using the land: Unit 2 Lesson 3, keeping animals: Unit 2 Lesson 2, Unit 3 Lesson 2.
5 What dangers are found on farms?	Machinery and tools can make a farmyard a dangerous place.	Dangers on the farm: Unit 3 Lessons 1 and 3.

National Curriculum coverage

Unit 1 Food we eat

National Curriculum links
- Show an awareness of places beyond their locality.
- Locate places on a map of the UK.

Unit 2 A farm study

National Curriculum links
- Use a large scale map of a small area.
- Obtain information from secondary sources.
- Use geographical terms.

Unit 3 A farm story

National Curriculum links
- Make a map of an imaginary place.
- Localities (farms) may be similar and have differences.

Scotland Environment Studies coverage

The units cover the following contexts and content for Understanding People and Places:

- Things we use and eat which come from distant places.
- Major physical and natural features in the locality.
- The uses of buildings and land in the local area.

UNIT 1 | Food we eat

Learning targets

On completion of this unit children should understand that:

1 ➡➡ food comes from plants and animals
2 ➡➡ some food is a mixture of things and is processed in factories
3 ➡➡ a meal contains a balance of different foods.

Before you start

Background knowledge

This section introduces farming plants and animals as the first stage of all food production, and gives children an opportunity to discover the types of food available and how we mix them for a balanced meal.

- Carbohydrates (sugars and starches) are our main source of energy.

- Proteins, mainly meat, cheese, cereals and pulses are body builders.

- Minerals and vitamins, many of which are in fruit and vegetables, have many functions for healthy living.

- Water is another essential.

The lesson about jam can link with other lessons on fruit on pages 159 and 161. The French breakfast in Lesson 3 can be used with Section 10 Unit 2 on Chinon (*see* pages 162–5).

Teaching points

We eat a variety of foods that are fresh or processed, and that come from plants and animals. You may have vegetarians or children with certain food allergies who need sensitive teaching during this unit.

Geographical skills

- Knowledge of the world beyond the locality
- Atlas skills

Vocabulary

farm, field, fruit, animal, plant, meal, factory

Resources for Lesson 1

Copymaster 21 On your plate, pencils, pens

Resources for Lesson 2

Copymaster 22 Making jam, paper, felt-tip pens, jug of water, sugar, bowl of fruit

Resources for Lesson 3

Paper, felt-tip pens, baguettes, jam, orange juice, hot chocolate, serviettes

Resources for the activities

The Little Red Hen, Ladybird Books; jam jar labels, large map of the UK, selection of different vegetables, cocktail sticks

Assessment indicators

- Can the children recognise their food as having animal and plant origins?
- Do they know that some foods are a mixture of ingredients?
- Can they design a meal with a balance of different foods?

Teaching the lessons

Lesson 1   ① ③

Introduction   10 min

After lunch talk to the class about the meals they ate. Show them a drawing on a paper plate of the school meal for that day. Discuss where the meal was cooked and where each item came from. Trace the origin of the food back through shops, to markets and farms. Can they trace it back as far as the field on a farm?

On your plate   40 min

The children need to colour and match the foods on

Copymaster 21 On your plate with their original plant or animal. Able writers can add labels to name each food and plant. They have an opportunity to create their own meal and show its origins. Differentiate the activity in the following ways.

1 Ask children to add clocks to show when they would eat each meal.

2 They can make graphs of lunchbox contents to show types of food included.

3 Link the activity with art to create 3D plates of food with art materials and dried foods such as peas, beans, seeds and pasta.

Summary 5min

Have a 'quick quiz' called 'Where does it come from?' Call out a food, e.g. cheese, and ask a particular child 'Where does it come from?' If the child answers correctly, he or she can do the next one, choosing a food and a person. If the answer is wrong or the child does not know the answer, the teacher becomes quiz master again.

Lesson 2 ②

Introduction 5min

Display a jug of water, a bag of sugar and a bowl of fruit. Ask for ideas on how the three things could be mixed together to make something else. Ask if children know how the three items can be changed into jam. (Through the use of heat.)

Making jam 30min

Using **Copymaster 22 Making jam**, children can cut out the stages in the jam-making process, or use them as a resource to make a flow line. This can be presented as a concertina book in the shape of a jam jar.

Children can fill in and label the empty jar on Copymaster 22 with their own design.

Differentiate for very young children by cutting out a large jam jar shape and asking them to draw or cut out fruit pictures to stick on the shape with sprinkles of sugar and some coloured paper for water drops.

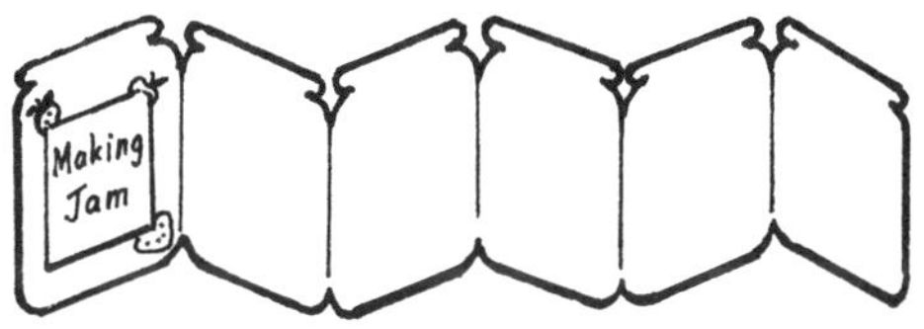

A concertina book

Summary 5min

Have a class brainstorm on all the things jam is used for and eaten with.

Lesson 3 ③

Introduction 10min

Talk about the variety of things children in the class have for breakfast and compare it with the meal of bread, jam, orange juice and hot chocolate a French child normally has. Explain that bread is made from wheat which is a cereal, so it is similar to the breakfast cereals we eat in this country. The French children have their milk in their hot chocolate drink, the orange juice has vitamins for good health. The sugar in the jam gives energy. Can they say where each of these items comes from? Is it a fruit, a cereal or a dairy product?

A French breakfast 30min

The task is to design a breakfast menu for a French café. The menu should be full of pictures to show each item in the meal. If possible, turn this into a practical event, producing baguettes, jam, juice and hot chocolate for a class breakfast. Plates are not used at breakfast in France; bread is just put onto a paper serviette on the table. Hot drinks are served in bowls without handles.

Summary 5min

Talk about each item on the menu and its origins. Can children work out why we have a mixture of foods at one meal? Talk about the fact that a mixture of foods are needed to keep us healthy.

Extra activities ① ② ③

Meals without meat

Make a list of food types (excluding meat) under the headings: Fruit and vegetable, Cereal products, Dairy products. Ask groups to make a packed lunch menu which includes one food from each category.

The Little Red Hen

Read or tell the story of *The Little Red Hen*. Use the sequence of breadmaking in the story for children to make their own picture story about breadmaking. Include growing wheat, harvesting it, milling it into flour, making bread dough and baking. Food shapes can make interesting looking books. The children's own books can be shaped like a loaf of bread.

Jam labels

Ask children to bring in jam jar labels and make a display around a map of the UK. Link places of manufacture with their labels. Traditionally jam factories are near fruit growing areas. Able children may be able to use an atlas index to find places.

Vegetable sculpture

Children can design a vege-person by building vegetables onto each other with cocktail sticks to make a model. A group of them make a colourful display for a harvest theme.

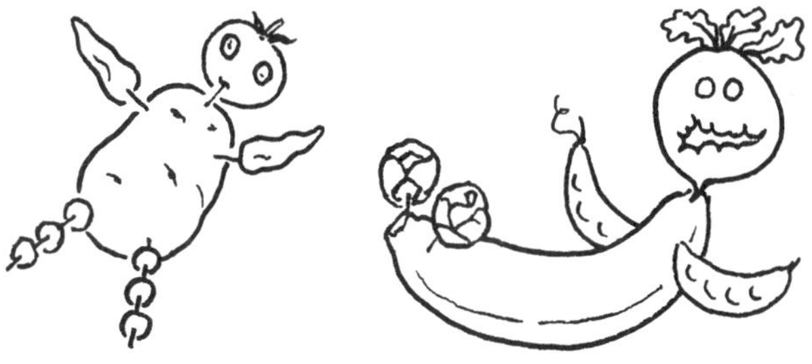

Vegetable sculptures

On your plate

Colour the food on the plate. Join each food to the correct picture around the plate. Colour the picture a matching colour.

Now you can do a plate of food in the same way.

The boxes show how jam is made.

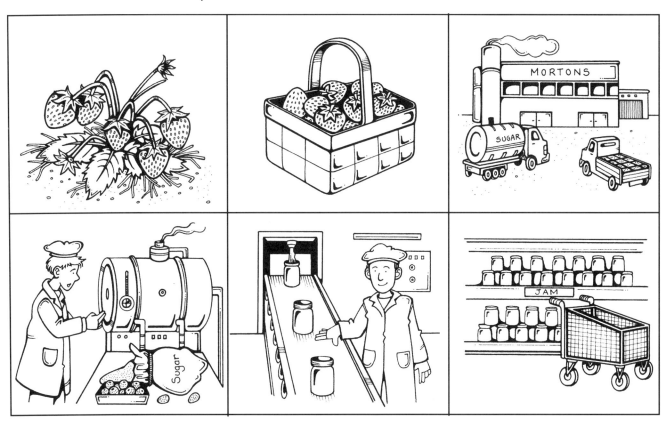

The label tells you about the jam.

This jar is waiting to be filled and labelled.

A farm study

Learning targets

On completion of this unit children should understand that:
1 ➡ farms are places of work
2 ➡ farmland and buildings have a variety of uses
3 ➡ maps are a source of information.

Before you start

Background knowledge

Lester Gosbee is the farmer at Manor Farm, Frittenden, Kent. His farm was originally a hop garden and apple orchard but, like most of the other farmers in the area, Lester has changed to sheep rearing as a more reliable source of income. An old orchard and a small block of hop-pickers huts, however, remain as evidence of past farming practices. Lester runs the farm with his sister. They share a sheep dip with neighbouring farmers. Travelling shearers visit at shearing time. His local market is at Ashford, about 12 miles away. In recent years he has diversified by building stables and letting them out, with grazing, to local horse owners and he has opened one field to members of the caravan club.

More information about Frittenden can be found in Section 9 (*see* pages 140–147).

Teaching points

Farms are places of work, with a seasonal pattern of jobs. Point out how the farmer allocates land for different uses, and follow one farm animal's yearly calendar to learn about seasonal changes.

Geographical skills
● Using maps and following a route
● Using geographical vocabulary

Vocabulary
farm, field, boundary, market, fleece, shearer

Resources for Lesson 1
UK map, Copymaster 23 Manor Farm, pens

Resources for Lesson 2
Paper, paints, felt-tip pens, glue

Resources for Lesson 3
Wilberforce Goes on a Picnic by Margaret Gordon; Copymaster 24 Farm talk, pencils

Resources for the activities
Paper, pens, black felt-tip

Assessment indicators
● Do the children know that farm work changes with the seasons?
● Can they name jobs done on a farm?
● Can they find out information from a map?

Teaching the lessons

Lesson 1 ② ③

Introduction

Introduce the farmer, Mr Gosbee and point out where Kent is on a large map of the UK. Frittenden is a small village, 10 miles south of Maidstone. (See map in Section 9 page 142.) Discuss the ways this area may be different from where your school is. Explain that one of Mr Gosbee's jobs is to walk around the farm each day to check that the gates are closed and that the animals are safe.

Manor Farm 30min

Using **Copymaster 23 Manor Farm**, choose one of the following tasks to suit ability of your class.

1 Draw a line on the map to show Mr Gosbee's route from the farm house to check the fields where animals are kept.
2 Draw a graph to show how many fields are used for a) sheep, b) hay, c) horses, d) grass, e) caravans, f) woodland.
3 Colour each field to show what it is used for and make a colour key.

Summary 5min

Talk about the parts of the farm which are still natural: the woodland and the large lake. Some locals fish in the lake, and swans nest there. The wood is full of bluebells in the spring. Do the children know why Mr Gosbee leaves these areas as they are, instead of using all the land for farming?

(Because he likes to encourage wildlife which are part of the ecosystems on the farm and to make the farm a pleasant place to be.)

Lesson 2

Introduction | 10 min |

Discuss the jobs Mr Gosbee does with his sheep. Try to divide them into the four seasons or at least get them into a sequential order. (Sheep farmers in different parts of the country work differently, depending on the breed of sheep and the weather.)

A year with sheep | 40 min |

Split the children into five groups: one for each season and one to make the background. Each group should prepare pictures of work with the sheep during their season. Associated pictures of tools, products, and weather symbols can also be drawn. When a group has finished they can build up a collage of seasonal activity on the master background of fields, hedges and trees.

Spring: lambing, lambs are marked with colour for identification

Summer: dipping to kill parasites in the wool, hooves are trimmed

Autumn: dipping, sheep are sold at market

Winter: sheep are kept in barns and shorn

Summary | 10 min |

Ask each group to tell the rest of the class about the season they have been working on.

Lesson 3 ②

Introduction | 10 min |

Read the story *Wilberforce Goes on a Picnic* by Margaret Gordon. Ask the children why Wilberforce likes it in the countryside? Explain that Mr Gosbee needed to find new ways to earn money from his farm so he found some people who like to be in the countryside but do not live on farms. He built stables for their horses and prepared a field for their caravans.

Changes at the farm | 30 min |

Each child in a group decides to take the part of one of the people on **Copymaster 24 Farm talk**. They make up a conversation about the farm and why they like spending their time there. The speech bubbles can be filled in with sentences typed on a computer and cut out. For a wall display, enlarge the speech bubbles and mount them around pictures of faces looking over a farm gate.

Differentiate by giving able children the task to do on their own, or introduce another visitor to the farm such as a fisherman or a birdwatcher.

Summary | 5 min |

Ask each child in each group if they would like to visit the farm and what would they be most interested to see.

Extra activities ① ②

Inputs and outputs

Mr Gosbee spends money on things for the farm. These inputs include winter food for sheep, chemicals for dipping, wages for shearers, building materials for stables and fence repairs, fuel for tractors, food for sheepdogs. He receives money for fleeces, sheep sold at market, caravan site rents, stable rents and apples sold at the gate. These are his outputs. Show this pictorially around a picture of a farm with arrows in and out.

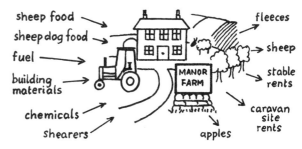

Inputs and outputs

A flock of sheep

Make a simple template of a sheep. Each child writes inside a sheep, a word, phrase or sentence about sheep on a farm. Outline each sheep with a black felt pen and glue them just overlapping to make a flock. Refer to the flock from time to time, asking individuals to read one of the pieces of writing.

The shepherd

Write a job advert for a shepherd. Think about the jobs he will have to do, and the sort of person that job would suit. As well as asking for particular qualities for the job, ask what the farmer can offer to attract somebody.

Farm visit

Try to visit a farm or a special children's farm so that your class can see animals being cared for in their home surroundings. If this is impossible, contact your nearest branch of the National Farmer's Union or Young Farmers Club. Either of these organisations may be willing to send a farmer to visit the school with a suitable talk and may even bring an animal for the children to see.

Mr Gosbee and his sister are sheep farmers at Manor Farm.

The map shows what each field is used for.
A dotted line shows a public footpath.

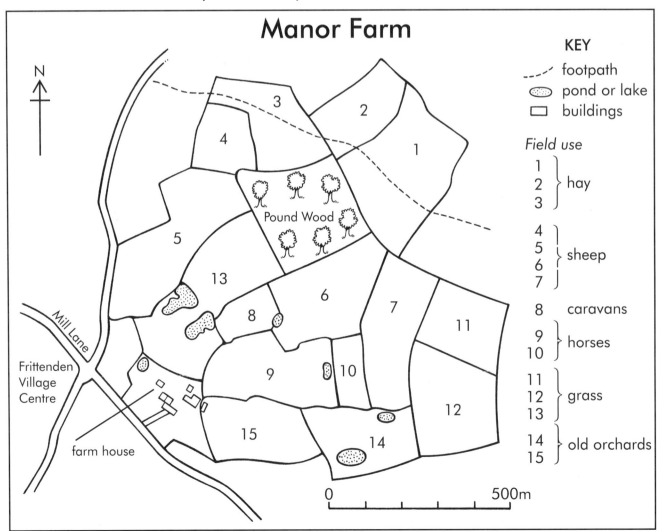

Manor Farm

N

KEY
- ⌇ footpath
- ◯ pond or lake
- ▢ buildings

Field use

1 2 3	hay
4 5 6 7	sheep
8	caravans
9 10	horses
11 12 13	grass
14 15	old orchards

Pound Wood

Mill Lane

Frittenden Village Centre

farm house

0   500m

What do the people in caravans say about the farm?

Mr Gosbee offers a stable for a horse.

These women buy apples at the farm.

UNIT 3 | A farm story

Learning targets

On completion of this unit children should understand that:
1 ➡➡ farms contain buildings which are used for different purposes
2 ➡➡ farm animals need food and shelter
3 ➡➡ there are dangerous places and machinery on farms.

Before you start

Background knowledge

Children often have a romanticised view of farms, unaware that it is one of the most dangerous workplaces and is not a suitable place for children to play unattended. The farm buildings included in *Rosie's Walk* by Pat Hutchins are the henhouse, the barn, beehives and a mill. The hazards which deter the fox from catching the hen include a rake, a broken fence, a haystack and a pond. The observation cards referred to in some lessons can be found on page 90 of Section 6. They include symbols to show the senses we use for observation: hearing, sight, smell and touch.

Teaching points

The amusing story of *Rosie's Walk* is used to highlight the variety of buildings found on farms but also the dangers of this place of work. Each animal has different needs in its environment.

Geographical skills

* Making a map
* Using symbols

Vocabulary

farmyard, barn, henhouse, mill, beehive, danger, shelter

Resources for Lesson 1

Large sheet of paper, felt-tip pens

Resources for Lesson 2

Copymaster 25 The henhouse, felt-tip pens, white, black or brown sugar paper, straw or yellow raffia, glue

Resources for Lesson 3

Copymaster 26 Red for danger, pens and pencils, red felt-tip pens

Resources for the activities

Observation cards, modelling materials, plastic farm animals and farm buildings, boxes, camera, music for Old Macdonald

Assessment indicators

* Do the children know about the different buildings found on farms?
* Can they recognise a dangerous situation from a picture in the book?
* Can they say why the hen needs a special shelter?

Teaching the lessons

Lesson 1 ① ③

Introduction   20 min

▓ Read *Rosie's Walk* to the class. Ask the children to recall the places Rosie passed on her walk. List them in order or attach pictures from the book, in sequential order, to a board. With older children, add the hazard which foils the fox. You should now have a long list of features on Rosie's route with everything in order.

A signpost map   30 min

∴ Sit a group around a large piece of paper. Each child chooses a building and a hazard to draw and cut out. In the centre of the large sheet one child can draw Rosie. The building pictures are glued around the hen,

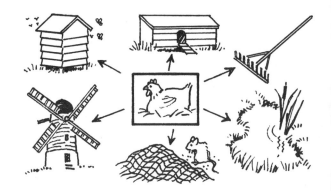

A signpost map

using the master list to help remember the order, with arrows pointing to each one. The hazards and fox can be added to make a more detailed signpost map.

Summary `10min`

▦ Pin the maps up, and ask children to suggest a title for them. Captions or labels could be added to tell what each farm building is used for.

Lesson 2

Introduction `10min`

▦ Use the storybook to show the children a picture of the henhouse. Discuss with them the reasons why Rosie needs a house like this. Ask questions such as 'Why has it got a small door?' 'Why would the farmer want to close the door at night?' 'How would he encourage Rosie to go inside?' 'What does he want the hens to do in the house?'

The henhouse `40min`

👤 Using **Copymaster 25 The henhouse**, children make a dot to dot 'map' of Rosie that can be cut out and embellished with paper feathers and felt comb. Instructions on the sheet explain how to make a nesting box with eggs. Completed nesting boxes can be built up to make a henhouse. Add a paper roof and a small ladder for a wall display.

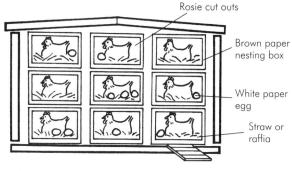

Rosie cut outs
Brown paper nesting box
White paper egg
Straw or raffia

A henhouse

Summary `5min`

▦ Can the children see why the farmer likes to have all his hens together in one safe place?

Lesson 3

Introduction `10min`

▦ Remind the children of the dangers the fox encountered in the farmyard. Ask them if they know any danger signs that are used on our roads. Emphasise that the colour red is used to indicate danger.

Farm dangers `30min`

👤 Children use **Copymaster 26 Red for danger** to find out about the use of the colour red to indicate danger. They are shown some danger signs and given an opportunity to find one for themselves.

Back at the farm, a farmyard scene shows some dangers. The copymaster can be used in different ways.

1 Colour red all the things that could be dangerous.
2 Put red crosses on all the things that are sharp/have engines/are heavy.
3 Make a danger sign to warn people about one of the dangers on the farm.
4 Make danger signs to warn the fox about the hazards on his route.

Summary `5min`

▦ Talk about potential dangers at school. Which things could be dangerous if we did not know how to use them properly?

Extra activities

Observation cards

Use the observation cards from Section 6 page 90 to think about the sounds, sights, and smells on a farm. As you read through the story, hold up a card and ask 'What would Rosie see here?' or 'What would the fox hear by the pond?' The children can record sights, smells and sounds under copies of the symbols on the cards.

Warning device

Rosie is always being followed by the fox. The children can design and make a device to warn Rosie that the fox is following her. Consider the noises the fox might make on different materials as he approaches the henhouse, or a device he trips to make a noise.

A model farm

Use plastic farm animals and buildings made from boxes to set out a farm for Rosie. Plan which buildings need to be close together and which can be further from the farm centre. Simple maps can be made of the models by setting the farm out on paper and drawing around each building. Take photos of the models from above to get a plan view. Remove the buildings and colour code or label each farm building. New walks for Rosie can be drawn out on the maps with arrows showing the direction she takes.

Old Macdonald

Use this well-known song to teach and reinforce knowledge of farm animals. At the end of the song, check whether the children know which homes the animals live in and what food the farmer gives them to eat. A signpost map, similar to Rosie's in Lesson 1 could be made with Old Macdonald in the middle and his animals around him.

The henhouse

Rosie is a hen. Start at number 1 and join the dots to make a hen. Cut out some brown and white feathers and a red comb and glue them on.

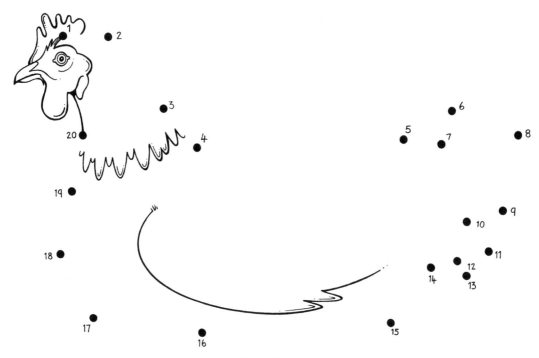

Make a nesting box for Rosie the hen.

1 Place Rosie on a piece of black paper. Don't glue her yet.

2 Cut some strips of brown paper and glue around Rosie to make a box.

3 Cut out an egg shape from white paper and tuck it under Rosie.

4 Glue some straw around the egg. Now glue Rosie and her egg in place.

26 | Red for danger

Colour this word **red**.

Red is a bright colour. It makes us notice things.

Why are these things **red**?

a post box **a fire extinguisher** **a rose**

the top of a tap **a traffic cone** **a road sign**

There are many things that could be dangerous in the farmyard. How many can you see?

JOURNEYS

Focus

Journeys include routes, reasons for travelling and forms of transport used. This section explores reasons for journeys by looking at animal movements around the school grounds. It considers local journeys and modes of transport by following a Teddy Bear's adventures. Direction of travel, and giving and following directions is developed in classroom activities by using directional vocabulary, such as 'left', 'right', 'turn', 'forwards' and 'ahead'. These directional lessons can be linked to PE and IT. Lessons on journeys occur in other sections, e.g.:

- journey of a letter (Section 3 Unit 2 pages 48–51)
- a postman's delivery journey (Section 2 Unit 1 page 31)
- a village trail Section 9 (Unit 2 page 142)
- going shopping Section 7 (Unit 2 pages 106–7).

Content

Unit 1: Animals
Unit 2: A bear's journey
Unit 3: Our journeys

Source material

The RSPB produce a wealth of educational materials for use in schools as well as lending films and videos. For a complete list, send a stamped addressed envelope to RSPB Educational Dept.,The Lodge, Sandy, Beds SG19 2DL.

Brainstorm

This brainstorm covers the lessons in Section 5 and can be added to for a cross-curricular topic.

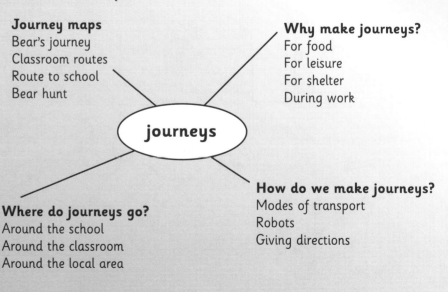

Journey maps
Bear's journey
Classroom routes
Route to school
Bear hunt

Why make journeys?
For food
For leisure
For shelter
During work

journeys

Where do journeys go?
Around the school
Around the classroom
Around the local area

How do we make journeys?
Modes of transport
Robots
Giving directions

Teaching plan

This can be used as a medium-term plan and provides a scheme of work on the geographical aspects of journeys.

Enquiry questions	Learning targets	Pupil activities
1 Why do we make journeys?	Journeys are made to obtain food, shelter, work and leisure.	Observe animals' reasons for journeys: Unit 1 all lessons; trace weekend journeys: Unit 2 Lessons 2 and 3.
2 What means of transport do we use?	We choose different transport for different journeys.	Record weekend modes of transport: Unit 2 Lessons 2 and 3.
3 How can we record journey routes?	Maps show routes of journeys.	School ground maps: Unit 1 Lesson 1; local area visit/maps: Unit 2 Lesson 3; robot and classroom journey/maps: Unit 3 Lessons 2 and 3.
4 Where do journeys take us?	Journeys take us from one place to another.	Animal observations: Unit 1 Lesson 1; bear hunt song: Unit 2 Lesson 1; robot routes: Unit 3 all lessons.

National Curriculum coverage

Unit 1 Animals

National Curriculum links
- Making real and imaginary maps.
- Fieldwork in the locality.

Unit 2 A bear's journey

National Curriculum links
- Use of local maps.
- Knowledge of the UK map.
- Ability to make a simple imaginary map.

Unit 3 Our journeys

National Curriculum links
- Can plan a short route and make a map.
- Use of geographical vocabulary.
- Practical activities in the school grounds.

Scotland Environment Studies coverage

The units cover the following contexts and content for Understanding People and Places:
- Kinds of traffic in the area and the need for safety procedures.
- Developing the mental map of familiar places.
- Using plans to find places.

Animal journeys

Learning targets

On completion of this unit children should understand:
1 ➡ that animals make journeys to find food
2 ➡ that animals need to search for shelter
3 ➡ how to make a simple route map.

Before you start

Background knowledge

Most animal journeys are undertaken in the search for food. Survival is the main reason for moving around. Secondary reasons include looking for shelter, escaping from predators, breeding and washing.

To encourage birds to visit the school grounds put up a bird table and provide a shallow bath. Visiting birds often have a circuit of feeding grounds, and if the same bluetit seems to come back every five minutes, it could well be a different one on its own feeding circuit.

Bird bath — Shallow container

Hedgehogs also have a feeding circuit and visit several gardens in their search for food and a place to hibernate.

Snails carry their shelter so their journeys are in search of food and a place to hide from predators. Their slimy trail, which helps them slide along the ground, leaves a route map to show where they have been.

Teaching points

Animals make journeys for food and to keep themselves safe. If you catch small creatures to study put them back where they are safe.

Geographical skills

- Observation in the school grounds
- Simple map making

Vocabulary

move, visit, search, food, shelter, safe

Resources for Lesson 1

Bird food, container suitable for a bird bath, tray of sand, paper and pencils

Resources for Lesson 2

Copymaster 27 A snail tank, pencils, pens, snails, large plastic container, damp soil, leaves, stones, twigs/branches, snails, muslin cover, black paper, art materials

Resources for Lesson 3

Large photographs of animals, Copymaster 28 Animal journeys, pencils, felt-tip pens

Resources for the activities

Snail, waterproof pen, *Rosie's Walk* by Pat Hutchins, paper, pencils, enquiry cards

Assessment indicators

- Can children watch and record an animal's movements?
- Do they know why the animal makes a journey?
- Can they make a simple route map?

Teaching the lessons

Lesson 1   ① ③

Introduction   [15 min]

Explain to the children about the plan to feed and give water to visiting birds. Take them outside and show them the bird table and bird bath. Put water in the bath and food on the table. If this is a new venture for your school, explain that it may take a day or two for birds to find out that food and water is available. If no bird table is possible, scatter food in a safe place on the ground. If you put it on and around a large tray of smooth sand, birds will leave their tracks behind.

Visits from birds   [30 min]

Position a group of children quietly behind a window where they can see the bird table and bath. Let them watch for five minutes, then change the groups over. During their observation time, ask them to notice where the birds come from, whether they go straight to the table or stop and look around from a safe place first, then where they go afterwards. After their observation time, ask them to draw a plan of the area they could see, and show with arrows and labels one bird's journey.

Differentiate by giving the children identification guides to find the type of birds that visited. Make it simpler by giving a ready drawn plan of the area for the children to put in the route.

Summary [5 min]

Ask the children where they think the birds came from and where they went after they ate the bird food. Check the sand tray for tracks and see if children can tell you in which direction the tracks lead.

Lesson 2

Introduction [5 min]

Explain that snails are living creatures that we want to find out about but not harm. Ask children to handle them as little as possible and only very carefully using a piece of card or a twig. If there is a place in your school grounds where there are snails (under logs, large stones, beneath walls, compost heaps, etc.) gather them with the children.

If you have to bring them inside, keep them in a large plastic box, on damp soil with some food. Use a cover which allows air in. The snails will be all right inside the box for two to three days.

Snail trail [30 min]

Copymaster 27 A snail tank shows a snail tank with all the things a snail needs in its life. Children can use the copymaster in a variety of ways.

1 Children can write labels to explain how the snail uses the items in the tank.
2 Trails can be drawn to show the snail's journeys to find food and water and to return to its shelter.
3 The snail's journeys can be mapped.

Observe a snail closely by placing it gently on a large piece of black paper, and waiting for it to emerge from its shell. Allow it to move across the paper and observe its slimy trail. Link with an art lesson to make a snail trail picture on black paper, with cutout leaves and silver trails made with white paint or glitter.

Summary [5 min]

Take the snails back to where they were found, or return them to the tank and wash hands.

Lesson 3

Introduction [10 min]

Remind children of the reasons for animal journeys: for food, shelter, washing, etc. Use some large

photographs of animals from magazines or books to ask 'Where do you think this animal is going?'

Journey quiz [20 min]

Copymaster 28 Animal journeys assesses whether children know the reasons why animals make journeys. In it's simplest form, the children match the animal to its destination. Activities using Copymaster 28 can be differentiated as follows.

1 Ask the children to cut out the animals and their destinations and pair them up. For each pair they can make a small map which shows the journey made, with the garden or countryside features passed on the way.
2 Children can make a route between the animal and its destination. Along the route they write the reason for the journey.

Summary [5 min]

Using the animal photographs, gather the children and bring together their ideas. What journeys might each animal make? Which journey is the most important? Are journeys different at different times of the year?

Extra activities

The snail returns

Find a snail's shelter in the school grounds. Take the snail out and make a waterproof mark on its shell. Put it down about a metre from its shelter. Leave it until the next day. Check the shelter to see if it has returned. If so, try again, putting it down a little further away. Continue until it no longer returns. How far will a snail go to return to its shelter?

Use a story

Many animal stories tell of creatures' journeys, e.g. *Rosie's Walk* by Pat Hutchins (*see* pages 66–8). Use whichever stories you have to make journey maps and to work out the reasons for each journey. Make a set of enquiry question cards to put inside each journey book you have. Where does the journey start? Why are they going? Where are they going? What is passed on the way? Set this activity as a group discussion.

Pets

Make a sheet about 'My Pet'. Where does it go? Make a map of its daily journey around the house, its walk, or its cage. Children without pets can work with a pet owner. Their questions will help get fuller answers.

Bees and butterflies

Make a colourful flower border with paper flowers. Cut out bees and butterflies which the children colour or paint and attach them to dotted lines that journey from flower to flower.

A snail tank

Everything a snail needs is in this tank.

plants   stones   air   wood   damp soil

The snail leaves a trail when it moves.

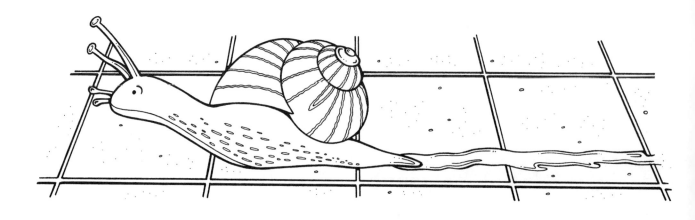

28 | Animal journeys

Where is each creature going?

hedgehog

bee

nest

pile of leaves

rabbit

bird

grass

flower

UNIT 2 A bear's journey

Learning targets

On completion of this unit children should understand that:

1 ➡ journeys go through different landscapes
2 ➡ journeys vary in length and time
3 ➡ journeys go to different destinations.

Before you start

Background knowledge

The bear's journeys are based on the adventures of a school mascot that went to Holland on a school trip. A family from Sweden who were staying in the same Youth Hostel took the bear to Sweden with them, promising to pass him on to other travellers. Each journey he made was written up in a log book in his rucksack, and each traveller sent the children a postcard. The school received cards from about ten countries, and the bear eventually came home by post from Australia with a rucksack full of small souvenirs and a diary full of adventures. This unit suggests some ways of initiating simple journeys with a class bear.

Teaching points

Journeys take you from one place to another. Animals, people and items can all make journeys.

Geographical skills

- Use of enquiry questions to explore places
- Simple imaginary maps
- Use of UK maps

Vocabulary

journey, route, feature, view, travel, transport

Resources for Lesson 1

Teddy bear, sacking, dark paper, felt-tip pens

Resources for Lesson 2

Copymaster 29 Map for a bear, felt-tip pens, teddy bear, small bag for the bear, word processed weekend report slip

Resources for Lesson 3

Copymaster 30 Bear's transport, local map

Resources for the activities

Bond, Michael *Paddington Bear*, address labels, very small bear that will fit in a toy car or truck, toy truck, road track playmat, Copymaster 47 from Section 8 Unit 2

Assessment indicators

- Can the children locate a place on a map?
- Can they draw a simple route map?
- Can they describe geographical features?

Teaching the lessons

Lesson 1 ①

Introduction 5 min

Before the lesson hide a toy bear in a big box covered with sacking or dark paper to resemble a cave. Tell the children that you have lost your bear.

Bear hunting 40 min

Teach them the 'Bear Hunt' song that goes like this, making up actions to go with it.

We're going on a bear hunt,
We're going to catch a big one. [Spread arms wide]
What a beautiful day. [Smile and make a sun shape with hands]

We're not scared. [Shaky voice and shiver]

Uh-uh a lake!
A wide cold lake
We can't go over it. [Shake head, making bridge shape]

We can't go under it. [Shake head, making tunnel with hands]

Oh NO!
We'll have to go through it!
Splish splash [Wade around room]
Splish splash
Splish splash

[Replace the lake with other features]

Long grass, Swish swish...
Snow drift, Stumble, slide...
muddy bank, Squelch, squelch...

Shh... shhh　　　　　　[Arrive at the cave]
What's that?　　　　　　[Tiptoe with finger to lips]
A *wet nose*
A *furry ear*
It's a *bear*!

Make a map to show the bear hunt journey, putting in the features seen on the route.

Summary　　　　　5min

Talk about other features you may come across and whether they would be obstacles to the journey.

Lesson 2

Introduction　　　　　20min

Introduce the bear as the class bear, a class mascot to share and join in class activities. Talk about the bear being at school on its own at weekends when the children are not at school. Someone will probably suggest that somebody should take it home. Mention the idea that the child who takes the bear home could buy a postcard or write the name of the places that they take it, so the class can trace the bear's journeys. Even if the child caring for the bear does not go anywhere significant, the bear will have made a journey to their house or a shop or park.

Weekend bear　　　　　20min

Copymaster 29 Map for a bear gives the children a reason to map their journey from school to their house and shows things the bear will pass on the way. The 'features' tick box encourages observation of their local environment. Discuss the presence of, and need for, these features and help the children to decide how they will show them on their maps. As the bear has a bag to pack, the activity also encourages children to think about what will be needed for a short stay. The bag could include a word processed note that the parents can help to fill in with the names of places visited.

MY WEEKEND

Date: _____

I went to: _____

I saw: _____

_____

Please send me to school on Monday.

Summary　　　　　10min

Decide who will take the bear for the first weekend. Put their name on a calendar to keep a record.

Lesson 3

Introduction　　　　　10min

When the bear comes back from his first weekend away, ask the child who took him home to tell the

class about his journeys: the places the bear went to and what he saw and did. Probe for local visits to shops, things seen, type of transport used and the length of the journey.

Bears get around　　　　　30min

Copymaster 30 Bear's transport shows the types of transport that a bear might use in the local area. Copymaster 30 can be used in various ways.

1　The children can make a diary of the bear's weekend, using the transport pictures to illustrate the journeys made.

2　They can make picture maps of some short and long journeys for the bear, e.g. a walking to the postbox, taking the train to the seaside.

3　After a weekend visit, some transport pictures and the weekend report slip can be displayed around a local map

Summary　　　　　5min

Use the weekend report slips and point to local places on a map. Talk about the best type of transport for different length journeys.

The bear's weekend journeys

Extra activities

This bear is lost

Use a Paddington Bear story by Michael Bond or picture of a bear to discuss the need for a label on bears (or on anything else that is going on a journey). Children design and make a label for the class bear.

Teddy Bears' Picnic

Ask some children to write invitations from your class bear to those bears who own a child in your class. Each child can draw a map so their bear can find its way to the picnic spot. Hold a teddy bears' picnic in the class or school grounds if there are no woods nearby.

Bears on track

Provide a really small bear that will fit in or on a toy vehicle. Children use a road track play mat to send the bear on a journey. Combine with work on direction. Working in pairs, on child can give directions while the other sends the bear on the journey.

Wilberforce

Use Copymaster 47 in Section 8 Unit 2 to trace a journey which starts in a town and ends in the countryside.

Map for a bear

This map shows the way from school to your house.

It shows things you pass on the way.

Tick the features you see on your route

school

home

Bear's transport

by car

walking

on a bus

on a train

by bike

on a boat

Our journeys

Learning targets

On completion of this unit children should understand that:

1 ➡➤ journeys take us from one place to another
2 ➡➤ directional vocabulary helps to describe a route
3 ➡➤ correct directions get us to our destination.

Before you start

Background knowledge

Directional vocabulary is covered in Section 6 pages 86–9. In this unit, however, it can be used to describe journeys and give directions. This topic is a good opportunity to combine geography with IT as the children pretend that they are programmable toys or robots and receive instructions from another child. They will soon see the need for accurate instructions using the correct vocabulary. Once they understand the need for clear instructions they can use one of the range of programmable toys.

Teaching points

The short journeys that each child makes are used to investigate the character and direction of journeys. Remind children that 'left' and 'right' can become confused if people are not facing the same way.

Geographical skills

- Promotes spatial awareness
- Use of directional vocabulary
- Following short routes.

Vocabulary

left, right, straight, turn, ahead, back, stop

Resources for Lesson 1

PE equipment, 'start' and 'finish' posts

Resources for Lesson 2

Copymaster 31 Follow the route, pencils

Resources for Lesson 3

Copymaster 32 Class furniture, classroom plan, various coloured crayons, chinagraph pencils or washable pens

Resources for the activities

Turtle, roamer, simple computer adventure game, pencil, paper, scissors, *Hansel and Gretel*, twigs, pebbles

Assessment indicators

- Can children use left and right correctly?
- Can they give directions?
- Can they follow directions?

Teaching the lessons

Lesson 1 ① ② ③

Introduction 10 min

The lesson can take place in the school hall or playground. Get some equipment ready to set up some obstacles and a start and finish post, not too far apart. Children should change into PE clothes.

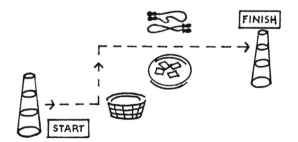

Robots 20 min

After a warm up period of running and changing direction on command, play one or two directional games.

1 Children jog around and run to north, east, south and west corners of the room which can be labelled with initials.
2 Play 'Simon Says', using left and right instructions.
3 Children march around and, on command, turn left or right.
4 Teach them the song and actions of 'You put your left arm in, Your put your left arm out', etc.

Now play robots around the apparatus. Position a child at the start and give instructions as they move, to reach the finish, e.g. 'Take two steps ahead. Stop.

Turn left.' Blindfold the children so that really have to listen to the instructions. Put the children in groups with similar apparatus and let them instruct each other to make a journey.

Summary `10min`

Talk about the vocabulary used to direct someone on their short journey. Which words did the children use? Which were the important words?

Lesson 2

Introduction `5min`

Choose a character that your class knows about, e.g. Wally from the *Where's Wally?* books or Spot the dog and draw a picture of one of them. Hide the character somewhere in the classroom. Several characters can be hidden to allow more children to try the routes. Explain to the children that the character is hiding and you will give instructions to find it.

A classroom journey `30min`

Choose a child and place them in the front or middle of the room. Give them directions to find the character, e.g. 'Walk halfway up the room and turn left. Go ahead until you reach the window and Wally will be under a book on your right.' Repeat the directions until the children get used to listening and remembering. Let other children try the activity.

Children use **Copymaster 31 Follow the route** to follow directions. Using a coloured pencil, they start at Person 1 and trace his journey – forward one square, turn right, forward two squares and where does he arrive? (Corner with sink.) Repeat with Person 2 to arrive at the sink again.

Differentiate by asking children to describe the journey they drew on the copymaster, using directional language to describe where they went.

Summary `5min`

Check that children ended at the correct finishing point (the sink) and ask them questions to check their knowledge of directional vocabulary.

Lesson 3

Introduction `5min`

Look at **Copymaster 32 Class furniture** with the children. Discuss whether you have those features in your classroom. If you have some important features which are not included on the sheet, the children can draw or cut out pictures of them. Sort the children into small groups to make classroom maps to mark journeys on.

My classroom `30min`

Children can cut out or draw classroom features and glue them onto a master sheet to form a class

plan, to include their own desk or table. Each child in the group uses a different colour crayon and marks their journey from their table to the waste paper bin. The children compare lengths of journeys. Who sits closest? Now they draw their journey to another point, say to the bookcase. Again they compare journeys. The teacher can encourage use of directional and distance vocabulary.

Differentiate by giving a classroom plan already made and covered in see-through film to use with chinagraph pencils or washable pens, or marking on a blank plan where to glue features. More able children can make individual plans.

Summary `5min`

Ask the children in each group what they have discovered about the journeys they made in the classroom. How do their journeys compare with other children? Are all journeys the same?

Extra activities

The turtle

Children can trace a route by moving the cursor across the screen. Printouts show the route taken and could be the starting point for a story about a journey.

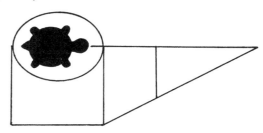

Computer games

Use a simple computer adventure game (e.g. 'Albert's House' or 'Find Spot') to practise directional activities and language. When the children have had their computer time, follow up by asking them to make a map of the journey they made in the game.

Footprints

Children can draw around their shoes and cut out footprints. When a large number of footprints have been made, ask a group of children to use them to show a route, e.g. to the secretary's office to help new children deliver messages, or to make a guessing game where one group sets the trail and followers guess where it goes as they follow the footprints.

Using a story

Hansel and Gretel chose an unsatisfactory way to mark a route. Get children to rewrite the story, or make a cartoon strip, leaving a better trail to follow. Give them some items they may have or might find on the way, e.g. twigs, pebbles, leaves, a handkerchief, a hair ribbon, a shoelace.

Follow the directions to make a classroom journey.

Journey 1

1

2

3

4

5

? _____

Journey 2

Move two squares forward.
Turn right.
Move four squares forward.
Turn left.
Move two squares forward.
Look ahead.

Where are you?

_____

Class furniture

chalkboard

table and chair

sink

bookcase

sand tray

playhouse

cupboard

toybox

SCHOOL GROUNDS

Focus

This section shows ways of studying the local area through three units based on work in the school grounds. Depending on the catchment area of your school, each child's local area may be different. Using the school grounds makes a common area with which both you and the children are familiar. It makes fieldwork frequent and viable without organising transport and disrupting the school day.

As with all place studies, the unit tries to answer enquiry questions that cover the range of human and geographical features normally found in a school and its grounds. Unusual sites may need an extra activity to cover any features not represented in this section.

Content

Unit 1: Direction
Unit 2: Quality
Unit 3: Improvement

Source material

Large scale local maps. Your county council office (usually the Transport and Environment Dept.) has an Ordnance Survey licence and can provide you with copies of your local area in a large scale. Ask for 1:1250 or 1:500.

Compasses

Buy the best quality you can afford. Orienteering compasses are reliable and easy to hold still.

Dried flowers and plant material

Collect seed heads in autumn, dried grasses in summer, driftwood from beaches.

Fir cones can be fixed to wires and bare twigs painted.

Brainstorm

This brainstorm covers the lessons in Section 6 and can be added to for a cross-curricular topic.

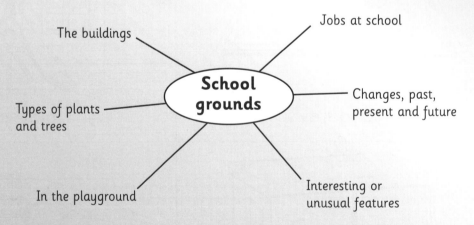

- The buildings
- Jobs at school
- Types of plants and trees
- **School grounds**
- Changes, past, present and future
- In the playground
- Interesting or unusual features

Teaching plan

This can be used as a medium-term plan and provides a scheme of work on a study of the local area.

Enquiry questions	Learning targets	Pupil activities
1 What are the school grounds like?	Children will know the main geographical features of the school.	Sketching school views: Unit 1 Lesson 3; observation trail: Unit 2 Lesson 1.
2 Who uses the school for work?	Different jobs are done by different people at a school.	Matching people to places: Unit 2 Lesson 3; job description: Unit 2 Extra activities.
3 How attractive is our school?	Children learn to form and express their views.	Assessing quality: Unit 2 Lesson 3; looking for places to improve: Unit 3 Lesson 1.
4 What changes can we make?	Everyone can help to improve their environment.	Making and displaying painted pots of plants: Unit 3 Lessons 2 and 3; decorating paving slabs: Unit 3 Extra activities.
5 What skills can we learn?	Use of photographs, a compass, directional vocabulary and simple maps.	Left and right, and compass work: Unit 1, all lessons; mapwork: Unit 1 Lessons 1 and 2; using photographs Unit 3 Extra activities.

National Curriculum coverage

Unit 1 Direction

National Curriculum links
- The main physical features of the locality of the school.
- Undertake local area fieldwork.
- Follow directions.

Unit 2 Quality

National Curriculum links
- Pupils will have opportunities to observe and record their ideas about the attractiveness of the school grounds.
- They can undertake studies that focus on geographical questions, based on fieldwork in the locality.

Unit 3 Improvement

National Curriculum links
- Investigate the quality of a locality, and know how that locality is changing and how its quality can be improved and sustained.
- Practical activities in the locality of the school.

Scotland Environment Studies coverage

The units cover the following contexts and content for Understanding People and Places:
- Some ways of maintaining a clean environment.
- Boundaries and their importance for safety.
- Developing the mental map of familiar places.

Direction

Learning targets

On completion of this unit children should understand that:

1 ➡➔ directions can be given using a variety of vocabulary
2 ➡➔ North, East, South and West are compass directions
3 ➡➔ landmarks help when giving directions and finding the way.

Before you start

Background knowledge

Where is North? Magnetic North is shown by the needle on a compass. It is to the west of true North or polar North and it changes a few degrees every year, due to magnetic influences. True north is found at the North Pole. Grid North is the north we put on maps, so that North and South are parallel to the sides of the paper.

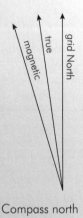

Compass north

Teaching points

Children will learn about direction. What is on your left and right changes as you move, but North remains constant.

Geographical skills

- Following directions
- Making maps and plans
- Fieldwork activities

Vocabulary

left, right, north, south, east, west

Resources for Lesson 1

Copymaster 33 Left and right, pencils, yellow and red felt-tip pens or crayons

Resources for Lesson 2

Globe, compass, atlases, Copymaster 34 Finding north, pencils, felt-tip pens, chalk

Resources for Lesson 3

Drawing paper, pencils, compasses

Resources for the activities

PE hoop, compass, paper, pencils, coloured counters, camera, tray, lemon and red paper

Assessment indicators

- Do children know their left and right hands?
- Can they name the points of the compass?
- Can they follow and give simple directions?
- Can they find features on a map of the school?

Teaching the lessons

Lesson 1 ❶ ❸

Introduction 15min

Sit all the children facing the same way to play a pointing game. Then ask a child to point to a feature in the room. Can another child describe where it is? 'Over there', 'Behind the computer', 'Under the desk'.

Introduce left and right into the game. Ask the first child to point to the clock. Ask the next child 'Is it to the left or the right of the door?' Then ask individuals to point to something to the right of the window, left of the door and so on.

Using left and right 20min

 Using **Copymaster 33 Left and right**, choose from these differentiated activities.

1. Use colour coding to help children remember which is left and right. Children colour Peter's left hand lemon and his right hand red.

2. Colour things on Peter's left hand side lemon and things on his right red.

3. Draw arrows radiating from Peter to named items on the picture. The result is called a signpost map with Peter representing the pole of the signpost.

4. Children can make a picture map of their desk showing some things on their left and right.

Summary `10min`

Ask children who sit opposite each other whether an item is on their left or right. Show children how, if they stretch their left hand in front of them so that they are looking at the back of their hand, and stretch their thumb out to form a right angle, their left hand makes the shape of 'L' for left. Explain that children who face each other have different things on their left and right.

Lesson 2

Introduction `20min`

Set out for each group a globe, a compass and some atlases open on full global maps. Tell each group that they are going to find out about North and where the North Pole is. Allow some free time for them to investigate and discover with these three resources. Point to an arrow you have fixed on the wall which points to North. Show each group how you used a compass to find out where north is.

Finding North `30min`

Use **Copymaster 34 Finding North** and choose from the differentiated activities below.

1 Allow children to have any side of the globe facing them. Then they can draw the globe and their view of the world on the copymaster, using colour to distinguish between land and sea.

2 Children can add features to the playground picture. They colour code four items and list them in the grid, adding each colour to make a key.

3 More able children can work in groups to make a plan of their own school playground, finding and adding the direction North. This is a good fieldwork activity, and directions can be chalked on the playground. They can add South, East and West arrows.

Lesson 3

Introduction `15min`

Remind the children how to use a compass. Show them how to hold the compass level until the needle settles. Gently turn the compass until the needle covers N for North. Point to North and then to the other directions. Discuss with the class how you can see different views by looking in different directions. Walk around outside and point out the features which surround the school. Let children practise using a compass to find out which direction they are facing.

School views `20min`

Using the compass, children find out which way they are facing and title their sheet with the direction they have chosen, e.g. 'Looking East'. They can sketch or paint the view of the school grounds.

Differentiate for able children by choosing views that use the compass points NE, NW, SE or SW.

Summary `5min`

Each child places their work around a compass rose to make a wall display.

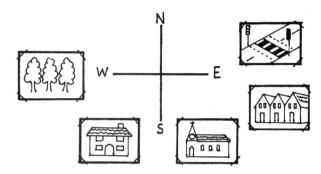

Compass rose

Extra activities

Compass practice

Put a selection of items collected in the school grounds in a hoop, with a compass in the middle. The children can draw the hoop and its contents. By drawing arrows from the compass to the objects they will create a signpost map. Items can be listed with their North, East, South or West direction.

Orienteering

Make large but simple maps of the school grounds. Take photos or use children's sketches of different features such as the waste bin, tree or gate. Put coloured counters at each feature for children to collect. Show a photo to a pair of children who go that feature and collect a counter. They return and place the counter on their map in the correct place. They continue until they have visited and mapped each feature. Before removing the counters they can mark features visited with coloured stars or symbols that they design.

Left and right days

On 'Left Day' try to incorporate 'leftness' into every lesson. Here are some ideas.

1 Children only put up left hands.
2 Play 'Simon Says' using the left side of the body.
3 Make left handprints and footprints.
4 Keep pencils on the left side of desk.
5 Label left sides of body, door, clock, cupboard.

The following week have a 'Right Day'.

Left and right tray

Line one half of a tray with lemon coloured paper and line the other half with red paper. Label the lemon side left and the red side right. Children can make and wear a lemon bracelet on their left and a red bracelet on their right wrists. Give them items one at a time, asking them to place them on the right or the left side of the tray. You could start the activity with only lemon and red coloured items

Left and right

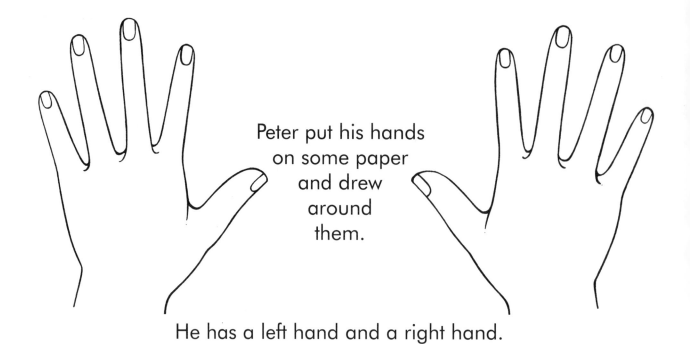

Peter put his hands on some paper and drew around them.

He has a left hand and a right hand.

left   **right**

This is a picture map of his classroom.

Peter is sitting at his desk.

Look at the things he can see.

Some are on his left and some are on his right.

34 | **Finding North**

Look at a globe and draw a picture of it.
Can you find the North Pole?
Mark the North Pole on your globe.

North is marked on this playground with an arrow. The arrow points to North.
Add these to the picture:
- a waste bin at the North end
- a football at the South end
- a tree at the West end.

Fill in the grid below.
At each compass point, write down something you can see in the playground. Colour it and show the colour in the end box.

	I can see	colour
N		
E		
S		
W		

☐ Tick this box when you have used a compass to find North in your playground.

UNIT 2 Quality

Learning targets

On completion of this unit children should understand that:
1 ➤➤ geographical features give the school its character
2 ➤➤ different areas have different uses
3 ➤➤ the attractiveness of a place can depend on design, tidiness and noise.

Before you start

Background knowledge

When they study the local area, children need to look at the way people and places interact. Use your knowledge of the school grounds to make various observations. What can be seen, heard, smelled, felt, etc.? Which areas are for leisure, work, transport, storage, or are out of bounds?

Teaching points

Focus on the enquiry question 'What is it like to be at this school?' Enquiry questions which probe into the child's first response draw out more thoughtful attitudes to the local area. 'What do you like about it?' 'Why do you think it is like that?' The first step is to observe the environment, the second to assess its quality.

Geographical skills

- Observation in the environment
- Making a trail map
- Using geographical terms

Vocabulary

school, grounds, environment, features, area, work, leisure

Resources for Lesson 1

A set of observation symbols on card, large sheet of paper, pens

Resources for Lesson 2

Large map of the school, self-adhesive labels, pencils, felt-tip pens

Resources for Lesson 3

Copymaster 35 School grounds report, Copymaster 36 How attractive is your school?, pencils

Resources for the activities

Copymaster 35 School grounds report, paper, pencils, self-adhesive labels

Assessment indicators

- Can the children recognise simple symbols?
- Can they follow a route?
- Do they know the main physical and human features of the school grounds?
- Are they able to express their views on their environment?

Teaching the lessons

Lesson 1 ① ②

Introduction [15 min]

Draw symbols on cards to represent 'look', 'listen', 'feel', 'smell', 'imagine'. Hold up each card in turn and ask the children for observations about things in the classroom. At first, you could restrict this to items on a table, then extend it to things anywhere in the room. When children are familiar with the idea, explain that they are going to discover the school grounds in this way.

Observation trail [25 min]

Walk around the school grounds with the class. Hold up your chosen observation symbol at stopping

places you have already prepared. Suggestions for stopping places:

Listen	secretary's office
Smell	kitchens
Feel	warm and cold surfaces
Imagine	trees in a different season
Look	shapes of windows and doors.

Ask questions at each stop, e.g. With the 'listen' symbol you could ask, 'What can you hear?' 'Is it a loud noise?' 'Does it disturb anybody?'

| LOOK | LISTEN | SMELL | FEEL | IMAGINE |

Summary `10min`

Back in the classroom, write down all the things the children can remember under each observation symbol on a large sheet of paper. This can be used as a resource for the next lesson.

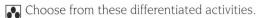
Lesson 2

Introduction `10min`

Display the list of observed features made at the end of your observation trail. Remind the children about the trail and talk about the features on the list, pinpointing the ones which give the school its character. This may be the play equipment, the quiet places or the outside influences of traffic or countryside.

Recording observations `20min`

Choose from these differentiated activities.

1   Children in different groups can draw one of the symbols used in the observation trail at the top of their page. If they draw the symbol for 'listen', then they draw all the things they heard underneath the symbol, and so on.

2   On large paper divided into four or five sections, members of a group record a feature for each observation symbol.

3   On a map of the school grounds, children draw observation symbols at the stopping places along their route. Around the map they can list or draw the features discovered on the trail.

Summary `5min`

Children recall the things they observed on the trail. Each group can be asked to decide which feature they liked most. A smiley face drawn on a self-adhesive label can be fixed to a large features list to indicate each group's views.

Lesson 3

Introduction `15min`

Enlarge **Copymaster 35 School grounds report** and hand it out to groups of children. Discuss the meanings of 'work', 'leisure', 'communication' and 'getting together' in the context of school life. You can simplify the word 'communication' by calling it 'sending messages' but refer to the range of methods, e.g. voices, letters, books, computers, etc.

Assessing quality `30min`

Distribute copies of **Copymaster 36 How attractive is your school?** for the children to complete. The children decide how areas of the school are used,

then fit them into the scales on the copymaster. They assess the attractiveness of each place and express their opinion in the sad and smiley faces boxes. Explaining the reasons for their choice of a favourite place or area completes an exercise in observing, recording and expressing their views.

Differentiate for slower workers by cutting up the sheet and making a simpler edition with one use of area box, e.g. 'work' and one scale, e.g. 'Is it tidy?'

Summary `5min`

Compare one of the scales to see if all the children had the same entries. Probe to see whether children know why not all the answers are the same.

Extra activities

Jobs at school

Using Copymaster 35 School grounds report, ask the children to find out about the jobs held by people at school or by people who visit the school.

The children can write a job description leaflet about one of the jobs, drawing the person at work with their name and job title on the front. Inside, children can record the person's hours of work, the tasks they do and the areas in the school where they work. If they can interview the person, they can add what the person says about their job.

Leisure

Use Copymaster 35 School grounds report to explain how to make a graph of favourite spare time occupations at school. The completed graph could be displayed and will complement work on the school grounds.

School boundaries

Walk around the school boundaries looking over them at the locality beyond. List the things which can be seen, either as words, pictures or symbols. Differentiate by providing a tick list of simple drawings for children to look for and tick. Back in the classroom, put the features seen into the following groups or sets: enjoyment; useful; workplaces; homes; transport. Some things will fit into more than one group.

I like it!

On a very large piece of paper ask a group to draw a picture of the school and its grounds. Ask them to mark on it the features observed during the topic. Give each child a strip of three self-adhesive labels. Ask them to draw a smiley face on each label, which can be peeled off and stuck on the picture in the areas they particularly like.

35 | School grounds report

Work
Children and adults work at your school.

Leisure
This graph shows how some children spend their leisure time.

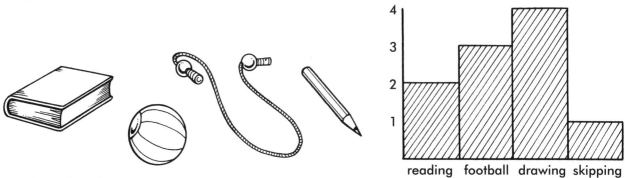

reading football drawing skipping

Communication
There are different ways to send messages.

Getting together
We do lots of things together.

| Work | Leisure | Communication |

How attractive is your school?

Where do these things happen?

⚽👟 _____   📚 _____

☎ _____   📝 _____

Fill in the boxes to compare parts of your school. 🙂 or 🙁 ?

🙂 tidy ⟵	⟶ untidy 🙁

🙂 quiet ⟵	⟶ noisy 🙁

The area I like best is _____

Improvement

Learning targets

On completion of this unit children should understand that:

1 ➡ our environment is changing and we can make changes to improve it
2 ➡ environments need looking after to maintain quality
3 ➡ communication and publicity help in the upkeep of environments.

Before you start

Background knowledge

Realistically, plans to improve the school environment have to take into account the age and ability of the children. Children learn that they can influence the attractiveness of their surroundings through some very simple ideas for improvement. This unit suggests a small project that the children can plan, design and put into action themselves, reporting and publicising their work. Acrylic paints are used because they are waterproof. Clothes will need protecting and brushes should be washed out before the paint dries.

Teaching points

Children will learn how simple measures can improve their surroundings and discover ways to communicate their ideas. To sustain the improvements made, children could adopt a 'housekeeping' role. This will make them into willing caretakers and encourage pride in the environment.

Geographical skills

• Use of large scale plan of school
• Use of computers
• Practical activities in the school grounds

Vocabulary

environment, improvement, change, paint, plants, pollution

Resources for Lesson 1

Gloss paint, decorator's brush and materials, pot plant, plant pots and jam jars, dried flowers and bulbs, Copymaster 37 Places for pots, pencils, clipboards, large scale plan of the school grounds

Resources for Lesson 2

Copymaster 38 Plant pots, pencils, waxed stencil paper, acrylic paint, fine brushes, plastic plant pots or jam jars, trowel, bulbs, compost or oasis, dried flowers/fresh grasses

Resources for Lesson 3

Paper, felt-tip pens, computer

Resources for the activities

Coloured paper, paints, paper and pencils, camera, card

Assessment indicators

• Do the children notice wear and tear on a building?
• Can they think of a way to improve their immediate surroundings?
• Do they realise that changes need constant care and upkeep?

Teaching the lessons

Lesson 1   ① ②

Introduction   10min

▨ Display a large pot of gloss paint along with a decorator's brush and materials. Add a pot plant, some empty plant pots and jam jars, dried flowers and bulbs.

Ask the children how you could you use these things in the school. Probe for repairing old paintwork, brightening up places, changing and adding colour.

Paint and plants   30min

⚃ In small groups, children take **Copymaster 37 Places for pots** and a clipboard to survey the school. They

inspect paintwork for wear and tear and note places which need improvement. The children should also look for places where pots of plants or flowers would brighten up a dull area and note this on their sheet too. On their return to the classroom, they write a short report of their findings, recommending the place most in need of a pot of paint or pot of plants.

Differentiate by asking more able children to mark the places on a large scale plan of the area surveyed.

Summary   10min

▨ Explain the need for a professional to paint the school building, but emphasise that the children can add the plants and decide which places most need plants or flowers.

Lesson 2

Introduction [10 min]

Divide the class into groups to do different tasks (unless you want a large number of decorated pots). The tasks could be separated into:

1   making a design and template to decorate a pot
2   painting the design onto the pot
3   planting a bulb/making a dried flower arrangement.

Pots of plants [35 min]

Children can select the information they need from **Copymaster 38 Plant pots**. Designers will need stiff paper or waxed stencil paper for their design, and will need help cutting out the template. Painters will need acrylic paint, fine brushes, plastic plant pots or jam jars. Plantsmen will need bulbs, compost, or oasis and dried flowers/fresh grasses.

Summary [10 min]

The finished pots and arrangements can be placed in the areas they were designed for and the children can talk about how they look and whether their efforts have improved and changed their surroundings.

Lesson 3

Introduction [15 min]

Discuss with the class how they would like to share the care of the plants. Consider the care of bulbs and flower arrangements and the need to tell the rest of the school. The children will need to find a way to communicate their improvement idea. This could take the form of an assembly, a wall display, or a computer written newsheet.

Spreading the word [30 min]

Children write their names on cut out flowers to make a bright rota board to remind carers of their job.

Rota board

Whichever method is chosen to 'spread the word', initially children should make a report sheet which answers the following questions.

● 'What did we do?'
● 'Why did we do it?'
● 'What do the pots look like?' (Include drawings.)
● 'How will we look after them?'

The work can be word processed for a newsheet, enlarged for a wall display or learned for an assembly.

Summary [5 min]

Choose the first few caretakers and put those 'flower heads' on the rota board.

Extra activities

Asking for help

Following a wear and tear survey of the school grounds, as in Lesson 1, there will be painting and maintenance tasks that children will not be able to do. This offers an opportunity for purposeful letter writing. First, children can write a short letter to the headteacher, outlining the thing they would like improved, and asking who they could write to about it. Secondly, follow up by writing, using the computer, a letter to the person suggested by the headteacher.

Paving slab pictures

Is there a school area with paving slabs, which could be brightened or added to? Large simple pictures of creatures such as ladybirds, or snails can be painted on them using acrylic paints. A simple template made by the teacher can be drawn around, and outlined in black paint before filling in with colours.

Before and after

Encourage the use of photographs as a way of recording work done. It can save laborious writing and teaches a useful skill. Children take a photograph of an area before any improvements or changes take place and another photo afterwards. These can be mounted side by side to show the practical work being done. They can simply be labelled or have captions added depending on the ability of the child.

Change the view

Take a set of photos which show areas of the school grounds where there is room for improvement, e.g. litter on the ground, an untidy place, a bare wall.

Mount the photos on a card with these questions:

● Is this area attractive?
● Would you change it?
● What would you do to improve it?

Children choose one area to make plans for improvement.

As you walk around the school, look for places where you can
see that some new paint is needed. You can also look for places
where a plant or some flowers would brighten the area.
Write the places that need a bright new look in the two pots.

My Report
This is what I saw _____

_____

_____

The best change to make would be _____

_____

_____

_____

38

Plant pots

Design

1

2

3
Does it fit?

4
Make a template

Paint

1
Choose

2
Fix on pot

3
Draw around template

4
Paint

Plant

1
Compost

2

3

4

Arrange

oasis

Pick fresh or collect dry plants

1

2

3

4

PERSONAL GEOGRAPHY

Focus

Geography is about people and places. All of us have experiences of places and groups of people which are special to us alone. Put together, this set of geographical images is unique to each of us – our personal geography.

The ideas and lessons which follow provide an approach to geography which gives each child a sense of their place in the world they know. It is, moreover, a stepping stone towards their discovery of the wider world beyond. The children will feel motivated to produce something unique and special, all about themselves and the people and places in their lives. You will have the opportunity to teach in a cross-curricular way, to follow the interests and opportunities spontaneously as they arise in class. You can explore beyond the confines of a topic while at the same time linking with the various subjects and requirements of the National Curriculum.

Teaching method

Each child makes a book about their personal geography. It can be compiled as one self-contained topic over a half-term, or can be a scrapbook to be added to occasionally over a longer period, i.e. over two terms, a school year or throughout their primary years with different tasks in different year classes. If the idea appeals to more than one teacher in a school, split the type of work to be covered between year groups to prevent repeating activities.

The lessons

The lessons are geography based. Although some seem to have little formal geography, they are building the foundation for geographical knowledge about places, transport, people's jobs, land use and geographical issues, while using and practising geographical skills. The set of lessons are in an order that shows some geographical progression but it is not necessary to use them all or to keep to the same order. They could be interspersed with work based on other curriculum subjects to make a wider ranging personal scrapbook.

Content

Unit 1:   All about me
Unit 2:   Out and about
Unit 3:   My world

Source material

This will be mainly from the children.

A set of local shop photographs or carrier bags which advertise the shops.

Brainstorm

This brainstorm covers the lessons in Section 7 and can be added to for a cross-curricular topic.

People I know
My doctor
Relations

Who am I?
Personal details
House, garden
Passport

Personal geography
me

My wider world
Letters from other places
Places where relations live
Souvenirs from distant places

Where I live?
Shops I go to
Favourite places
A local issue
Improving places I know

Teaching plan

This can be used as a medium-term plan and provides a scheme of work for a topic on personal geography.

Enquiry questions	Learning targets	Pupil activities
1 Who am I and where do I live?	Knowledge of own individual identity and address.	Passport making: Unit 1, Lesson 1; observation of house and garden features: Unit 1 Lessons 2 and 3.
2 What is my local area like?	I live in a place that I am familiar with.	Shops in the area: Unit 2 Lesson 1; expressing views on quality of the environment: Unit 2 Lessons 2 and 3.
3 What do I know about the whole world?	I have links with some faraway places.	Using envelopes: Unit 2 Lesson 1; investigating where people and goods originate: Unit 3 lessons 2 and 3.

National Curriculum coverage

Unit 1 all about me

National Curriculum links
- An opportunity to investigate their surroundings.
- Development of knowledge and understanding about places.

Unit 2 Out and about

National Curriculum links
- Use of enquiry skills and questions.
- Understand that environmental quality can be changed.

Unit 3 My world

National Curriculum links
- Local area knowledge.
- Fieldwork in the local area.
- Use of maps and atlases.

Scotland Environment Studies coverage

The units cover the following contexts and content for Understanding People and Places:

- Daily lives of some children elsewhere compared with their own.
- Developing the mental map of familiar places.
- Making models of known places and story settings.
- Using plans to find places.

UNIT 1

All about me

Learning targets

On completion of this unit children should:

1 ➤➤ know their own address
2 ➤➤ be able to offer an opinion on a particular place
3 ➤➤ be able to describe the features of a small area they know well.

Before you start

Background knowledge

The school will have each child's date of birth and address but the rest of the information for this unit will come from the children themselves. Stories that involve people's addresses, such as *Katie Morag Delivers the Mail* by Mairi Hedderwick, will help set the context for this work. The catchment area of your school may be wide so check that your geography resources include maps that cover where everyone lives. Sets of photographs of shops, signposts and other local features will also be useful.

Teaching points

This unit focuses on the child's own house and garden and concentrates on observation and developing a sense of belonging to a place. Some children may know very little about their address, house, journeys, etc. At the beginning of a topic like this a letter home will explain why the children are coming home with so many questions and encourage parents to help their children find and bring information and resources to school.

Geographical skills

- Knowing one's address
- Using a quiz sheet

Vocabulary

house, address, birthday, personal, garden, special

Resources for Lesson 1

Paper, pencils, felt-tip pens, paint, a passport

Resources for Lesson 2

Copymaster 39 My house, pencils, felt-tip pens, paper 'window frames', fabric, glue

Resources for Lesson 3

Stories about gardens such as Jennings, Linda *Fred's Garden*, Hodder and Stoughton, 1987; Hughes, Shirley *Sally's Secret*, Bodley Head, 1973; paper felt-tip pens

Resources for the activities

Copymaster 40 Title pages, felt-tip pens, envelopes, trays of sand, dried flowers from pot pourri, bark, stones

Assessment indicators

- Do the children know their date of birth?
- Can they say their address?

Teaching the lessons

Lesson 1   ①

Introduction |15 min|

▦ Answer the question 'Who am I?' by presenting yourself in such a way that the children have a model to copy. Standing in front of the class, or filling in a questionnaire on the board, tell your name, date of birth, address and any 'distinguishing' or special features. (Although they are fun, distinguishing features are no longer used on passports.) Children who already know these facts can try to present themselves following your example.

Personal details

Name _____
Birthday _____
I come from _____
My address is _____
_____
Special features _____

Passport page

Who am I? `25min`

 The children can fill in a personal details sheet and make it into a passport page with a self-portrait or a real photo. Link with an art lesson to draw and paint self-portraits.

Summary `10min`

 Discuss who needs to know personal details, e.g. a doctor, the school and customs officers and show an example of a passport around the class.

Lesson 2

Introduction `10min`

Ask children to close their eyes and imagine a room in their house – the room should be special to them in some way. Ask them to imagine looking around and noticing some of the things in the room. They should think about the things they like in the room, what the room is used for and what makes it special to them.

My house `30min`

 Use **Copymaster 39 My house** as a planning draft. Children can plan a larger collage here and use their ideas to make a fabric collage of their special room. The copymaster includes a poem for children to add a line, which reveals some of the things in their room. To make large pictures for display, prepare some paper with empty window frames made of brown or white paper glued on each sheet. The children paint or make a fabric collage of the view into their special room. Strips of material glued on each side can simulate curtains.

Summary `10min`

Ask some children to read out their poems and show their pictures to the class. Develop the picture gallery into a game called 'Guess who lives here?' with names on labels for children to fix to the pictures with Blu-tak®. Play the game for a few minutes at the end of session.

Lesson 3

Introduction `15min`

Use a story to introduce this idea. Two suggestions at different levels are *Fred's Garden* by Linda Jennings, or *Sally's Secret* by Shirley Hughes.

Tell the children that, as they listen to the story, they should think about what Fred/Sally liked or disliked about the garden and what they used the garden for.

My garden `25min`

 Discuss what a particular garden is like for the different people or animals that use it. Ask the children how they use their gardens. Draw out answers such as playing games, gardening, storing things, family events, feeding birds and drying clothes. Query whether different members of the family use the garden for different things.

Ask the children to make a picture that shows different uses of their garden. They could use paper you have already divided into sections for a number of different uses or make a collage picture of the different garden activities.

Summary `5min`

Discuss which are the most common garden activities and which are unusual. Use a writing session for a piece of descriptive writing about their garden.

Extra activities

Making a book

Here are some ideas for presenting work:
1 a topic scrapbook where finished work can be glued in as it is completed
2 a concertina book, with each face showing one aspect of personal geography
3 a box that contains the work in a notebook, or home made book with a collection of photos, models, stamps, postcards, etc.

Some ideas for a title page can be found on **Copymaster 40 Title pages**.

Addressing letters

Reinforce knowledge of a child's address by frequent practice. If children are to take letters home from the school, let them spend some time writing their address on the folded letter or envelope. If you make cards for special festivals, make and address envelopes too.

Tray gardens

Sand gardens made in shallow trays give each child a chance to create their own garden. Rake the sand into patterns and decorate with dried flowers from pot pourri, bark and stones. This is an ancient Japanese garden design.

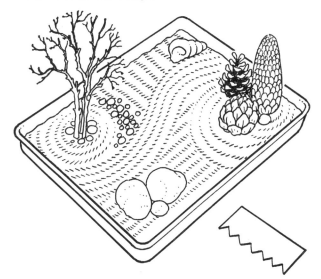

Japanese sand garden

Time differentiation

Special needs children should be encouraged and helped to produce the same work in this unit. They may need differentiation by time rather than by task.

My house

Looking through the window at a special room.

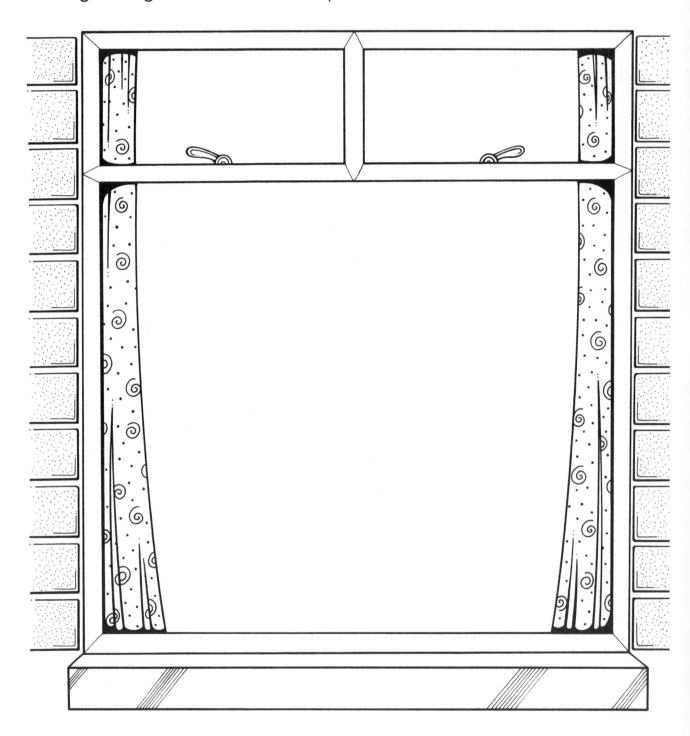

Looking through the window.
What do I see?

_____

In a special room for me.

Title pages

It's me

by _____

My world

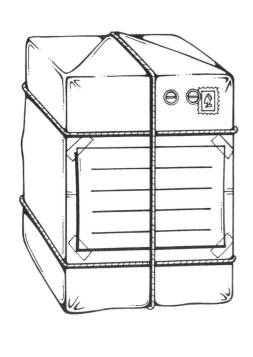

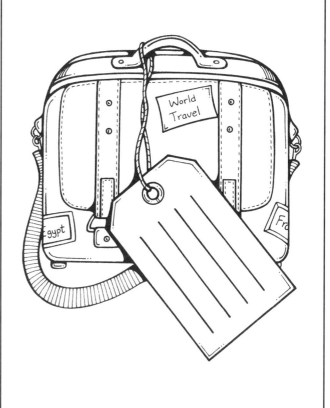

Out and about

Learning targets

On completion of this unit children should understand that:

1 ➤➤ local journeys are made to go shopping
2 ➤➤ some places are more attractive than others
3 ➤➤ there are some things they may like to change in their area.

Before you start

Background knowledge

Investigate the nearby shopping areas that the children are likely to use so you are able to talk to them about the range of shops they are likely to visit. A set of photographs of the shop fronts in the nearby shopping area and close up photos of bank and chain shop logos will help children to remember which ones they visit and reinforce their local area knowledge.

Teaching points

This looks at the local places children use and visit and their opinions about the quality of their environment. Children will have different views and values. Use this opportunity to encourage them to listen and respect the ideas of others.

Geographical skills

- Knowledge of the local area
- Fieldwork

Vocabulary

shop, journey, transport, favourite, problem, change

Resources for Lesson 1

Copymaster 41 Going shopping, Copymaster 42 Types of shops, pencils, felt-tip pens, photos of local shops, High Street business logos

Resources for Lesson 2

Paper, paint, word processor, labels

Resources for Lesson 3

Paper, felt-tip pens

Resources for the activities

Paper, felt-tip pens

Assessment indicators

- Can the children describe a local place or feature?
- Can they express an opinion?
- Do they know that different shops sell different goods?

Teaching the lessons

Lesson 1 ①

Introduction [10 min]

At the simplest level, talk with the class about a shop they visit and what mode of transport they use to get there. Extend the discussion by asking about landmarks seen on the journey and the things bought at the various shops visited. Children may profess to seeing nothing on the way. Find out what play activities they do on their journeys and build this into the work. With young children, you may like to restrict the theme of going shopping to one type of shop or, if they are older or more able, extend it to give them more choice.

Going shopping [30 min]

Fill in **Copymaster 41 Going shopping** with pictures, labels, sentences and/or shop logos. The first box can include the mode of transport, the road to the shops with some of the features passed on the way. Differentiate by asking the children for varying amounts of detail. Some children may be able to add a signpost showing the distance, others may draw only the vehicle they travel in.

The shopping basket can be linked to one type of shop or contain items from a range of shops, whatever is appropriate to the children's shopping experiences. Use **Copymasters 42 Types of shops** to help the children with which items are bought in which shop.

Summary [10 min]

Show a selection of pictures or photos of shop and familiar High Street business logos to assess whether children recognise the local ones.

Lesson 2

Introduction `10min`

Use some of these enquiry questions to encourage children to think about and tell the others about their favourite places. 'Where is it?' 'What's it like?' 'Why do you like it?' 'What do you do there?'

My favourite place `30min`

Each child can paint a picture of their favourite place. They can use a word processing programme to print out labels which answer the enquiry questions and glue them on or around their picture. Younger children can print simple labels such as 'beach', 'sea',' pier', to glue onto their picture. Differentiate by asking more able children to turn their labels into captions, e.g. 'The beach is sandy with rockpools'.

Favourite places

Summary `10min`

Discuss with the class the variety of types of places that are favourite. If there is a spread of locations, a block graph could illustrate your class preferences and link with data handling in a maths session.

Lesson 3

Introduction `15min`

Use this opportunity to encourage children to think about a local issue and express their views on it. Choose a simple idea such as litter in the street or cars speeding past the school and allow a free discussion. Differentiate by allowing groups or individuals to mention other things that bother them.

Something bothers me `30min`

Children can title their work 'The problem' and show by pictures or a combination of words and pictures what the problem is. Under the next heading, 'What I would do', they can show their idea for solving or helping. This can also be in picture form for the youngest children. You may want to adapt the introduction to the lesson so that children work on the problems they are most interested in or affected by.

Summary `5min`

A rounding up time for the teacher to reveal all the suggestions that were made and for the class to decide which ones would work. If the children have been working in groups, let each group present their problem and suggestions for improvement to the rest of the class.

Extra activities

Improving my plot

Here is an opportunity for children to imagine having a free hand at changing their garden or an area of land in their neighbourhood. If there is a wasteland or an empty plot in the area, visit it with the class and let them suggest how it should be developed. If there is nowhere obvious, then their own garden or a part of the school grounds could provide the focus for improvement or change.

The wasteland

My doctor

Children can create a profile of one of the important people in their life outside their family. Enquiry questions get the children thinking on the right track. Here are some to use. 'What is your Doctor called?' 'Where is the surgery?' 'What is the waiting room like?' 'How does your doctor find out what is wrong with you?' 'What things does your doctor do in his or her job?'

I like living here

A brainstorm about all the things children like about living in their area. In the centre of the piece of work put a picture (or a photograph or postcard) of the place where they live. Around the picture fix large speech bubbles. Write a reason for liking the area in each of the bubbles. This could make a class display or individual pieces of work on a smaller scale.

Signpost maps

Children make a signpost map of the places or shops they visit in the area. In the centre of the paper they draw themselves in a circle with arrows radiating outwards from the centre to pictures of places they visit. They could start with the school and then add other places they go to outside school hours.

Going shopping

Getting to the shop

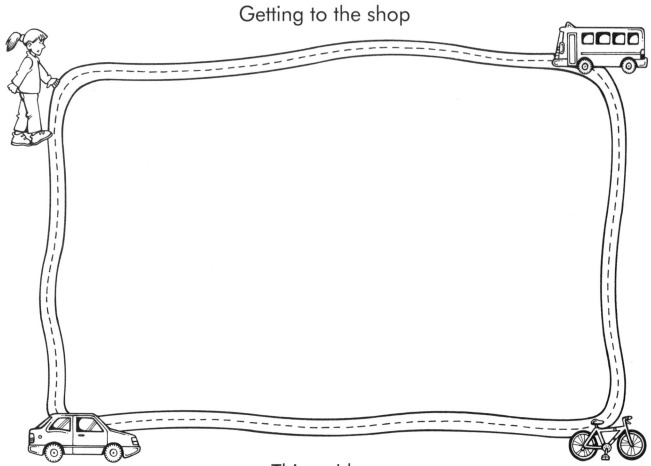

Things I buy

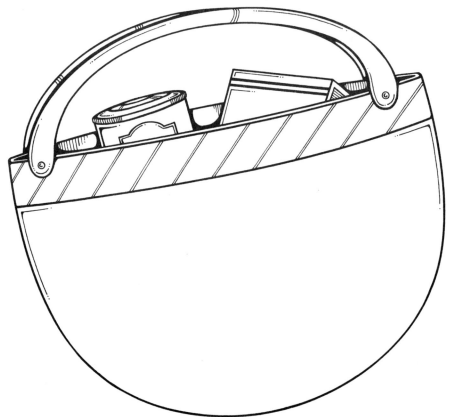

Types of shops

There are all sorts of shops. They sell different sorts of things. Here are some you may have seen in the town.

Newsagent
sells:
- newspapers
- sweets
- cards.

Bakery
sells:
- bread
- cakes
- sandwiches.

Butcher
sells:
- meat
- sausages
- cheese.

Shoe Shop
sells:
- shoes
- boots
- socks.

Supermarket
sells:
- food and drinks
- cleaning materials
- pet food.

Drycleaner
cleans:
- clothes
- duvets
- rugs.

Greengrocer
sells:
- fruit
- vegetables
- plants.

UNIT 3 | My world

Learning targets

On completion of this unit children should:

1 ➤➤ understand that where they live is a part of a bigger world
2 ➤➤ know people who live in different parts of the country
3 ➤➤ have been to and know about other places which are different.

Before you start

Background knowledge

The first lesson reinforces the work on addresses and builds on general knowledge about the postal system. As in an earlier unit, the success of this unit depends on children bringing information and items from home. A letter explaining your needs for the topic will encourage family help and interest. You can supply a range of maps and some artefacts for those children who do not remember to bring things.

Teaching points

Items from other places which interest the child can lead to discovering places on maps. Looking for small places on maps is difficult so stick to nearest cities or counties when helping children find where someone lives.

Geographical skills

- Use of atlases and maps
- Making simple maps
- Using enquiry skills

Vocabulary

personal, travel, souvenir, relations, friend

Resources for Lesson 1

Copymaster 43 Through the letterbox, used envelopes, map of the UK, atlases

Resources for Lesson 2

Road atlas, Copymaster 44 I know someone from…, pencils, felt-tip pens, wall map

Resources for Lesson 3

Artefacts from home such as souvenirs, stamps, coins, clothes, postcards; paper, felt-tip pens

Resources for the activities

Paper, pencils, felt-tip pens, artefacts, globe

Assessment indicators

- Are the children familiar with a UK map?
- Can they locate personal places on a UK map?
- Can they address an envelope?

Teaching the lessons

Lesson 1   ①

Introduction   15min

Introduce and prepare for this task a week ahead. Show children envelopes which have come to the school with different postmarks on them. Use a large map of the UK to point out where the letters originated and draw lines on the map to link them to the school. Ask children to bring in some envelopes which have been sent to their house and are from different places. (After Christmas is a good time for this.)

Through my letterbox   40min

Copymaster 43 Through the letterbox shows an envelope addressed to a school with labels to all the important features. Make some blank envelopes for children to fill in. You can use them for children to copy the details of envelopes that have come to your school or for children's own envelopes. Children can cut out and glue postmarks from a collection of envelopes, around a map of the UK, using an atlas to find each town. They can link each town to their own home town with a line.

Differentiate by using a county map for local postmarks, discovering the main postal towns of your area. Children may discover that they tie up with postcode initials, e.g. CT for Canterbury, ME for Maidstone, TN for Tonbridge (all in Kent).

Summary   10min

Let each child match a postmark (real or homemade) to a UK map on the classroom wall.

Lesson 2

Introduction 15min

Tell the children the name of a place in the UK where you know someone. Point to it on a wall map. Ask if they know someone who lives in another town. Armed with a road atlas or class atlas, you could look up each location and point to the place on the wall map.

I know someone from... 30min

For their personal geography book, each child uses a photocopy of **Copymaster 44 I know someone from...** and marks one or two places where they know someone on the map of the UK. They can use the two boxes provided on the copymaster to label the places, e.g. 'Granny Jones lives in Norwich'. The copymaster can be mounted onto larger paper if necessary to give more room for children's contacts. More able children can use an atlas to add a geographical location, e.g. 'Norwich is in the east of England'. Photos of the people or places could be added to further sheets.

Summary 10min

Use a wall map to ask children to point and name the place where they know someone. Can they point to the school's location?

Lesson 3

Introduction 15min

Use a 'show and tell' session for children to bring in artefacts that are from home but originate in other places. This could include souvenirs, stamps, coins, clothes, or postcards. Encourage children to talk about their item, describing its material, function and origin. What clues are there about its origins? Labels and style often give clues.

Show and tell 25min

Children can record their knowledge about an artefact with a sketch. Their answers to a set of questions, e.g. 'What is it?', 'What is it made from?', 'What clues tell you where it comes from?', 'What would you like to know about it?', etc. can be added to their sketch and will show their level of observation.

Artefacts from other places

Summary 10min

Each child makes a label for their artefact saying what it is, if it is not obvious, and where it comes from. The artefacts can be displayed.

Extra activities

I have been to...

Ask the children about a place they have visited, why they went there and what they remember about the place. The children make a stand up card. On the front they draw a picture of a place they have been and inside they answer the enquiry questions: 'Where have you been?', 'Why did you go there?', 'What is the place like?' The cards can be displayed around a map or globe for other children to read before putting with their personal geography work.

After a school visit

Each child will have been to the same place but will have different memories of the visit. There can be a standard starting point for the work, such as 'On Monday I went to the Old Manor Theme Park'. Depending on the ability of the children, you can ask for pictures or written replies to starter sentences, such as:

- The first thing I saw was…
- The best ride was…
- The journey was…

It's my world

Give each group a globe. The children draw the globe in the middle of their sheet of paper. Around the outside they draw images of other places and also of their own area. They can include wildlife, homes, food, people, holidays, flags, etc. – whatever they are interested in. Extend more able children by using research books, CD-Roms or by asking them to name the countries that their images show.

My world

The postman brought a letter.

a stamp on the envelope

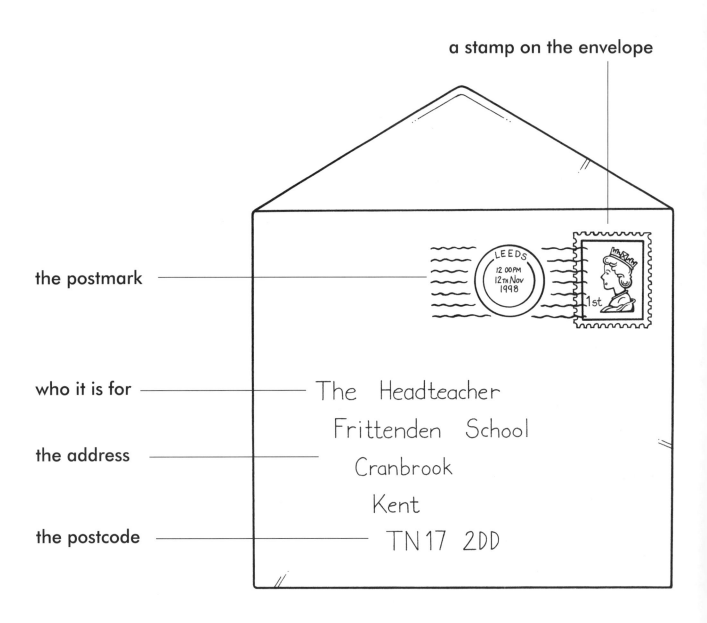

the postmark

who it is for

The Headteacher

Frittenden School

the address

Cranbrook

Kent

the postcode

TN 17 2DD

This letter came from Leeds.
It was sent to a school in Kent.

I know someone from...

THE ENVIRONMENT

Focus

The quality of the environment is fundamental to our continued enjoyment of the world. Many things threaten the world as we know it. Children need to be able to explore and discover the environments of the world and to realise for themselves the need for careful management for the future. This section looks at environments from different angles. Litter is a unit which offers practical involvement in the local environment. The work on the Country Code explores how to protect and sustain an attractive working environment. Zoo animals looks at the interaction between men and creatures and their changing environment. The seashore and rainforest units investigate the features of two particular environments. Each unit in this section could either make a topic on its own or be linked to one of the locality studies in this book. A combination of the lessons and units could make a topic on 'Environments' while individual lessons could be used to link with topical events, artwork, language work or RE.

Content

Unit 1: Litter
Unit 2: Country Code
Unit 3: Zoo animals
Unit 4: Seashore
Unit 5: Rainforest

Source material

Scoffham, Stephen and Thomas, Sue *Primary Colours: A world of Ideas*, Stanley Thornes (Publishers), 1997. This teacher's resource book contains further ideas for lessons. See the sections on 'A place in the rainforest', 'A place at the seaside'.

Environmental groups can be approached for up-to-date information and teaching aids.

World Wide Fund for Nature, Panda House, Weyside Park, Godalming, Surrey GU7 1XR.

Brainstorm

Each unit is quite different and, as the whole section would not be used as one topic, the brainstorm asks enquiry questions for each topic to answer. One example is given for each.

What is the environment like?
Plants and animals found

Is this environment attractive or unattractive?
Litter survey

The environments – a theme

How is this environment changing?
Rainforest trees cut down

How can the environment be managed?
Following the country code

Teaching plan

This can be used as a medium term plan and provides a scheme of work on an environmental theme. Children's activities will need to reflect the particular theme being studied. If linked to a locality study the two plans can be combined.

Enquiry questions	Learning targets	Pupil activities
1 What is this environment like?	Can identify plants and animals found in the environment.	Fieldwork identification: Unit 4; use of photos: Unit 5.
2 Is this environment attractive?	Can form and express a view on the attractiveness of a place.	Artwork representations: Unit 5; sorting and reporting on rubbish: Unit 1.
3 How is this environment changing?	Knows that people can affect and change environments.	Litter surveys: Unit 1; endangered species study: Unit 3; use of trees: Unit 5.
4 How can the environment be managed?	Can suggest ways to improve environments.	Recycling, making bins: Unit 1; making notices: Unit 2.

National Curriculum coverage

Unit 1 Litter

National Curriculum links
- Makes maps of real places.
- Investigates the quality of the environment.
- Discovers how the environment can be managed and improved.

Unit 2 Country code

National Curriculum links
- Use geographical terms.
- Make a map of an imaginary place.

Unit 3 Zoo animals

National Curriculum links
- Knowledge that environments are changing.
- Knowledge that environments need to be sustained and managed.

Unit 4 Seashore

National Curriculum links
- Use of geographical terms.
- Awareness of changing environments.
- Knowledge that environmental quality needs management.

Unit 5 Rainforest

National Curriculum links
- Express views on an environment.
- Knowledge that the environment is changing.

Scotland Environment Studies coverage

The units cover the following contexts and content for Understanding People and Places:
- Some ways of maintaining a clean environment.
- Developing the mental map of familiar places.
- Making models of known places and story settings.
- Using plans to find places.
- Major physical and natural features in the locality.
- The uses of buildings and land in the local area.
- Daily lives of some children elsewhere compared with their own.
- Things we use and eat which come from distant places.

Litter

Learning targets

On completion of this unit children should understand how to:

1 ➡ observe and record findings during fieldwork
2 ➡ find and add locations to a simple map
3 ➡ suggest a way to improve their surroundings.

Before you start

Background knowledge

Rubbish is a collection of items which we do not want. Litter is discarded rubbish which makes an area untidy. Litter can be a whole school topic to make the community more aware of caring for their immediate environment. If your school is already litter free then take on the challenge of a nearby park, the entrance to an old people's home or the area in front of the school gates. Your local council will have information on where the recycling banks in your area are.

Teaching points

This unit focuses on observation and mapping techniques while finding simple ways to prevent litter around the school. Children should only collect litter wearing protective gloves and under supervision.

Geographical skills

- Making and using a simple map with a key
- Using a survey sheet to record findings
- Observation in the local area

Vocabulary

litter, rubbish, waste, disposal, survey, recycle

Resources for Lesson 1

Copymaster 45 Litter survey, site plan, clipboards, pencils, felt-tip pens, word processor

Resources for Lesson 2

Empty cereal boxes, fabrics, papers and junk, art materials, scissors

Resources for Lesson 3

Ten green bottles, PE hoop, Copymaster 46 Empty bottles, paper, pencils

Resources for the activities

Protective gloves, paper, pens, word processor; Foreman, Alan *Dinosaurs and All that Rubbish* , Puffin, 1974

Assessment indicators

- Can the children find a place on a map?
- Do they understand the need to care for the environment?
- Do they use litter bins?

Teaching the lessons

Lesson 1 ① ②

Introduction 10 min

Use the class rubbish bin to stimulate a discussion which answers these questions:

- 'What do we put in here?'
- 'What is rubbish? What is litter?'
- 'How does rubbish become litter?'
- 'Is there any litter in our school grounds/ park/ street?'
- 'How did it get there?

Explain that our survey is a way to find out what and where the problem is.

Finding the litter 45 min

 Copymaster 45 Litter survey provides a simple litter survey that can be filled out on any site chosen. Each group will also need a simple plan of the site with some landmarks to help them work out their location. You may want to send different groups to different places on the site so that each group just checks out one or two locations. Using Copymaster 45, children record the amount of litter found. (More able children can be asked to devise their own symbols and key.) Results from the whole site can be collated to give an overall picture. With young children, you may want to do the whole site together, picking out places with varying amounts of litter to do the survey.

Summary `10 min`

As a class, write a report on your findings. Write on the board the sentences you all agree with. Ask for a statement of what you investigated. Follow that with what you found. Where does the biggest problem occur and why is that? Where is there no litter and why? Finish the report with a suggestion of what needs doing and a way of doing it. One group could word process and print the report so that everyone can have a copy.

Lesson 2 ③

Introduction `10 min`

Ask children to use a box, such as an old cereal packet, to design a small litter bin for their table or the library corner.

A monster litter bin `40 min`

The top of a used box will already be open. Children may need help with large scissors to cut this open top to make it like the mouth of an animal or a monster. Once this has been done, children can freely design their bin. If they need some guidance, enquire whether their creature has eyes, hair or scales, ears, and tongue so as to stimulate their thoughts on what they will include. There should be a collection of fabrics, papers and junk art materials for them to use.

Monster bins

Summary `5 min`

There may be places around the classroom and school where these bins could be used. Remind children about the litter survey from Lesson 1 which may show where they are needed.

Lesson 3 ③

Introduction `15 min`

Place ten green bottles in a row on the table and sing 'Ten Green Bottles' with the class. As each bottle 'falls' off the wall put it into a PE hoop or a box labelled either 'Bottle Bank', 'Dustbin' or ' Litter'. Explain that the 'Litter' may be anywhere, in the street, park, countryside, beach.

Recycling `30 min`

Using **Copymaster 46 Empty bottles** choose a task to suit the age and ability of your children.

1 Give each child a cut out of a bottle. Ask them to write on it what happens to the bottle when it is empty.

2 Give each child a green bottle shape. Ask them to cut a jagged edge on it and mount it on their page, finishing the sentence: 'This bottle is dangerous because…'

3 Using paper folded to make a concertina book, children can make a flow diagram, of the life of a bottle starting with being sold, then being used, thrown away and then…?

Summary `10 min`

Discuss the best place for bottles to go when they are empty. Sing 'Ten Green Bottles' again and this time let the ten bottles 'fall' into the bottle bank.

Extra activities ① ③

What's in the bin?

Using protective gloves, spread the contents of the class bin out onto a large sheet. Ask the children to name the types of things in there: paper, apple cores, broken pencils, plastic, etc. Separate the waste into two piles: things that can be used again and things that cannot. Ask children to draw these two groups or invent a way to use one item again.

Local recycling

Children write the slogan and draw the pictures for a handout to encourage local people to use the nearest recycling centre. The handout should include the location of the recycling banks and outline what facilities it has.

Using a story

Read D*inosaurs and all that Rubbish* by Michael Foreman. Use the story to create a drama role play, a poem or a 'Before and after' display that shows the effect of rubbish and pollution on the world.

Nature recycles

Teach the children about one of the ways recycling occurs in the natural world.

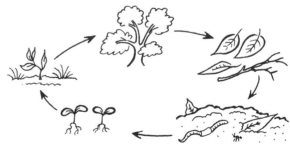

Water cycle

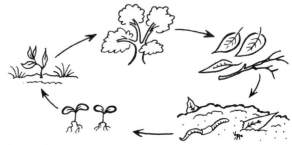

Plant cycle

Litter survey

Where is the litter? How much litter is there?

Survey	Place 1	Place 2
What litter is there?		
Where is it? (In, under behind?)		
Could it do any harm?		
How much litter? (One piece, two or three, more?)		

These bins show a way of recording how much litter was found.

 no litter

 two or three pieces

 lots of litter

How much litter did you find?

Place 1	Place 2	Another place?

Use pictures of bins on your map to show how much litter you found. Show them in the key.

Empty bottles

Bottles come in all shapes, colours and sizes.
They contain all sorts of things.

Lots of things happen to empty bottles.

Near where you live there will be a bottle bank for empty bottles.

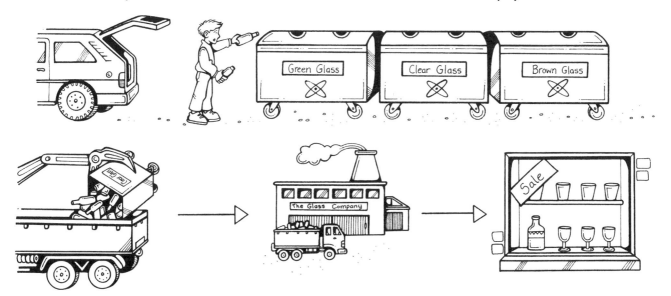

When the bottle banks are full, they are emptied into lorries and
taken to a factory to be made into recycled glass. The glass can be
made into more bottles and other things made from glass.

The Country Code

Learning targets

On completion of this unit children should know:

1 ➡️ some of the differences between a town and the countryside
2 ➡️ how gates are used
3 ➡️ some plants and wildlife to be found in the countryside.

Before you start

Background knowledge

The Country Code published by the Country Commission, 71 Kingsway, London WC2B 6ST gives this advice:

- Take your litter home.
- Take special care on country roads.
- Keep dogs under close control.
- Leave gates as found.
- Guard against all risk of fire.
- Leave livestock, crops and machinery alone.
- Keep to public footpaths across farmland.
- Respect wildlife.
- Use gates and stiles to cross fences, hedges and walls.
- Help to keep all water clean.
- Make no unnecessary noise.
- Enjoy the countryside and respect its life and work.

Teaching points

Some children never go into the countryside, even those who live nearby. Assume little or no knowledge about country matters.

Geographical skills

- Use geographical vocabulary to describe features

- Undertake fieldwork
- Make a pictorial plan or map

Vocabulary

country, farm, wood, pond, hedge, stile, gate

Resources for Lesson 1

Wilberforce Goes on a Picnic by Margaret Gordon; Copymaster 47 The picnic basket, felt-tip pens, items for fieldtrip/picnic, hamper or bag

Resources for Lesson 2

Paper, pencils, collage materials, photos of gates

Resources for Lesson 3

Copymaster 48 In the hedge, clipboards, green Binca® fabric, paper, string, twine, glue, twigs, modelling materials, hedge specimens

Resources for the activities

Paper, poster paints, felt-tip pens, nature specimens, counters, dice

Assessment indicators

- Can the children tell one Country Code rule?
- Can they identify a common flower, bird and tree?

Teaching the lessons

Lesson 1 ①

Introduction 20min

🎬 Read the story Wilberforce Goes on a Picnic by Margaret Gordon. Use the pictures in the book to stimulate a discussion on the differences between town and country. Find out who has been on a picnic and discuss what it is like – what you do, where you go and what you eat.

Ideally, take your class on a fieldtrip with a picnic to walk and sit in the countryside. If you use a footpath which crosses a farm it would be courteous to inform the farmer of your visit.

A country picnic 30min

👤 Using **Copymaster 47 The picnic basket**, ask the children to think of suitable foods to take for outdoor eating in the countryside. They can write or draw their ideas in the picnic basket. Suggest that they consider the problems of the sun melting chocolate, wasps liking sweet things and the difficulty of eating with a knife and fork outdoors. If there are things you wish them to bring on a fieldtrip, add them to this activity, and send the copymaster home as preparation for the visit.

Children can complete a picture map with features that show the change from town to country.

Summary `5 min`

Compare menus. Ask how you will carry the picnic if you are going for a walk. What bag would be the easiest to carry over stiles? When would a hamper be suitable?

Lesson 2

Introduction `10 min`

A series of photos or drawings of different gates would help answer questions such as 'Why do we have a gate at school?', 'Why do some people's houses have gates?' 'Why does a field have a gate?' Lead the children to consider that gates a) keep people out, b) keep people or animals in, and c) allow movement from one place to another.

The farm gate `30 min`

Ask each group to make a collage of their group looking over a gate into a farmer's field that they would like to cross on a footpath. There can be animals or crops in the field and a footpath alongside. There is a notice on the gate. Children can decide what it might say. Each child adds a picture of their own head looking over the gate and an item for the field, e.g. animals, wildlife, farm machinery or people.

Discuss the notice. Is it a request, a warning or does it convey some information? What type of things would the farmer put on a gate? The notice can be word processed, printed or handwritten.

Summary `10 min`

Display the work. Discuss the notices on the gates. What has each group chosen to write, and why?

Lesson 3

Introduction `10 min`

If there is a suitable hedge near your school, take the children to look at it. Otherwise fill a vase with a range of hedge plants such as hawthorn, holly, ivy, bramble and hazel. Explain that small plants grow under a hedge, and climbing plants grow up through it. The more species of plants in the hedge the more wildlife it will shelter. Farm animals shelter behind the hedge. Ask the children which creatures they think would use it for shelter.

Weave a hedge `30 min`

Combine use of **Copymaster 48 In the hedge** with experience gained from a short fieldtrip to a local hedge to provide a pictorial hedgerow display. Use green Binca® embroidery fabric for the background. Ask each child to use Copymaster 48 to help them provide material for the picture. If each child produces two twigs of hedgerow and one creature you should be able to build up a hedge rich with wildlife. The hedge can be three-dimensional, using bare twigs and paper leaves. Finished twigs can be placed on the background

and sewn in using string or garden twine. Creatures can be tucked or glued into the hedge. Add a footpath sign and a stile to give your hedge boundaries.

Summary `5 min`

Ask children at different times to identify the creatures and plants in the hedgerow display.

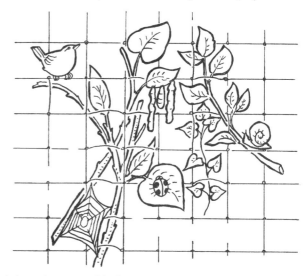

A three-dimensional hedge weaving

Extra activities

Close the gate!

Design posters which ask walkers to close the gate as they use a footpath through a farmer's field. Use the poster design to reinforce knowledge of some plants and creatures by asking children to decorate their poster with footpath wildlife.

Wildlife on a wall

A group of children can make a simple map of a wall in or near the school grounds. They draw the brick pattern and put coloured spots on places on the wall where some plants or creatures are found. They make a very large key, using the coloured spots matched to large pictures of the wildlife found. Label pictures with the name of the plant or creature.

A nature table

Some classes will have few children who have visited the countryside. Make a nature table which could last over a term and be forever changing. Start with simple specimens such as flowers and twigs from trees. Encourage children to bring in and label specimens. Add new things every two or three days. Gradually bring in unusual and fascinating specimens, e.g. a log showing annual rings or broken snail shells left by a thrush.

Country Code

Children can design and make a simple board game, that snakes from the town to the countryside picnic spot. As counters move forward on the throw of a dice, good Country Code behaviour is rewarded with extra turns and jumping spaces. Bad code behaviour results in missing turns and moving back spaces.

The picnic basket

Fill the picnic basket for a trip to the countryside.

As well as lunch, pack a game that can be played outdoors.

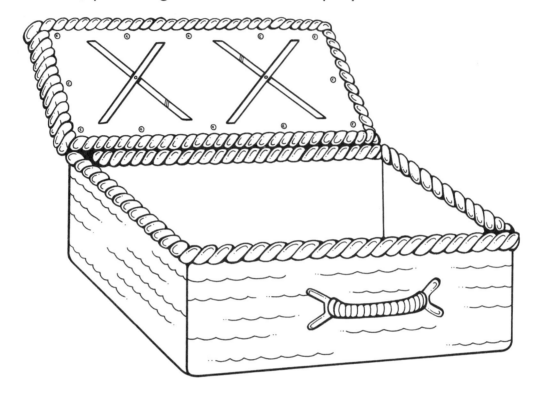

Finish the map. Can you show buildings and other things that could be seen on the way to the countryside?

Footpath

ivy

hawthorn

holly

hazel

These plants grow in a hedge.

Their leaves help us to get to know them.

wren

robin

blackbird

These birds nest or find food in a hedge.

A bird book will show you their colours.

ladybird

spider

'Hedge Brown' caterpillar and butterfly

lacewing

These insects and small creatures live among the leaves in the hedge.

primrose

violet

lords and ladies

These flowers grow under a hedge for shelter.

Zoo animals

Learning targets

On completion of this unit children should understand that:

1 ➤➤ zoos and sanctuaries keep wild animals captive
2 ➤➤ some animals are becoming extinct
3 ➤➤ maps show features of a place.

Before you start

Background knowledge

Parks and sanctuaries are being opened around the world to help protect wildlife. Animals in danger of extinction are bred in captivity and released into the wild, e.g. The Otter Trust in Norfolk, Howletts Gorilla Breeding in Kent and the Woolly Monkey Sanctuary in Cornwall.

In some zoos, animals are caged unsuitably and suffer in captivity.

Teaching points

Wild animals live in special habitats which may be declining. It is difficult to reproduce those habitats in captivity. Protecting endangered species shows the benefits of keeping animals in captivity.

Geographical skills

- Use of globes and atlases
- Making an imaginary map
- Research using secondary sources

Vocabulary

extinct, endangered, zoo, sanctuary, protect, breed

Resources for Lesson 1

Campbell, Rod *Dear Zoo*, Macmillan Children's Books, 1998; Copymaster 49 Dear zoo, pens, reference books, atlases, globes, world map

Resources for Lesson 2

Animal outlines, books, pens

Resources for Lesson 3

Copymaster 50 The lion is loose!; card, dice; magnets; modelling materials such as Plasticine®, balsa, lollipop sticks, corks, Blu-tak®, mesh, matchboxes, drawing pins

Resources for the activities

Paper, pencils, felt-tip pens, scissors

Assessment indicators

- Do the children know the name of an endangered species?
- Can they follow a route on a map?

Teaching the lessons

Lesson 1 ❶

Introduction [10min]

▓ Read aloud *Dear Zoo* by Rod Campbell. Which children have been to a zoo?

Zoo animals [30min]

👤 Using **Copymaster 49 Dear zoo**, children research one zoo animal. Make available atlases, globes and some information books about wild animals and their habitats. Researching some habitats may prove difficult. Food, water and shelter are an animal's main needs and the children should try to find out about them.

Summary [10min]

▓ Pin the children's work around a map of the world. Attach strings to the countries the zoo animals come from. What do the children notice?

Lesson 2 ❶

Introduction [10min]

▓ Draw outlines of some endangered species. Ask the children if they know which animals you have drawn. Explain why each one is in danger of becoming extinct. It is usually because its habitat is being destroyed or it is being killed for its skin or horns. You could include as few or as many as you wish from this list: tiger, rhinoceros, blue whale, panda, polar bear, fruit bat, tree frog, African elephant, natterjack toad, koala, sea turtle, swallowtail butterfly.

Endangered animals [30min]

👤 Ask children to draw their own outline or use a prepared template of an endangered species. Ask them to fill the animal shape with their ideas on why the animal is in danger, how they feel about it, and what could be done to save it. It may be a good idea for younger children to all work on the same animal following your talk about its life. The rhino would be an example. 'It lives in Africa. It is killed by poachers for its horn which is used for ornaments and dagger handles. Some people think its horn is medicinal.' Older children can use reference books to research information on other species.

Enlarge these animal outlines for use as templates

Summary 5min

Select children to read out their ideas. Is there an idea that can be followed up in another lesson?

Lesson 3 ① ③

Introduction 10min

Explain that the group are going to make a game for the rest of the class to play. This fun game teaches about the features found in a zoo, so ask the children for the types of buildings they would find in a zoo park. Small models will be needed, so allocate tasks to children. Here are some they may wish to include – cages, signpost, shop, ice-cream kiosk, zookeeper's office, lake, visitors, animals.

Magnetic Zoo map 30min

Provide a base board for a game of 'Magnetic Zoo' with at least 8 x 16 squares. The size of square will depend on model sizes, but 4cm square should be adequate. **Copymaster 50 The lion is loose!** gives ideas and instructions for making a variety of simple zoo models. Children may have different ideas or may adapt these to their own specifications. Drawing pins are magnetic and are used to make the base of magnetic people, who may be caught by the lion, whose base contains a magnet. The aim of the game is for the zookeeper (Player 1) to land on the same square as the lion (Player 2) and catch him before he eats too many people! The game is played by each player throwing a dice and

moving the number of squares around the board and around the obstacles. The lion tries to catch people. The zookeeper tries to catch the lion. Children may wish to develop different rules.

Summary 15min

When children have played the game ask them to make a map of the zoo and put in the route the lion took while trying to escape from the zookeeper.

Extra activities ① ② ③

Map a zoo

Make imaginary maps based on a discussion about the animals found in a zoo and the facilities for visitors. Children can make their maps pictorial or plan view and make a guided route.

Getting information

Children could write letters to different organisations, such as the two listed below, to find information on endangered species.

1   Elefriends, Cherry Tree Cottage, Coldharbour, near Dorking, Surrey RH5 6HA.
    This organisation works to protect African elephants against the ivory trade and is targeted at children.

2   The Whale and Dolphin Conservation Society, 20 West Lea Road, Weston, Bath BA1 3RL.

Looking after animals

If you have a school pet, make a lesson around the care of that animal. Each child draws the shape of the cage or hutch. Ask the children to make cut outs of the animal, its food and bedding to glue into the hutch. A speech bubble from the animal could ask for something to be remembered, e.g. a budgerigar may ask 'Please remember to put my cover on at night'.

Space for pandas

The bamboo forests where pandas live have been reduced by a quarter. To understand what this means ask them to draw a forest of bamboos. Some cane items would help with the artwork. Now ask them to fold their work into four and cut off three quarters and throw it away. This is the small forest that is left. It could be mounted next to a panda picture.

Diminishing bamboo forests

123

Draw a zoo animal in the cage.

Open the door... so we can see this animal in the wild.

Find out about its home in the wild.

What can you find out about its life?

_____

_____

_____

_____

_____

_____

_____

_____

_____

_____

50 The lion is loose!

How to make models for a game of Magnetic Zoo.

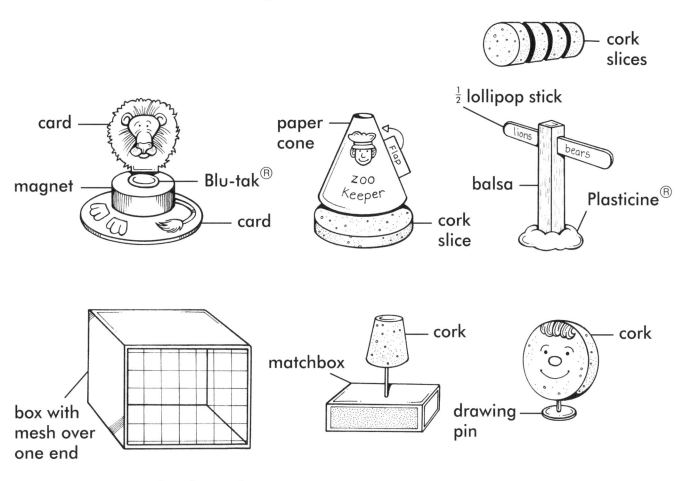

How to set up the board

Ask your teacher for a base. Add some ideas of your own.

Ask your teacher how to play the game.

THE ENVIRONMENT

UNIT 4

Seashore

Learning targets

On completion of this unit children should understand that:

1 ➟ the seashore is a habitat for creatures and plants
2 ➟ the seashore is a place for holidays
3 ➟ the sea washes things up onto the shore.

Before you start

Background knowledge

There are four main kinds of beach: rocky, sandy, muddy and shingle. Different plants and animals live in these different habitats. Rocky shores provide a habitat for shells, seaweeds, fishes and crabs. Sandy and muddy shores are good for birds, for shellfish that live under the surface and for plants in sand dunes. Shingle shores have little plant growth as they are constantly moved by the tides, but there will be plenty of washed up items, such as shells, seaweeds and egg cases. Barnacles and seaweeds are found on breakwaters. Tides are caused by the positions of the moon and sun in relation to the Earth. The sea comes up and goes down the beach twice every day. Before a visit to the seashore, check the tides to make sure that what you want to see is uncovered.

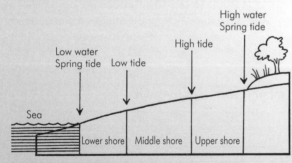
Zones on the shore

Teaching points

The shore is always changing because of tidal action. Animals and plants on the shore are adapted to and need a salty environment.

Geographical skills

- Use of vocabulary associated with coastal features
- Use of secondary sources

Vocabulary

beach, cliff, tide, rock, sand, waves

Resources for Lesson 1

Tank of garden snails, Copymaster 51 Empty shells, shell templates, paper, pencils, scissors

Resources for Lesson 2

Fishing net, bucket, reference books on seashores, bowl, blue poster paint, straws, A4 paper, black paper, Copymaster 51 Empty shells, cane, mesh, glue

Resources for Lesson 3

Items washed up on a beach such as shells, seaweed, driftwood, rope, bottle, can; tray of sand; Copymaster 52 Washed ashore, pencils, felt-tip pens

Resources for the activities

Squared graph paper, glue, coloured pencils, net, brown card, flat shells, sand tray

Assessment indicators

- Can the children draw a seashore scene?
- Can they group items into natural and manufactured sets?
- Can they match creatures to a habitat?

Teaching the lessons

Lesson 1 ①

Introduction 10min

Show the children some shells of different sizes and species. Ask the children to tell you what they know about them. Ask if they know why the shells are

empty, and talk about the creatures that live in shells. Set up a tank of garden snails for observation on how shell creatures move and use their shells.

Empty shells 30min

Copymaster 51 Empty shells shows shell creatures in their natural habitat with other rockpool creatures and plants. The sheet also explores some of the different things that happen to empty shells. A discussion with groups of children may bring out more ideas. Ask the children to draw a large shell shape and, inside the shape, to draw pictures and write about what happened to this shell when the creature inside died. Link this with language work to write poems about empty shells.

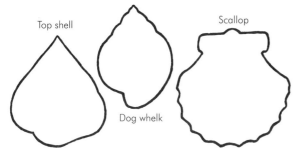

Top shell
Scallop
Dog whelk

These shell outlines can be enlarged and used as templates

Summary
☐ 5min

Read one or two pieces of work and display some shell work behind a display of empty shells.

Lesson 2
①②

Introduction
☐ 10min

Bring a fishing net and a bucket to a class discussion and tell the children you are going to the beach for a day out. What do they think you are going to do when you get there? Talk about the creatures you might catch in the rockpools, using pictures or information books to show what they are like. Explain that they need salt water to live in so you will return them at the end of the day.

Rock pools
☐ 30min

Find a bowl the size of A4 paper. Make a strong mix of water and blue poster paint. Provide children with straws and ask them to blow as many bubbles on the water as they can. While the bubbles are still high, gently lower the A4 paper on to them. The bubbles will burst leaving blue circles on the paper. Cut the paper into an uneven shape and mount on black paper to provide a rocky background. Using Copymaster 51 Empty shells and reference books, children can research some rockpool creatures to draw, cut out and glue onto the pool to make a group picture. A fishing net can be made from a cane and a piece of mesh and suspended over the picture.

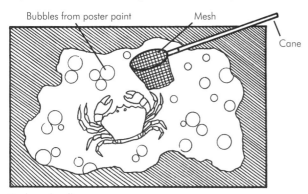

Bubbles from poster paint   Mesh
Cane

Rockpool collage

Lesson 3
①②③

Introduction
☐ 10min

Bring a plastic carrier bag containing items found washed up on the strandline by high tide. On a table covered with a layer of clean sand from the sand tray, gradually add the things from your bag, asking children to identify them and to tell you how they got onto the beach. Include natural items such as shells, seaweed, driftwood, and manufactured items such as rope, a bottle, a can and the empty plastic carrier bag.

Washed ashore
☐ 30min

Copymaster 52 Washed ashore asks children to identify things washed up on the beach and group them into 'natural' and 'manufactured' items. They are asked to choose an item and write down their thoughts about whether it is harmful and what eventually will happen to it. Differentiate by giving some children an opportunity to record how attractive or not the beach is when the tide has washed things up.

Summary
☐ 5min

Ask the children for ideas on how to reduce the amount of things washed ashore by the sea. As a class you may like to write a Beach Code – the seashore equivalent of the Country Code to encourage holiday makers to leave the beach clean.

Extra activities
①②③

Shell maths

Use some flat shells to introduce work on area. Ask children to draw around the shells on squared paper. Explain that to find out how much space the shell uses, count the squares. Whole squares count as one, half squares and larger than one half also count as one, but ignore squares less than a half. Compare different species or sizes of shells of the same species.

Acrostics

An acrostic poem focuses children on the vocabulary of a topic. Choose a seashore word and make an acrostic of seashore features. Decorate with creatures of the shore, e.g.:

Caves
Rockpool
Anemone
Beach

Experiment with sand

Use the sand tray to make damp sand. Feel and talk about the differences between dry and wet sand. Make a wet sandcastle. Let it dry out. What happens to the sand castle? Make prints in the wet sand. Blow on wet sand and dry sand to see what happens. Can children relate this to the beach? What happens on the beach when the wind blows? Can they make sand dunes in the sand tray?

51 | Empty shells

This is where shells live.

What happens to empty shells?

1 a home for a hermit crab   2 collected by a child

3 washed up by the sea and crushed into sand

Washed ashore

Can you name all the things washed up on the beach?

1 _____ 2 _____ 3 _____

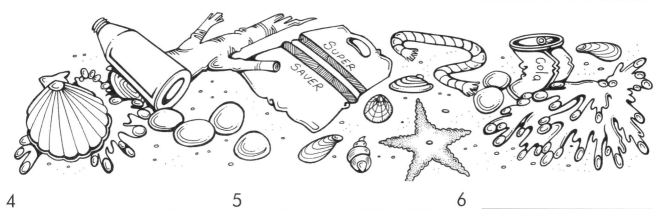

4 _____ 5 _____ 6 _____

Can you sort them into two groups?

natural things	rubbish

Choose one thing from the picture.
Why is it on the beach?
It is harmful?

_____

_____

_____

_____

_____

Rainforest

Learning targets

On completion of this unit children should understand that:

1 ➤➤ the rainforest is a rich environment containing trees and creatures
2 ➤➤ people live in the forest and find food there
3 ➤➤ the forest provides wood for making things.

Before you start

Background knowledge

Rainforest trees create a dense layer of foliage called a canopy. Very tall trees grow through the canopy. Parrots and toucan live there. In the canopy thick leaves cut out the light. Monkeys and sloth live there. In the shadowy layer, trees struggle towards the light. Butterflies and snakes live there. On the forest floor it is dark and gloomy. Insects, frogs and larger animals roam there. It is always hot and wet, large swamps and many rivers exist. Few people live in the dense forest but the edge of the forest is used by farmers, loggers and native villagers.

Teaching points

Children observe and research a fragile environment to discover the diversity of species of creatures to be found there. Trees take a long time to grow and we need them to keep oxygen in the air.

Geographical skills

- Use of geographical vocabulary
- Use of atlases and globes
- Use of photos and pictures

Vocabulary

forest, animals, jungle, unusual, rare, timber

Resources for Lesson 1

Bodsworth, Nan A Nice Walk in the Forest, Bodley Head; images of the rainforest, cheeseplant, paper, coloured feathers, glue, pens

Resources for Lesson 2

Copymaster 53 Food in the forest, Brazil nuts, cinnamon, honeycomb, mangoes

Resources for Lesson 3

Copymaster 54 Timber!, paper, pens, pencils

Resources for the activities

Cheeseplant leaf template, thick wax crayons white and green paper, pens, pencils, world map

Assessment indicators

- Can the children draw a rainforest scene?
- Do they know how wood is used?

Teaching the lessons

Lesson 1   ➊

Introduction   15 min

You will need a set of pictures, photos or a video to show the children the diversity of life in a rainforest. There is an amusing book called A Nice Walk in the Forest by Nan Bodsworth which could be used with this lesson. Show the children pictures and help them to imagine the hot wet jungle atmosphere where these animals and plants live. Cheeseplants grow in rainforests so, if you have one, bring it in for the children to see.

The forest   30 min

Make a template of a cheeseplant leaf 15–30cm long. Children can use it to cut out leaves, draw around and colour to make leaves or paint and press onto paper like a leaf print. Each child will need a large sheet of background paper to glue two or three overlapping leaves onto. Then they can make a bird or creature from your resource pictures to tuck into their 'forest'. Coloured feathers from a feather duster make a bright tail for a parrot or humming bird. Huge forests can be made if groups or the class combine their leaves and creatures.

Rainforest collage

Summary ⌗ 5 min

 Use the pictures to ask the children the names of the creatures of the rainforest. What do they find interesting about the different birds and animals?

Lesson 2

Introduction ⌗ 5 min

 Bring to a class discussion some things to eat that come from a forest such as Brazil nuts, cinnamon, honey and mangoes. Look at each one and taste at least one of them.

Food in the forest ⌗ 30 min

Copymaster 53 Food in the forest shows a forest dweller collecting honeycomb from a wild bees' nest in the hollow of a tree. The fire at the base of the tree creates smoke which soothes the bees, just as a beekeeper would. Assuming that you have talked about honey in the introduction to the lesson, children are asked to work out what the rainforest dweller is doing. The box below the person is to be filled with pictures of other food collected in the forest.

Differentiate by asking children to add other things collected in the forest. This might include leaves for thatching, water, dyes for decoration, wood for fires, canes for basket making. Either link this unit to a locality study such as Sri Lanka (*see* pages 170–77) or provide resource books.

Summary ⌗ 5 min

 Pass around pieces of honeycomb (available from health food shops) for children to look at or taste.

Lesson 3

Introduction ⌗ 5 min

 Ask questions so that children share their knowledge. What is a forest? What can the forest be used for? Who uses trees? What do they use them for? Explain that different people use wood and land for different things.

Timber ⌗ 40 min

 Copymaster 54 Timber! shows a logger cutting trees for export and a farmer cutting trees to clear the land. Both of them have reasons for cutting down the trees. The thought bubbles tell what will happen to the land or the timber.

Choose a task to suit the ability of the groups or pairs.

1 Pairs can turn the thought bubbles into speech bubbles to say what will happen.

2 Children in a group can each provide a fallen tree trunk for a pile of logs picture. On each tree trunk they can write what will happen to the log.

3 A group of children can draw the farmers' process from cutting trees, to burning them, hoeing land, planting and growing.

Logging collage

Summary ⌗ 5 min

 Ask the children if they can tell you how the rainforest is changing.

Extra activities

Jungle book

Use the cheeseplant leaf template to make pages for a book. Cut the same number of green and white leaves. Ask each child to draw an animal or bird on a white leaf shape. Alternate white and green pages so that each new creature appears from behind a green leaf. The green leaves could have characteristic slits in them so there is some clue of what is behind.

Made of wood

Outside, show the class how to make rubbings from a wooden gate, post or fence which shows the patterns of wood grain. Let the children use thick wax crayons to try it out for themselves. Inside the classroom ask the children to look for wooden items which show the grain in the wood. They can sketch an item and the pattern they have found on it.

The rainforests

Put a selection of all the work done on rainforests around a map of the world. Work with groups of children and, after looking on a globe or in an atlas for countries that still have some rainforests left, join the pieces of work to the locations with lines of trees, monkeys or parrots. Stress to the children that different countries have different plants and animals in their rainforests. Countries include The Gambia, Brazil, St Lucia, Sri Lanka, New Zealand and some Pacific islands.

He lights a fire.
He climbs the tree.
What is he doing?

_____

_____

_____

_____

_____

What other things does he collect in the forest?

Timber!

These people both work in the forest.

They are changing the forest.

This is a farmer.

This is a logger.

AROUND THE UK

Focus

This section introduces the UK as a nation of four countries. The first unit provides lessons which will familiarise children with the map of the UK and will start them looking at the variety of features to be found here. This unit can either be used in isolation or as an introduction to a contrasting locality study in the UK.

Both the locality studies are small places and can be studied in their entirety. For most children who live in towns and cities these places will provide a contrast to their own area. It is possible to choose other villages and islands and use the same lessons, adapting details of buildings and people's jobs to suit your own chosen locality.

Content

Unit 1: The UK
Unit 2: Frittenden village
Unit 3: Working in Frittenden
Unit 4: Iona, Scotland
Unit 5: Living on Iona

Source material

Frittenden and Kent:

- Tourist Information Centre, Cranbrook, Kent
- Kent Museum of Rural Life, Aylesford, Maidstone, Kent
- Argyll and Islands Tourist Board, Albany Street, Oban, Argyll PA34 4AR
- Craignure Tourist Information Centre, Isle of Mull, Argyllshire

Red Fox publish Mairi Hedderwick's Katie Morag books

Large PVC wall maps of the UK are available from Arnolds.

Brainstorm

This brainstorm shows how to make a 'web' for any chosen place. The headings cover study of a contrasting locality, wherever it may be. Underneath each heading is an example for Frittenden and an example for Iona. The small web shows the brainstorm for the UK unit on its own.

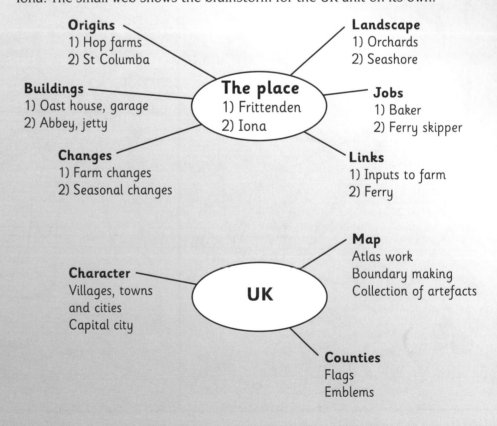

Origins
1) Hop farms
2) St Columba

Landscape
1) Orchards
2) Seashore

Buildings
1) Oast house, garage
2) Abbey, jetty

The place
1) Frittenden
2) Iona

Jobs
1) Baker
2) Ferry skipper

Changes
1) Farm changes
2) Seasonal changes

Links
1) Inputs to farm
2) Ferry

Character
Villages, towns and cities
Capital city

UK

Map
Atlas work
Boundary making
Collection of artefacts

Counties
Flags
Emblems

Teaching plan

This can be used as a medium-term plan and provides a scheme of work for any place. Details on the activities may need to be changed to suit the locality chosen.

Enquiry questions	Learning targets	Pupil activities
1 What is this place like?	Every place has its own character based on its physical features and land use.	Use of maps, pictures and artefacts to research the character of a place.
2 Who lives here and what do they do?	People in different places have different jobs. Daily life depends on facilities in the area.	Role play people's lives. Farm studies. Looking at the effect of weather.
3 How is the place linked to other places?	Roads, rail, ferry routes link places together.	Use maps to research journeys made. Discover methods of transport.
4 How is the place similar or different to where I live?	People in different places lead different kinds of life.	Compare a local farm or leisure opportunities. Draw contrasting views.
5 How is the place changing?	People and the weather change places.	Look at origins of a place and compare with present day. Study effects of farming changes and tourism on people's jobs.

National Curriculum coverage

Unit 1 The UK

National Curriculum links
- Awareness of the UK.
- Awareness that places exist within broad geographical contexts, e.g. within a town, a country, a nation, etc.

Unit 2 Frittenden village

National Curriculum links
- Study of a contrasting locality.
- Knowledge that environments are changing.
- Use of maps with different scales.

Unit 3 Working in Frittenden

National Curriculum links
- A contrasting locality study.
- Human features of a locality.
- Knowledge of how land and buildings are used.

Unit 4 Iona, Scotland

National Curriculum links
- A contrasting locality study.
- Use of maps and secondary sources to obtain information.

Unit 5 Living on Iona

National Curriculum links
- A contrasting locality study.
- Mapmaking skills.

Scotland Environment Studies coverage

The units cover the following contexts and content for Understanding People and Places:
- Major physical and natural features in the locality.
- The uses of buildings and land in the local area.
- Using plans to find places.
- Daily lives of some children elsewhere compared with their own.
- Things we use and eat which come from distant places.

The UK

Learning targets

On completion of this unit children should understand that:

1 ➤➤ we live in a part of the UK
2 ➤➤ the UK consists of four countries
3 ➤➤ villages, towns and cities are different types and sizes of settlement.

Before you start

Background knowledge

The UK is a political nation made up of England, Scotland, Wales and Northern Ireland. The British Isles are a geographical collection of islands that includes all of Ireland, the Channel Islands and the Isle of Man.

The national flag is the Union Jack, made up from the flags of the four countries and the nation's capital is London. Each individual country has its own flag and capital city.

Teaching points

The country we live in is part of a larger nation called the UK. By keeping this study of the UK on a geographical basis, children of different nationalities should not feel discriminated against.

Geographical skills

- Use of maps, globes and atlases
- Making simple maps
- Knowledge of the map of the UK

Vocabulary

nation, country, England, Scotland, Wales, Northern Ireland

Resources for Lesson 1

UK wall map, blank maps of the UK, enlarged copies of the country flags, collections of items from each of the four countries

Resources for Lesson 2

Copymaster 55 Village, town or city?, paper, pencils, felt-tip pens, glue, scissors, map of the local area

Resources for Lesson 3

Copymaster 56 London, tourist brochures of London, pencils, UK map

Resources for the activities

The Town Mouse and the Country Mouse, large outlines of flags, wax crayons, card, PE cones, glue

Assessment indicators

- Can the children mark a local town on a map of the UK?
- Can they name the four countries which comprise the UK?
- Can they recognise the four UK countries on a map?

Teaching the lessons

Lesson 1 ❶ ❷

Introduction [10 min]

▦ Use a wall map of the UK. Explain about the way the land and sea have been coloured differently. Point out the boundary lines between the four countries. Eire can be explained as a country which borders the UK, just as France shares a border with Belgium. Locate your own town and talk about its position in relation to the UK countries.

Mapping the UK [30 min]

▦ Work with a group and show the children how to colour a blue line around an island to show the coastline. Explain that this saves colouring of all the

sea. Help the children to mark the country boundaries on a blank map of the UK and let them suggest ways of showing each country on their map, and your own town. They may like to look at atlases to see what methods have been used there. The country flags can be enlarged for the children to add to their maps. Older children or those with more general knowledge may be able to add symbols of each country such as a thistle, a kilt or Ben Nevis for Scotland and so on.

Summary [5 min]

▦ Collect items from each of the four countries and display them on a wall map laid out on a table. Ask children to bring things to add to the collection that they can put on the correct part of the map.

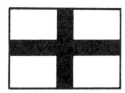
England

Wales

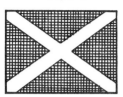
Scotland

Northern Ireland

Flags of the four countries

Lesson 2

Introduction [10 min]

 Use your own city, town or village as an example and let the children tell you its features. Probe for its buildings, shops, services (banks, fire station, offices, hospitals. leisure facilities, and transport networks. Now talk about the other two types of settlement and discuss whether they have more features or fewer than the type of settlement where you live.

Villages, towns and cities [30 min]

 Working in groups of three or six, and using **Copymaster 55 Village, town or city?,** children can create a set of three collages of the different types of settlement – villages, towns and cities. By cutting up pictures from the sheets they can build a settlement collage to show the buildings and transport found in each size of place. Cut outs of the signposts can be added and labelled with nearby places, chosen to fit each collage.

Summary [10 min]

 Look at a local map with each group and ask the children if they can find the names of some towns, villages and a city that they have been to or know about. Point out the way that the mapmaker shows the difference in size between the three types of settlements.

Lesson 3

Introduction [5 min]

Brainstorm 'London' with the class. Find as many images as you can of the capital of the UK. Use pictures or postcards to stimulate ideas. Ask questions such as 'Who lives there?', 'How do people get around?', 'Which famous buildings are there?'

London [30 min]

 Children can use **Copymaster 56 London** in a variety of ways. Differentiate by choosing tasks to suit the ability of the children.

1 Draw lines from the map to each of the features of London. Draw a route on the map as you visit some of the places.

2 Write a letter/postcard to a friend to tell them about a place you visited in London. Tell them its name and what it is like.

3 Make a page for a brochure called 'It's in London' and describe one of the capital's features.

Summary [10 min]

 Use the wall map of the UK to locate London and your own town. Find the other capital cities of the UK: Cardiff in Wales, Belfast in Northern Ireland and Edinburgh in Scotland. Explain that London doubles as England's and the UK's capital.

Extra activities

Town and country mouse

Read or tell the children the story of *The Town Mouse and the Country Mouse*, about the two mice who visited each other but found it difficult to adapt to the different life led by the other. Two big mice cutouts could be surrounded by speech bubbles that give impressions of life in a town and life in the country.

I live in the UK

This lesson would be suitable for foreign children recently arrived in the UK as well as those with some learning difficulties. Make a large Union Jack for each group of children. Number each panel on the flag and number some pots of wax crayons to match. When they have coloured the flag 'by number', each child makes a picture of a place they know. It can be local, a place visited or a famous place. Their drawings should be labelled and glued onto the Union Jack.

Flags

Use the idea above, extending it to include all the flags of the UK. Children can select a flag to colour and to research something about that country to represent on their flag. This would make a colourful bunting to hang in the classroom or hall.

Saints

Link with RE by telling the stories of St Patrick, St George, St David and St Andrew. Children can act out the saint's stories and make a banner for each saint showing the country flag and the saint.

Village, town or city?

Put the name of a village, a town and a city on the signpost.

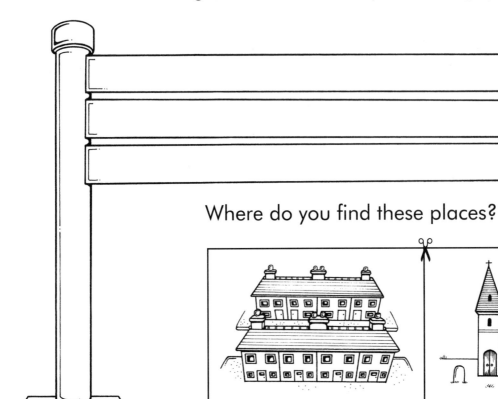

Where do you find these places?

Ways to travel in towns, cities and villages.

Here is a map of London. It shows some of the city's important and interesting places.

The numbers on the map match the numbers on each picture.

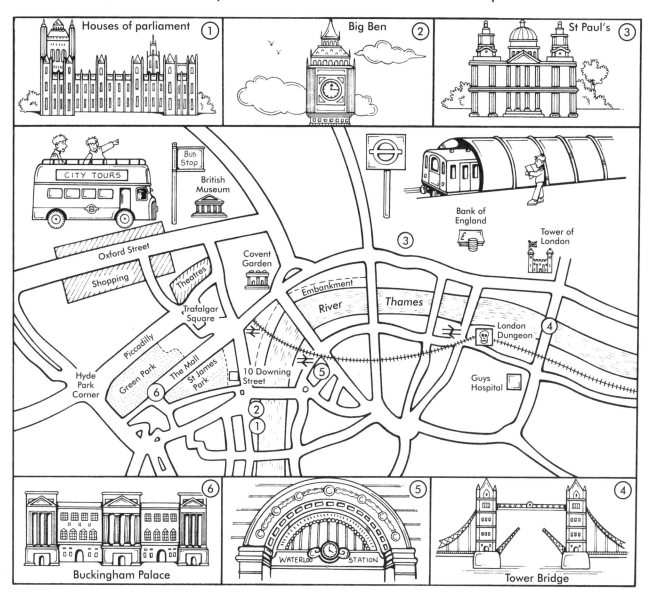

These labels tell you something about the places on the map.

1 The Prime Minister and members of Parliament meet here.

2 You can hear this famous clock chime on television and radio.

3 This cathedral was built by Sir Christopher Wren.

4 Traffic stops and the bridge is raised to let boats through.

5 Eurostar trains which go through the Channel Tunnel start here.

6 This is the London home of the Queen.

Frittenden village

Learning targets

On completion of this unit children should understand that:

1 ➡➤ a village is a small settlement with only a few services
2 ➡➤ Frittenden's origins are in farming
3 ➡➤ over time people's jobs and the use of buildings change.

Before you start

Background knowledge

Frittenden is a country village in Kent's 'Garden of England' area of orchards and hop farms. It has been affected by farming changes over the years. As hops became cheaper to import, all of Frittenden's oasthouses, which were used for drying the hop flowers for the brewing industry, have changed use. Some have become storage barns but most have been converted into unusual round homes. Old orchards have either been replaced by new low-growing trees or the farmer has changed to sheep rearing.

The village has a three-class school, village hall, a pub, a small garage and a village store. Many years ago it had a collection of small shops. An old mounting block (used to help people mount their horse) still remains at the garage which used to be the village forge.

One bus a week takes villagers ten miles to the north to Kent's county town of Maidstone for its Tuesday market. A local supermarket sends a free bus once a week. There is a farm study of a Frittenden farm in Section 4 (see pages 62–5).

Teaching points

By following a village trail made by the local schoolchildren this unit will look at the features of the village and trace some of its origins. Places change as modern methods and new ideas replace old ways of farming and working.

Geographical skills

- Use of a variety of maps with different scales
- Using secondary sources to obtain information
- Use of geographical vocabulary

Vocabulary

village, trail, country, field, forge, oasthouse, footpath

Resources for Lesson 1

Copymaster 57 Village trail map, pencils, felt-tip pens

Resources for Lesson 2

Copymaster 57 Village trail map, outline drawings of an oasthouse, pencils, felt-tip pens

Resources for Lesson 3

Horse shoe, item made from cast iron, hammer, coal, car part, spanners, safety glasses, petrol can, an electrical tool, Copymaster 58 Forge Garage, Copymaster 57 Village trail map, pencils

Resources for the activities

Copymaster 57 Village trail map, paper, felt-tip pens, card, PE cones, cane

Assessment indicators

- Can the children trace a route on the map?
- Can they explain the difference between a village and a larger settlement?
- Can they explain why a building may have a

Teaching the lessons

Lesson 1 ① ②

Introduction ⏱ 10 min

⚫⚫ Sit with a group, each child having **Copymaster 57 Village trail map** to look at. Introduce the village of Frittenden as a place that is different from your area but may have some features which are the same. Ask the children what they can find out by looking at the map. Encourage them to comment on the open spaces, the farms, the small number of buildings. Trace the walk around the village with them and stop and name each of the features and buildings represented or labelled.

A village trail ⏱ 30 min

👤 Children can use the map and information on the copymaster in different ways. Differentiate by setting tasks suitable for ability groups.

1   Draw a line to show the route taken around the village trail. Mount the map and draw countryside symbols around the edges.

2   Colour code roads red, ponds blue, houses black, etc. and make a key.

3   Use the map to make a list of the places where people work in Frittenden.

4   Ask the children to choose one place that interests them. Can they write some enquiry questions to show what they would like to know about it?

Summary

Ask the children about their discoveries in Frittenden and compare the features mentioned with your local area. 'Both areas have a shop, but are they different?' 'Both areas have a school, but are both small, Victorian buildings?'

Lesson 2

Introduction

Introduce a child at Frittenden School. His name is Craig Smith. He lives in an oasthouse behind the village store. The house used to be a farm building when the farmers in Frittenden grew hops. They used the oasthouse to dry the hops to make beer. Draw an outline of the oasthouse and point out how it was used. Now Craig's family live there. Most of the rooms are round. Craig's dad is a builder so he can paint and mend the cowl which is very high.

An oasthouse

The oasthouse

Locate some oasthouses on the village map. Find a way to mark them. Draw two pictures or fill in two ready prepared outlines:

- the oasthouse with farm work all around, smoke from the top and a man with a truck full of hops
- the oasthouse with children playing in a garden, windows added with curtains, a parked car.

Children can title each picture, label the differences or write captions about the change of use, depending on their ability.

Summary

Use an example of a building that has had a change of use near you to point out a local example to your class. It may be a shop, cinema, or empty premises waiting for a change.

Lesson 3

Introduction

Make a simple collection of a horse shoe, an item made of cast iron, a hammer and some coal. Alongside it put a part of a car, some spanners, safety glasses, a petrol can, an electrical tool or similar items from a garage. Discuss with the children how transport has changed from using horses to using vehicles. In Frittenden village there used to be a forge. Can the children guess what it is used for now?

Forge Garage

Children use **Copymaster 58 Forge Garage** to trace the change from horses to vehicles in Frittenden. There are spaces for 'Then' and 'Now' pictures to show the change of use of the building, and also the change from horse to vehicle transport.

Summary

Can each group tell you about the changes that have taken place at Forge garage? Which two old things still remain? (The name and the mounting block.)

Extra activities

Place names

In Frittenden the following road names tell you something about the features of the road: Mill Lane, The Limes, Chestnut Close. House names in the village reveal their origins: The Old Bakehouse, Cherry Tree Cottage, Weaver's Den, Ivy House. Ask children to draw house plaques to match the names.

Book of buildings

Take each building picture from Copymaster 57 Village trail map and enlarge it. Children take one building each and identify it on the map. They write it's name and write or draw pictures to show what it is used for. Put all the work together into a book with the village map at the front.

A village sign

Most of the villages in this part of Kent have a village sign which shows pictorially the character of the village. A group of children can make a village sign for Frittenden. Each child draws a feature of the village and together they assemble them as a collage on a piece of card. Finished signs can be attached to a cane and stood in PE cones.

Village trail map

This map shows a trail made by children at Frittenden School to show visitors some of the places in the village.

Start at the school and follow numbers 1–6.

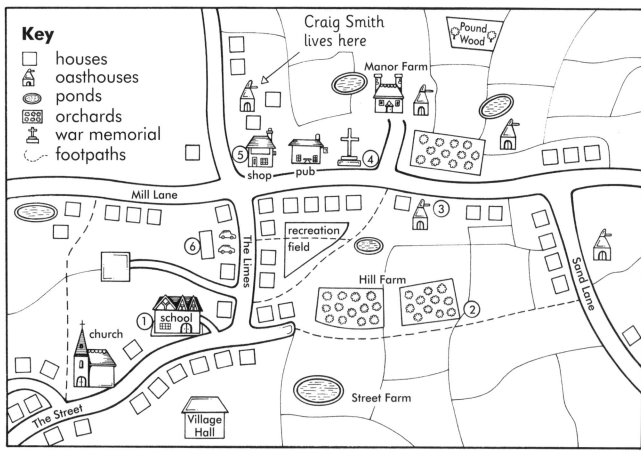

Farming

100 years ago   today

Repairs

at the forge   at the garage

What remains

What else reminds us?

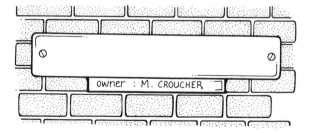

owner : M. CROUCHER

the mounting block

Can you find the meanings of these words?

- forge _____
- mechanic _____
- blacksmith _____
- garage _____

Working in Frittenden

Learning targets

On completion of this unit children should understand that:

1 ➡➡ different people have different jobs
2 ➡➡ some jobs provide a service, some make or produce goods
3 ➡➡ not all services are available in a village.

Before you start

Background knowledge

In Frittenden there are a mixture of old, uncommercial orchards with large trees and newer orchards with dwarf trees for easy picking and pruning. Mainly apples, but some pears are grown in Frittenden. There has been a baker in Frittenden for a long time. Recently the baker bought the village store and has combined the bread shop with groceries and a post office. He also sells stationery and is an agent for dry-cleaning. Other people who work in the village are employed in a plant nursery, the school, an old people's home, the pub and on farms. A lot of residents commute to London which is about an hour from a station three miles away, in Staplehurst. The mobile library visits the village hall once a week on Thursdays. Old people and the junior classes from the school are the main borrowers. Cranbrook, the nearest town with banks, a supermarket and small High Street shops, is five miles away.

Teaching points

Villages provide some essential services and a few places of work but most villagers need to visit nearby towns for work and shopping.

Geographical skills

- Using secondary sources
- Asking enquiry questions

Vocabulary

work, service, goods, market, mobile, orchard, library

Resources for Lesson 1

Copymaster 57 Village trail map, paper, pencils, felt-tip pens

Resources for Lesson 2

Shopping basket, purse, coat, used envelopes, Copymaster 59 The village store, pencils, pens

Resources for Lesson 3

Copymaster 60 In the orchard, pencils, pens, English apples

Resources for the activities

Paper, felt-tip pens

Assessment indicators

- Do the children know which jobs are common to all places?
- Do they know the types of jobs to be found in a small country village?
- Can they ask questions to discover details about a job?

Teaching the lessons

Lesson 1 ① ② ③

Introduction   10min

Use the village trail map on Copymaster 57. Make an OHP transparency of it and project it onto the wall. If you have not got this facility, enlarge the map as much as possible. Ask the children to point out places on the map where people work. Do they know any places where people work which do not seem to be in Frittenden? Encourage answers by referring to places of work near your school.

Working in Frittenden   30min

Ask all but one group to make a poster, entitled 'I work in Frittenden'. Each child in the group should draw a picture of a person at work in one of the places, showing the type of work they do. The people can be cut out and mounted on the poster with captions such as 'I work at the school. I am the secretary.' More able children can write a full job description, or write their views on working in the village, with its advantages and disadvantages.

The extra group of children should make a different poster that shows some jobs that cannot be found in the village, entitled 'Jobs in other places'.

Summary `10 min`

 Look at all the posters together. Discuss the jobs in Frittenden. Can these jobs be done in most places? Which ones are not found in towns and cities? Now look at the jobs in other places. Can the children suggest why these jobs are not done in Frittenden?

Lesson 2 ① ②

Introduction `10 min`

 Bring a shopping basket, containing a purse, some addressed envelopes and a dirty coat to the classroom. Tell the class that the farmer's wife, is going to Mack's Stores. She needs to buy some things for breakfast tomorrow and deal with the things in her bag. The children can tell you the things she may want to buy for breakfast and what she will need for the letters to be posted. They may need to be told about agencies for dry-cleaning.

The village store `35 min`

Able children can start the activity by making a shopping list so that nothing is forgotten. With young children, this could be done pictorially as a huge wall display. **Copymaster 59 The village store** asks children to draw items that are for sale in the frame of the shop window. They are then asked to find out about Mack's job. They will need to think up some questions to ask him about breadmaking, the postbox, the people he employs and his working hours. These can be written in speech bubbles and glued onto the copymaster.

Summary `5 min`

 Between yourself and the children you could try to answer some of the questions they have put to Mack to find out about his job.

Lesson 3 ① ②

Introduction `5 min`

 Remind the children about the four seasons and some of the changes that occur. Explain that a farmer's job changes with the seasons because of the changing weather.

In the orchard `40 min`

Children can use **Copymaster 60 In the orchard** to trace seasonal work in an orchard. The four seasons pictures can be copied onto a seasons box, which can vary in size, to make a pencil container or a bin for apple cores! The orchard picture shows picking aids, apple carriers and bulk bins, beehive (for pollination), and a cold store/packing shed. Children can fill in the spaces around the orchard with workers, apple bulk bins, labels and captions.

Season's box

Summary `5 min`

 Cut up some English apples, and have a tasting session to round off the work. Discovery, Cox and Jonagold are regional varieties.

Extra activities ① ②

Apple tree

In large cut-out apples, children can draw one of the things that happens to an apple during its growth, harvest and sale. If you can arrange to get the whole apple story covered, then hang them in a flow line to show the sequence of events, or hang them on a cut-out of an apple tree.

A survey of jobs

Ask children to bring to school the title of a job of one member of their family. Arrange these jobs into sets, depending on the range you get. You may have jobs under titles such as building, office, transport, shop and sales, computers, farming, horticulture, factory manufacture, food. The range can be displayed in graphs or Venn diagrams.

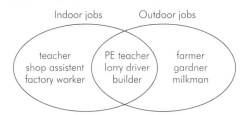

Venn diagram

Unusual jobs

Choose a few unusual jobs that children will find exciting, e.g. hot air ballooner, astronaut, clown, lifeboat crew. Research these jobs with the children working in groups. Ask them to draw themselves doing this job and describe how they feel about the job they do. Each group can present their unusual job to the rest of the class.

Jobs charades

Whisper the name of a job to a child. Ask them to act the job to the rest of the class. Children can guess the job that is being acted. If they find this very difficult let them use some words as clues, e.g. a shopkeeper may say 'We close at 5 o'clock'.

59 | The village store

What can you buy in the village store?

Draw some of the things Mack sells in the shop window.

MACK'S STORES

OPEN

This is Mack. He is a baker.

Draw some things that a baker makes.

The village store is a post office and a grocery shop too. Think of some questions you may like to ask Mack about his job there.

_____

_____

_____

_____

In the orchard

Different things happen in the orchard in different seasons. The pictures show you the work the farmer does in each season.

winter	spring	summer	autumn
pruning	pollinating	thinning	picking

In autumn the apples are ready to pick. It is the busiest time of the year.

There are spaces in the picture for you to add some words.

Iona, Scotland

Learning targets

On completion of this unit children should understand that:

1 ➡➡ people live in different sorts of places
2 ➡➡ places develop from different origins
3 ➡➡ people and the natural environment give a place its character.

Before you start

Background knowledge

Iona is a small island, three miles long and one and a half miles wide. It is situated a short distance off the south-west tip of Mull, a larger island in the Inner Hebrides, on the west coast of Scotland. For 14 centuries Iona has been a focal point in the Christian world. St Columba came to Iona in AD 563 from Ireland, and by the seventh century Iona was the centre of Christianity for Europe. Pillaging by Viking and Danish pirates in the eighth and ninth centuries wiped out religious buildings, and nothing very much remains earlier than the thirteenth century except for sculptured stones carved by monks. In 1938 the Church of Scotland formed the Iona Community, a group who have rebuilt and restored the ancient buildings, keeping Iona a place of pilgrimage.

Teaching points

Places are changed by the people who live there. Iona is an island with religious origins.

Geographical skills

- Use of maps as resource material
- Answering enquiry questions

Vocabulary

island, saint, pilgrim, abbey, monks, Celtic, monument

Resources for Lesson 1

Copymaster 61 St Columba of Iona, paddle, blue crêpe paper, Irish and Scottish flags, pencils, pens

Resources for Lesson 2

Copymaster 62 Celtic art, long strips of coloured paper, pencils, felt-tip pens

Resources for Lesson 3

'Fingal's Cave' by Mendelssohn, sea sound effects, Copymaster 61 St Columba of Iona, Copymaster 63 The ferry, Copymaster 64 On Iona, pencils, felt-tip pens, crayons

Resources for the activities

Balloons, *papier mâché*, black polythene, Plasticine®, outline map of Iona
Copymaster 61 St Columba of Iona

Assessment indicators

- Can the children locate a place on a map?
- Can they use resources to answer an enquiry question?

Teaching the lessons

Lesson 1 ① ②

Introduction ⏱10min

▦ Read this short account of the story of St Columba.

Columba lived in Ireland, and went to a school run by monks who trained him to become a priest. He travelled around Ireland, setting up monasteries and building churches. There were many battles in Ireland. Columba led one battle and many people were killed. The church leaders were angry with him. They told him to go out and find a new land to tell people about God.

He set off with 12 followers in a small boat called a coracle. They stopped at several islands on their way, but from each one he could still see Ireland, so he sailed on until he reached Iona. He saw a bay with steep cliffs, lots of rocks, and a small beach with some hills behind. He climbed the hill and looked out to sea. He could no longer see Ireland so he decided to stay. There was nowhere to sleep and no church so there was plenty of work to do. Columba started to teach people all over Scotland about God and he started over 100 churches. The monks on Iona carried on Columba's work and Iona became an important centre for Christians. Pilgrims travelled many miles to visit the island because Columba had started the Abbey there.

Explain that you would like the class to act out the story of St Columba's journey to Iona.

St Columba `45min`

 The drama role play needs to answer these questions: 'Who is St Columba?', 'Why did he leave Ireland?', 'How did he cross the sea to Iona?' 'What did he find when he landed on the island?' 'How did he develop the island?'

You could split the class into groups and ask each group to act out the answer to one enquiry question. Children holding banners with the questions written on them could introduce each section. The map on **Copymaster 61 St Columba of Iona** will give some ideas on answering the questions. Whether you use silent acting or spoken parts will depend on the ability of the children. Some ideas for props:

- a coracle: a moving circle of children holding hands, with Columba inside holding a paddle
- the sea: strips of blue crêpe or tissue, flapped to make waves
- Ireland and Scotland: flags from Unit 1 stood in PE posts.

Summary `10min`

 Practise and perform during an assembly or to another class.

Lesson 2

Introduction `5min`

 Use the map to locate the stone crosses on Iona. Explain that these are ancient monuments carved from stone by the monks. You may like to compare it with monuments in your area, such as war memorials, statues, or commemorative plaques.

The designs are Celtic, so circles and knots are strongly represented.

Celtic art `40min`

 The colouring activity on **Copymaster 62 Celtic art** gives the child the opportunity to get a sense of the pattern of circles used in Celtic art. The children are given the opportunity to draw a freehand map and to use symbols to mark Iona's stone crosses. One activity involves making coils of rolled paper and forming patterns of circles. The circles can be joined by strips of paper. For this activity the children will need long strips of coloured paper, cut fairly narrow, to approximately 1cm on a paper cutter. Differentiate for less able children by making one large classroom cross where each child makes a circle of paper and adds it to the master collage. More able children can form the paper circles into flowers or animals.

Summary `5min`

 Children can title their picture with a reference to Iona, such as 'Iona has Celtic crosses' or 'The monks carved the cross with circles'.

Lesson 3

Introduction `15min`

 Talk with your class about the features seen around the coast. Include waves, rocks, cliffs, other islands, caves and beaches. Iona has white beaches made from broken shells. Talk about the sounds the sea makes on rocks, on the beach, when it is rough and when it is calm. Play some music or sound effects connected with the sea. 'Fingal's Cave' by Mendelssohn, was inspired by his visit to Iona and a trip to Fingal's Cave on nearby Staffa.

Viewpoints `30min`

 Children paint pictures of a view of Iona, with the sea in the foreground or background, adding some of the coastal features discussed with the teacher. The children may like to hear the music while they paint.

Summary `10min`

Put up a gallery of pictures, called 'Views of Iona', and ask each artist to introduce their picture to the class.

Extra activities

Coracles

 Make a boat that floats. Children can design their own coracles or try this idea. Cover a blown up balloon with *papier mâché*. When dry, cut it in half to produce two boat shapes. Waterproof the coracle by stretching black polythene over the bottom. Fold it over the edges of the balloon boat and staple near to the rim. It may need to be weighted with Plasticine® for balance.

Caves

Start children off on a story where something is carried into a cave by the waves. Let them write their own story about the rocks, the waves, the dark cave, and what it feels like to be in a cave. The spouting cave on Iona sends a plume of water 100 feet into the air in rough weather. This could be incorporated into the story as part of the adventure.

St Columba's island

After reading the story of St Columba, give each child an outline map of Iona. Show them how to colour the outline of the island blue to represent the sea. Inside the map, ask them to draw part of the story. In the sea around the map they can draw the coracle bringing St Columba to Iona. Some children may be able to label the map and the pictures.

St Columba's diary

Children can write a diary account of St Columba's first days on Iona. They should record what he found there and what plans they think he would have had. You may want to discuss with the children the 'necessities' of life – food, water and shelter – and how might Columba planned to provide for them.

There were no buildings when Columba arrived.

You can see that many of the places on Iona are named after Columba and his monks.

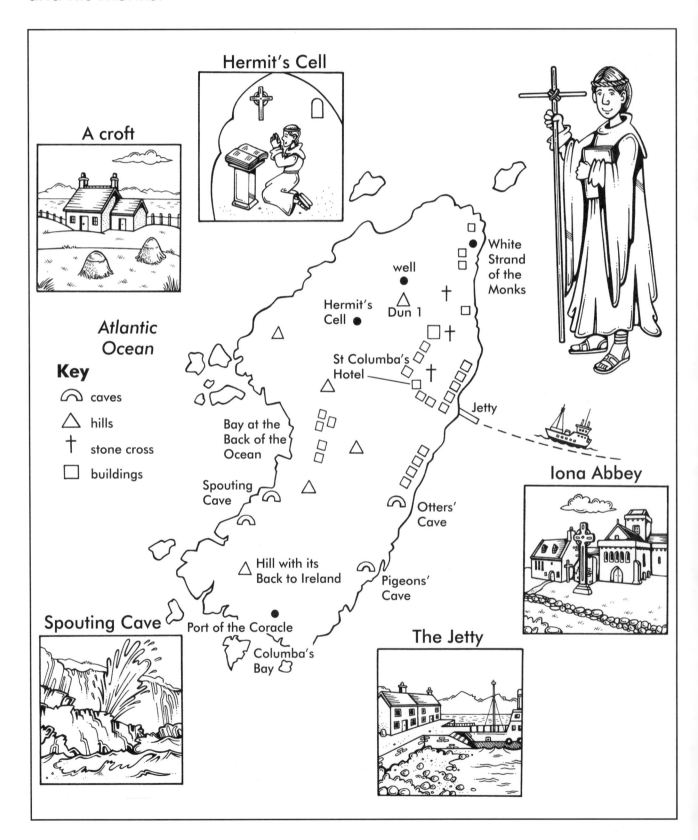

Hermit's Cell

A croft

Atlantic Ocean

Key

⌒ caves

△ hills

✝ stone cross

☐ buildings

well

Hermit's Cell ●

Dun 1

White Strand of the Monks

St Columba's Hotel

Bay at the Back of the Ocean

Spouting Cave

Jetty

Iona Abbey

Otters' Cave

Hill with its Back to Ireland

Pigeons' Cave

Spouting Cave

Port of the Coracle

Columba's Bay

The Jetty

Celtic art

Colour the patterns on the stone cross.

Draw a map of Iona.

Mark the crosses on your map.

Island of Iona

To make your own celtic pattern:
- take a strip of paper
- roll it up
- hold the top with glue between each layer
- now make some more
- make them into a pattern
- stick them onto card with thick glue.

1

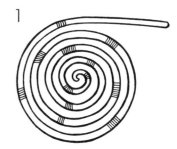

2

Glue

3

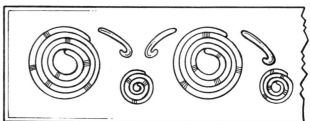

Living on Iona

Learning targets

On completion of this unit children should understand that:

1 ➡➤ the weather affects everyday life on an island
2 ➡➤ people choose island life for different reasons
3 ➡➤ island life depends on transport by boat.

Before you start

Background knowledge

Iona is linked to Mull by ferry to Fionnport – about a ten-minute crossing. Mull is also an island, so another ferry crosses to Oban on the Scottish mainland from Craignure. Tobermory, on Mull, has the main shops and services. A mobile bank comes to Iona once a week for half an hour. Buses run to Craignure and Tobermory from the ferry at Fionnport. The nearest doctor is on Mull. The nearest hospital for serious cases is on the mainland and is reached by helicopter or lifeboat. Rough Atlantic seas can make boat journeys impossible. Wet weather is common because of its westerly position but hot summers are frequent. Most jobs are linked to tourism and the abbey. There are about 70 homes on the island, of which 20 are in the village with the jetty and post office. There is a small primary school. Secondary age children cross to Mull and generally go to Tobermory. Some small farms (crofts) keep sheep and grow grass for hay.

Teaching points

Stress the smallness of the island, its distance from any large town or the type of facilities in your area which are taken for granted, and the islanders' dependence on transport by boat.

Geographical skills

• Communication of ideas
• Using geographical terms
• Making simple maps

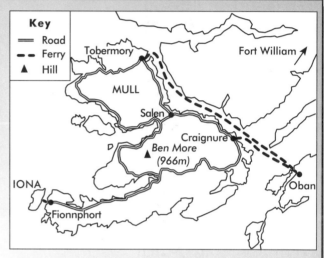

Iona, Mull and the Scottish mainland

Vocabulary

jetty, ferry, tourist, mail, artist, hotel, croft

Resources for Lesson 1

Copymaster 63 The ferry, pencils, felt-tip pens

Resources for Lesson 2

Copymaster 64 On Iona, pencils, felt-tip pens

Resources for Lesson 3

Paper, pencils, felt-tip pens, crayons, UK map

Resources for the activities

Hedderwick, Mairi *Katie Morag and the New Pier*, or *Katie Morag Delivers the Mail*, Red Fox, 1994; paper, pencils, felt-tip pens, crayons

Assessment indicators

• Can the children give a reason why the ferry crosses to Iona?
• Can they give a reason why holidaymakers visit Iona?

Teaching the lessons

Lesson 1 ③

Introduction [5min]

▨ Talk about the meanings of the following words used in this lesson.

ferry, jetty, skipper, passenger, gangway

This could be used as a dictionary exercise in a language lesson.

The Iona ferry [40min]

▣ Use **Copymaster 63 The ferry.** The ferry is depicted at Fionnport on the island of Mull in the afternoon. It is filling up with passengers for Iona.

152

The children look at the picture and try to work out who each passenger is, where they may have been and why they are going to Iona. Categories of people on the ferry include tourists/pilgrims, islanders coming back from work, school and shopping. Goods and services such as the mail, the mobile bank, sheep in a pen and milk crates are also arriving. The ferry skipper is on the boat. Children make a list of passengers and goods. Then they choose one passenger and one item and draw and write about why the journey is made.

Summary `10min`

 Talk about the things which are not available on the island, that the islanders need to go to Mull or the mainland for, e.g. doctor, dentist, hospital, shoe shop, cinema, a market.

Lesson 2 ②

Introduction `10min`

Explain that only a few people live on Iona but many come to visit, especially in the summer. Help the children to think of reasons why it would be a good place for a holiday, and what jobs the islanders do. **Copymaster 64 On Iona** shows its attractions and facilities.

People on Iona `30min`

Using Copymaster 64, choose one of the following activities according to the children's ability.

Things to see

1 Children can draw a map of Iona and decorate it with things seen on the island.
2 Children can make a poster advertising a day trip to Iona.

People at work

1 Ask children to do a 'profile' of one person's job with drawings and an account of what they do.
2 Children make a Venn diagram of 'Indoor jobs' and 'Outdoor jobs'.

Summary `5min`

Talk to the class about their views on whether Iona would be a nice place to work. What job would they like to do there?

Lesson 3 ①

Introduction `10min`

Check that your class are aware of the names and pattern of seasons through the year. Use the wall map of the UK and show where Iona is in relation to your home area. Point out that, although the seasonal pattern is the same all over the UK, in the north winters tend to be longer and harsher. Show the children the Atlantic Ocean from which Iona has little shelter, and explain that the sea brings winds and rain to the island.

Weather on Iona `30min`

Split the class into two groups. Explain that one group will think about winter on Iona and the other group about summer on the island. Brainstorm the things found in each contrasting season.

Winter	Summer
Snow	Swimmers in the sea
Cattle with long shaggy coats	Beach games
Farmers giving hay to cattle	Puffins flying
Stormy sea	Café open
Boatmen in oilskins	People in shorts
People in wellington boots	Tourists arriving
Cancelled ferry notice	Boat trips
Gift and art shop closed	Artist painting outside
Power cuts and storm damaged buildings	

Each group makes a composite picture of the contrasting activities on the island, one mounted on a background of calm sea, the other on rough seas.

Differentiate by adding spring and autumn. These two seasons should include people preparing for the summer tourist trade and preparing for winter storms.

Summary `5min`

Ask one or two children to present their picture to the other group and explain about the seasonal activities taking place on the island.

Extra activities ① ② ③

Katie Morag stories

Read one of the stories by Mairi Hedderwick to the children. Each story gives a true image of an island in the Hebrides and can be used to create the atmosphere of Scottish island life. Choose pages from the book to set simple enquiry questions that ask for a picture and sentence answer, e.g. 'What is the jetty like?', 'What can you find on the beach?'

Katie Morag's problems

Katie Morag Delivers the Mail, and *Katie Morag and the New Pier* are both stories which show problems that can arise on a small island like Iona. Choose one of the stories and, after reading it to the class, ask 'What if... ?'An example from *Katie Morag Delivers the Mail*, could be, 'What if Katie had broken her arm when she fell in the stream?' This could lead to work on how she got to hospital on the mainland, with a sequence of drawings showing her journey by tractor, ferry to Mull and helicopter to Oban.

Postcards

End the locality study by making postcards which show an aspect of life on the island. Messages on the back should show something the children have learned about the island, and can be used for assessment.

153

Look at all the people who are waiting for the ferry.
Work out who they are and why they are going to Iona.

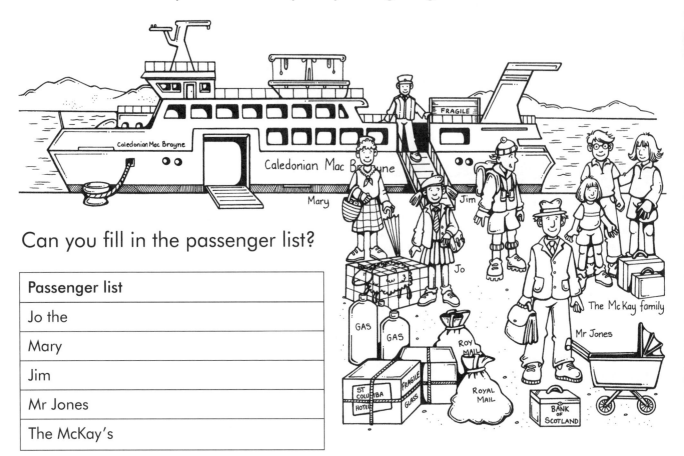

Can you fill in the passenger list?

Passenger list
Jo the
Mary
Jim
Mr Jones
The McKay's

Choose one person.

Write their name in the box. Write or draw
where they have been or what they are
going to do on Iona.

Choose one item.

Draw it in the box.
Why is it going on
the ferry?

On Iona

Things to see

the abbey	seabirds	art gallery
shells on beaches	highland cattle	seals

People at work

post man	boatman	farmers
hotel workers	artist	abbey guide

PLACES OVERSEAS

Focus

Unit 1 looks at the world as a wider place and discovers some international links related to the food we eat. It introduces the use of atlases and globes to locate places and has cross-curricular links with science and food technology. Unit 1 can be used as an introduction to the place studies. The rest of the section covers two place studies, either of which could be chosen as a contrasting locality.

France is in the nearest foreign country for many British children; some French language is often known in the school and food links are quite common. Many children will have some rudimentary knowledge of 'Frenchness'. The units on Chinon provide an opportunity to build on a little knowledge and perhaps dispel any incorrect ideas or stereotyping that may have been introduced elsewhere.

Sri Lanka has been chosen for its size and its island completeness. It has strong links with the UK through its exports and tourism. It is far enough away to be exotic and therefore very interesting with its different culture, climate and wildlife.

Content

Unit 1: World cookshop
Unit 2: Chinon, France
Unit 3: Journeys in Chinon
Unit 4: Sri Lanka
Unit 5: Conservation in Sri Lanka

Brainstorm

The brainstorm gives headings to suit any locality study, and has separate lists for the two locations in this section.

Source material

Chinon place study

Tourist maps and brochures:

- The French Tourist Office, 178 Piccadilly, London

Books for children:

- Perrault, *The Sleeping Beauty*
- Aesop, 'The Fox and the Grapes' and 'The Crow and the Cheese'
- Williams, B *Joan of Arc*, Cherry Tree Books, 1989

Teacher resource books:

- Scoffham, Stephen and Thomas, Sue *Blueprints: Infant Geography Resource Bank*, Stanley Thornes Publishers, 1994

Sri Lankan place study

Geography Junction 'Take two' Resource Pack, Channel Four Publications

Sri Lanka Tourist Board, 53 Haymarket, London SW1Y

Books for children:

- Bennett, Gay *Sri Lanka*, Beans Books, 1984
- Tzannes, Robin and Paul, Korky *Sanji and the Baker*, OUP, 1993

Many Oxfam shops sell Sri Lankan decorated elephant ornaments and other goods.

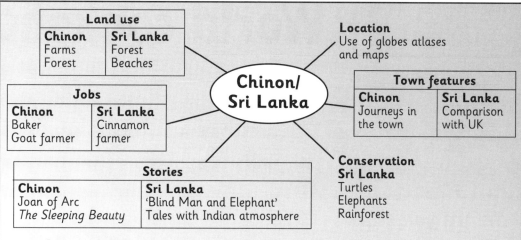

Land use	
Chinon	**Sri Lanka**
Farms	Forest
Forest	Beaches

Location
Use of globes atlases
and maps

Chinon/ Sri Lanka

Jobs	
Chinon	**Sri Lanka**
Baker	Cinnamon
Goat farmer	farmer

Town features	
Chinon	**Sri Lanka**
Journeys in	Comparison
the town	with UK

Conservation
Sri Lanka
Turtles
Elephants
Rainforest

Stories	
Chinon	**Sri Lanka**
Joan of Arc	'Blind Man and Elephant'
The Sleeping Beauty	Tales with Indian atmosphere

Teaching plan

This can be used as medium-term plan and provides a scheme of work for any locality studied. Many of the activities can be adapted to other places. Whichever locality is studied, the same enquiry questions and learning outcomes can be used.

Enquiry questions	Learning targets	Pupil activities
1 What is this place like?	Discovery of the geographical and human features of a place.	Information from maps: Unit 2 Lesson 1; landmarks: Unit 3 all lessons; island life: Unit 4 Lessons 1 and 2; wildlife: Unit 5 Lessons 1 and 3.
2 Where is this place?	Children will learn to use globes, maps and atlases to discover locations.	Locating places for mapwork: Unit 1, all lessons, Unit 2 Lesson 1, Unit 3 Lessons 1 and 3, Unit 4 Lessons 1 and 2; simple coordinates: Unit 5 Lesson 2.
3 What is it like to live in this place?	Children can compare homes, jobs and lifestyles with their own locality.	Job profiles: Unit 2 Lesson 2, Unit 3 Lesson 3; farms: Unit 2 Lesson 3, Unit 5 Lesson 3; towns' features: Unit 2 Lesson 1, Unit 4 Lesson 2.
4 How is this place linked to other places?	Children will recognise goods they use coming from different places.	Discovering links: Unit 1 Lessons 1 and 3, Unit 3 Lesson 3, Unit 4 Lesson 3.
5 How is it changing and why?	People change their environments by farming, building and tourism.	Environmental concerns: Unit 5 all Lessons.

National Curriculum coverage

Unit 1 World cookshop
National Curriculum links
- Develop an understanding about different places.
- Awareness of the world beyond their locality.
- Use of globes, maps and secondary sources.

Unit 2 Chinon, France
National Curriculum links
- Identify geographical features on a map.
- Contrasting locality study.

Unit 3 Journeys in Chinon
National Curriculum links
- A contrasting locality study
- Use pictures and symbols on a map.
- Use geographical vocabulary.

Unit 4 Sri Lanka
National Curriculum links
- A contrasting locality study.
- Use secondary sources to obtain geographical information.
- Discovering the world beyond our own locality.

Unit 5 Conservation in Sri Lanka
National Curriculum links
- Environments are changing.
- Quality of environment can be sustained and improved.

Scotland Environment Studies coverage

The units cover the following contexts and content for Understanding People and Places:
- Using plans to find places.
- Using the globe as a representation of the world.
- Things we use and eat which come from distant places.
- Daily lives of some children elsewhere compared with their own.

World cookshop

Learning targets

On completion of this unit children should:

1 ➤➤ know how to use a globe and map to identify places
2 ➤➤ be aware of the world outside the UK
3 ➤➤ recognise that there are links between countries.

Before you start

Background knowledge

The recipe in this unit uses demerara sugar from Barbados, sultanas from Greece, oats from Scotland, golden syrup from East Anglia, cocoa from Ghana and margarine from Holland. These products are also made in other countries so check the labels for origins before the lesson. You can substitute other recipes to suit your cooking facilities, but always try to include a global spread of countries. Sugar is an interesting ingredient. It is made from cane (West Indies) or beet (UK) and is processed into many forms. It also occurs naturally in honey.

Teaching points

The children explore the location of places around the world by discovering the origins of everyday foods. Every country needs to import the food it cannot grow itself. This is mainly due to the varying weather conditions that different plants need.

Geographical skills

- Use of globes and maps
- Global awareness
- Research using secondary sources

Vocabulary

world, market, crops, fruit, ingredient, country

Resources for Lesson 1

Copymaster 65 Chocolate and sultana flapjacks, ingredients, globe, world map, pencils, felt-tip pens

Resources for Lesson 2

Green grapes, sultanas, product containing sultanas, map of Europe, world map, postcard, Copymaster 66 What is a sultana? paper, pencils

Resources for Lesson 3

Plasticine®, atlas, can of fruit, picture references, paper, coloured pencils

Resources for the activities

Paper, pens, clipboards, scrapbook, food labels

Assessment indicators

- Can the children recognise the shape of the UK on a map?
- Can they find named countries on a globe or map?
- Can they explain the use of colour coding on their own maps?
- Can they name some foods that are imported into the UK?

Teaching the lessons

Lesson 1 ❶ ❷ ❸

Introduction [20min]

▨ Sit the children around a display you have made of the ingredients for 'Chocolate and sultana flapjacks'. (The recipe is on **Copymaster 65 Chocolate and sultana flapjacks** and makes about 30 flapjacks.) With a globe and/or a world map show each ingredient and read from the packaging where it comes from. Let children try to find the places on the globe and map.

World cookshop [40min]

 Split the children into six groups. Each group will take turns to cook and also to produce a world map

surrounded by pictures of the flapjack's ingredients. Children should frame each picture with a colour that matches the colour they have used for the country on the map, e.g. Ghana and cocoa coloured green. Small countries can be shown up with a coloured arrow. Differentiate by ensuring that boys have equal opportunity to cook and serve food, and to take part in the clearing up afterwards.

Summary [10min]

▨ Taste the flapjacks. Ask children about their maps, questioning them on their colour coding to see whether they understand this early key making skill, e.g. 'Why is there a green frame around the cocoa pod and tin?'

Lesson 2 ② ③

Introduction   15 min

Display a bunch of green grapes, sultanas and a product with sultanas in it. Show the children a map of the world and a map of Europe. Remind them where Greece is, and show them a postcard or holiday brochure depicting a hot weather scene. Probe for their views on the weather there and what fruits they think could grow there. Ask for ideas for the reason for sultanas and grapes on the same display, or pictures of grapes on sultana packaging.

Sultanas   30 min

Each group will need **Copymaster 66 What is a sultana?**, a small dish of water and some sultanas. The activity reconstitutes sultanas to look almost like grapes again. It may take some time to work, so an early lesson would give afternoon or next morning results. The second part of the sheet shows four pictures in the stages between growing grapes on vines to making sultana flapjacks. The children cut out the pictures to make a concertina book, a flow diagram or a storyboard with captions.

Summary   5 min

Each group completes their sultana investigation results. Ask the children questions to see whether they realise that water has been absorbed by the sultanas.

Lesson 3 ② ③

Introduction   10 min

Explain to the children that you want to make a fruit stall, with fruits from all over the world. The fruits can be made from Plasticine® or Playdough® and each one must have a label showing the country it comes from. Show how to use a reference book, atlas, computer or label on a can of fruit to discover the country of origin.

Models of fruit from around the world

The fruit stall   30 min

Children choose a fruit to model from a list you have prepared. Include fruits which allow the children to research the country of origin from the resources available. Children model a fruit, with materials in the classroom. Pictures, photos or real fruit will help model makers. Then they need access to the resources to research the country of origin of their fruit. They design and make their own label, to show where it was grown.
Differentiate by asking more able children to draw their fruit on a world map matching it to its country.

Summary   5 min

Talk to each child, assessing whether they have researched their fruit correctly, and help them find the country on a world map. Display their fruit on a made-up fruit stall. Use the fruit stall in maths for shopping work.

Extra activities

Market stall survey

Take the class to visit a local market stall, greengrocer or supermarket. At the fruit stall, list all the fruits for sale and put them into different categories: tropical, tree, citrus, soft, fruits we like, fruits we dislike and fruits never tasted. You may be able to arrange for the manager to talk to the children about one or two fruits and how they are stored and where they come from.

World recipes

Make a class recipe book a world theme. Each double page has a world map on one side with the countries of the food origins marked with different colours. On the opposite page is the recipe with each ingredient coloured to match the countries on the map. This could be an ongoing activity to add to every time your class has a cooking session.

Food labels

Encourage children to bring a can label or food package to school. Children can mount a food packaging label on coloured paper. Using the words on the label they can title their picture and copy the name of the country it comes from. Each mounted label can be fixed around a large map of the world and an arrow or piece of wool of the same colour can join the label to its country of origin.

Country research

From the work on recipes and fruit, each group of children can choose a country to research. Give them some enquiry questions to help them look for particular information. You might include: 'Does this country have a flag?' 'Where in the world is it?'. Do you know some words of its language?', 'What food crops grow there?' 'What interesting thing have you found out about this place?'.

159

Chocolate and sultana flapjacks

Ingredients

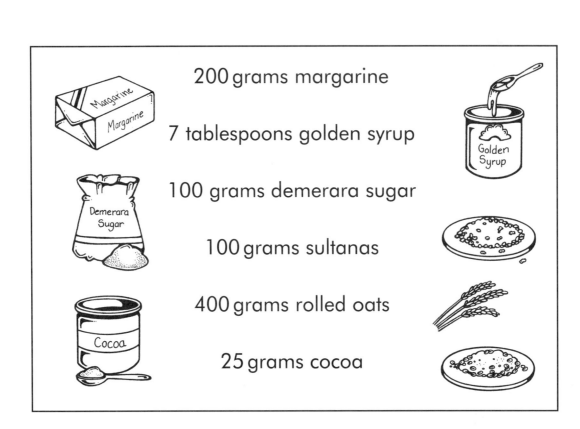

200 grams margarine

7 tablespoons golden syrup

100 grams demerara sugar

100 grams sultanas

400 grams rolled oats

25 grams cocoa

Method

1 Weigh the ingedients.

2 Melt the margarine, sugar and syrup in a pan.

3 Stir in the sultanas, oats and cocoa.

4 Put the mixture in two 20cm greased, square cake tins.

5 Cook for 25 minutes at 180°C. Cut into squares while warm.

6 Serve when cool.

What did you do to help make the flapjacks?

What did they taste like?

Can you decorate the border of the recipe card to show something about the ingredients and where they come from?

What is a sultana?

1 Take four or five sultanas.

2 Put them in a small dish of water.

3 What do you think will happen?

_____
_____
_____
_____

4 Much later.
What happened?

_____
_____
_____
_____

The sultana story

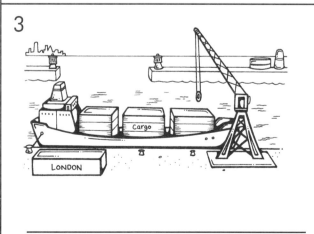

UNIT 2 | Chinon, France

Learning targets

On completion of this unit children should understand that:
1 ➤➤ maps show where a place is and what it is like
2 ➤➤ places overseas have similarities with our own area
3 ➤➤ different crops are farmed in different places outside our own area.

Before you start

Background knowledge

Chinon is a small medieval town in the Loire valley, famous for its wines, its links with Joan of Arc and its old chateau. It is 180 miles from Paris, 360 miles from Calais. The nearest city is Tours, 40 miles away. The town contains old timbered buildings, cobbled streets and typical French squares with restaurants and shops. The castle is high above the town with views of the River Vienne and farmland. Occupations in the area are in tourism, wines, goat's cheese and in the nuclear power industry which uses water from the Loire for its processes.

Teaching points

This unit focuses on where Chinon is and what is it like, and compares a bakery and some farms with those in your local area. Places are different but, as people have similar needs, we can find similarities (e.g. in the food industry) as well as differences (e.g. language).

Progression

Using a feature such as a baker's shop, where things can be recognised is an easy link for children. They can then explore features which are different and new.

Geographical skills
- Use of maps to identify features
- Use of geographical vocabulary

Vocabulary

France, country, river, castle, vineyard, baker, farmer

Resources for Lesson 1

Copymaster 67 Where is Chinon?, pencils, pens

Resources for Lesson 2

French shop front outlines, Copymaster 68 The baker's shop, pencils, pens

Resources for Lesson 3

Grapes, wine, sunflower seeds, oil, hulled seeds, bird feeder, milk, goat's cheese, paper, pencil, string

Resources for the activities

seeds, pots, compost; red, white and blue paper; felt-tip pens, glue

Assessment indicators
- Do the children know that Chinon is a town in France?
- Do they know that Chinon has some things the same as their town (baker, streets, cafés)?
- Do they know that Chinon has things that may be different (river, castle, vineyard)?

Teaching the lessons

Lesson 1 ❶

Introduction [10 min]

▨ Introduce the idea of leaving the UK for another country in Europe. Talk about methods of travel. Show the children a map showing where Chinon is in France. Which would be suitable ways to get there? The nearest airport is Nantes; the main railway station is Tours.

Introducing Chinon [30 min]

👤 1 Each child can draw the method of travel they would prefer and glue it to their map on **Copymaster 67 Where is Chinon?**, over the question 'Which way would you travel?'

Differentiate by elaborating on journey details, e.g. by car from home, by train through the Channel Tunnel to Paris, change to French railways to Tours, take a bus from Tours to Chinon.

2 Using the picture map on Copymaster 67, children can list the geographical features and buildings found in Chinon and adding grid references.

Summary [10 min]

🎲 Play the memory game 'When I went to Chinon I saw a castle'. The second child says, 'When I went to Chinon I saw a castle and a café...'. The third child says 'When I went to Chinon I saw a castle, a café and a river...' and so on until all features are exhausted.

Lesson 2

Introduction 15 min

 Ask the children where their family buys bread. Probe for all the outlets where bread can be bought. Explain that this is just the same in Chinon but there are more small bread and cake shops. They are called *la boulangerie* if mainly for bread, and *la pâtisserie* if for bread and fancy cakes. Show them two shop fronts on large paper headed with the two shop names.

 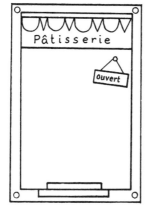

Shop frontages

The baker's shop 45 min

 Copymaster 68 The baker's shop is divided into two sections. Differentiate by choosing the appropriate activity.

The cake

1 Use the information to write the baker's diary for one day.
2 Make a decorated sign for the shop door showing the opening hours.

The bread

1 Cut out the bread and cakes and glue them onto large paper under the correct shop front picture.
2 Each child makes their own shop picture to show goods for sale.
3 Children match names of bread and cakes to the pictures.

Summary 10 min

 Use the large shop front pictures to tell the children the French names for the goods. Point to each one in turn and see if they can remember the names. This would be a good time to comment on the way we have used French words in our language to describe bread and cakes.

Lesson 3

Introduction 15 min

 Make a simple display of the following:
1 a bunch of grapes and a bottle of wine
2 a sunflower or a packet of sunflower seeds, a bottle of oil, a dish of hulled seeds and a bird feeder
3 a jug of milk and some goat's cheese.

Talk about each raw material and where it comes from, probing for farms. Ask what each item is made into and where it is processed. (Most Chinon wine is from small vineyards and made on site, or nearby in the town. Goat's cheese is also made on the farms.)

Farming 45 min

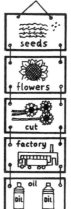 Ask children to make a flow diagram to show what is produced in one of the farms and to sequence the simple stages of production. Children can make individual flow pictures and join them to make a horizontal or vertical diagram with string.

Summary 5 min

 Help each child display their flow diagram on the wall or hang as mobiles.

Extra activities

Speaking French

A good way for slow learners to feel a real sense of achievement.

How to greet people in French:

Shake hands and say *Bonjour* (Good day)
Introduce yourself and say *Je m'appelle* (My name is…)
To say goodbye use *Au revoir*

Children can take turns walking around the group, shaking hands and introducing themselves.

Symbolic French flags

Make large individual French flags with blue, white and red paper glued together. Choose symbols that make you think of France from the work in the unit, e.g. baguettes, grapes. Draw one or two, cut them out and glue them onto the flag. Add a flagpole, with the blue stripe next to the pole. Explain that the French flag is called *le tricolore*, meaning it has three colours: red, white and blue.

Growing sunflowers

Plant three or four seeds in a 3" pot of compost. Water them and cover with a polythene bag, keeping them on a windowsill until the seedlings emerge. Take the cover off and, when large enough to handle, pot on individually into pots. Plant out after the end of May in borders or growbags with stakes if in an exposed site. Water well throughout the summer. Measure and record growth weekly. Dried autumn seed heads provide a lot of seeds for feeding birds.

Where is Chinon?

There are lots of ways to travel.

To get to France you have to cross the English Channel.

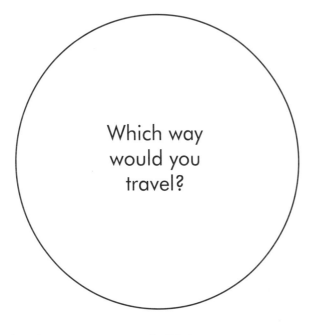

Which way would you travel?

A picture map of Chinon

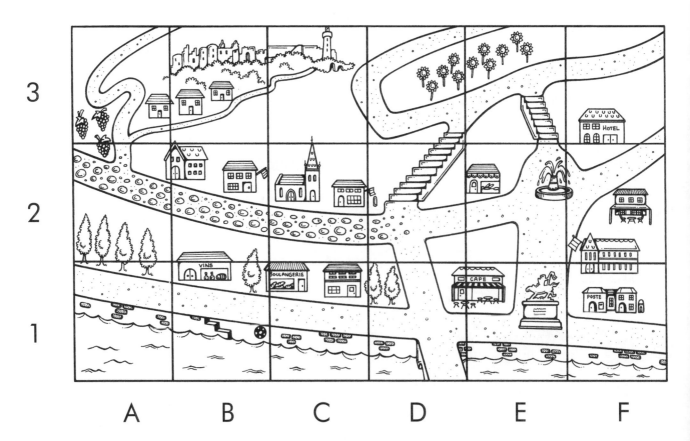

The places on this map tell you what Chinon is like.

The baker:
Pierre Berlan

Name of shop:
Le Petit Chateau

Opening hours: 7 am to 7 pm
Closed from: 12 to 2 pm

The shop sells bread, baguettes, croissants, tarts, éclairs, gateaux, choux buns, sweets.

The bread is baked at the back of the shop. Pierre lives upstairs above the bakery.

baguettes

croissants

éclairs

choux buns

tarts

bread

gateaux

petit pain

Journeys in Chinon

Learning targets

On completion of this unit children should understand how:
1 ➤➤ to follow a route on a map
2 ➤➤ journeys take you from one place to another
3 ➤➤ Chinon's landmarks give the town its character.

Before you start

Background knowledge

- Joan of Arc was born in 1412 during a time of war between England and France. When Joan was 13 she had a vision which told her to go and help the King of France. The Dauphin (heir to the French throne) was hiding in the chateau at Chinon. Joan told the Dauphin her plan. She was fitted out with armour and sent to Orléans, where she won the battle against the English. The Dauphin was crowned in Reims cathedral in 1429. People were afraid of her power and she was captured and burnt at the stake as a witch. In 1920 she was made a saint and 24 June is now a French national holiday in her honour.

- Written by Perrault, the fairy tale of *The Sleeping Beauty* is set in the Chateau Ussé, just north of Chinon through the Chinon forest. The Prince rode through the forest from Chinon while hunting and discovered the sleeping castle.

- The goat's cheese farmers come to Chinon for the market on Thursday's. They set up stalls in the town square to sell their cheeses. Most of the cheese farms are on the outskirts of the town south of the river.

Teaching points

Some journeys are for work and some for leisure. There are short and long journeys as well as many modes of transport. The use of journeys helps to reinforce the features and characters of a place and to give practice in map skills.

Geographical skills

- Following a route on a map
- Using directional vocabulary

Vocabulary

journey, route, direction, landmark, travel

Resources for Lesson 1

Copymaster 67 Where is Chinon?, Copymaster 69 Joan of Arc, pencils, OHP, transparencies

Resources for Lesson 2

Perrault's *The Sleeping Beauty*, collage materials

Resources for Lesson 3

Copymaster 70 Going to market, pencils, felt-tip pens, paper

Resources for the activities

Aesop's fables 'The Fox and the Grapes' and 'The Crow and the Cheese', French road map, tourist map of the Loire Valley, Copymaster 70 Going to market, pencils

Assessment indicators

- Can the children follow a route on a map?
- Can they recognise landmarks on a map?
- Can they sequence a journey from start to finish?

Teaching the lessons

Lesson 1 ① ② ③

Introduction [10 min]

▦ Tell the children the story of Joan of Arc, elaborating on the detail of her visit to Chinon. Enhance this part of the story with a description of the town, her journey through the streets and what she would pass on the way to the chateau.

Use an enlarged map of the town from Copymaster 67 and let the children trace the route as you describe it. Use an OHP to make a huge wall map, by projecting a transparent photocopy of the map.

Joan of Arc [30 min]

▣ Use **Copymaster 69 Joan of Arc** and differentiate by choosing tasks suited to ability groups.

1 Children can cut out the story captions and use them to sequence the route through the town,

interspersing them with their own pictures of landmarks passed on the way.

2 They can draw their own picture map of Joan's route or use the map on Copymaster 67 and label it with captions and arrows to show her route.

3 Write a newspaper article about Joan's visit to Chinon and illustrate it with a map or sketch of the town.

Summary 10min

Children show their work and describe Joan's journey.

Lesson 2

Introduction 15min

Tell the story of *The Sleeping Beauty*. Use geographical vocabulary to describe the Prince's hunting trip in the forest. Include: overgrown, Chinon forest, clearing, bridge, barrier. At the end of the story tell them about the link with Chinon.

The Sleeping Beauty 30min

Supply each group with a selection of art materials to produce a collage of the Chinon forest, It can include the chateaux at Chinon and Ussé, with the Prince and his hunting party along the route. The forest could feature a stream, a bridge, trees, fallen logs, deer, boar, pheasants. Frame each collage with geographical vocabulary shown in the picture and/or symbols of Chinon.

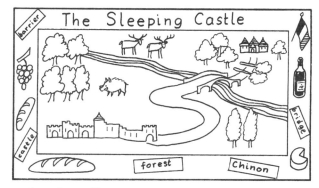
Art collage of forest

Summary 5min

Let each group tell you about their collage, pointing out the landmarks the Prince would pass on his trip.

Lesson 3

Introduction 10min

Tell an introductory story, such as 'Today it's Thursday and market day in Chinon. The goat farmer, Monsieur Lomax is taking cheese to market. As he leaves, his wife asks him to go to the Post Office for

stamps and to bring home some bread. He loads the cheese in his refrigerated van and sets off ...' Continue the story with references to things he passes on the way and notices in town.

The goat farmer

The children use **Copymaster 70 Going to market** to record the way the farmer spends market day. The pictures of places he visits can be used to make a flow diagram of his day at the market. Arrows can join the events in order to make a simple sequencing activity. Differentiate by choosing an appropriate activity.

1 Cut out the places and make them into a flow picture with clocks next to each one, to show the passage of time through the farmer's day.

2 This can be a map making exercise with landmarks. Ask children to make their own map to show Monsieur Lomax's route on market day. The pictures can decorate the map. Captions added to their map will tell the story of his day.

Summary 3min

Ask children about Monsieur Lomax's day at market. Do they know why he has a refrigerated van?

Extra activities

Role play

Choose one of the journeys you have used in this unit. Make a short role play asking the children how they can show the landmarks which were passed on the way. They may choose children or furniture to represent landmarks, or may simply refer to them in conversation during the journey.

Aesop's fables

Two Aesop's Fables, 'The Fox and the Grapes', and 'The Crow and the Cheese', can both be used for journey maps and links with products found in Chinon. Use pictures of buildings from Copymasters 67 and 70 to add to the picture maps.

On the river

Use a large map of France, a French road map or a tourist map of the Loire Valley to discover places up- or downstream from Chinon. Tourist maps show chateaux, road maps show towns, cities, railways and airports. Children can use this as a search game if you give them a tick list of what to look for.

Flow diagram

Using Copymaster 70, children can cut out four places visited or passed by the farmer going to market. Using '1st', '2nd', '3rd' and 'last', they can label the pictures and glue them in sequence on their own piece of paper. They can add their own of the farmer with his cheese for sale.

Joan of Arc

This short story tells you about Joan of Arc's journey into the castle at Chinon. The pictures show you scenes of the town as Joan would have seen them.

It is the year 1429. Joan travels to Chinon with a plan to save France from their enemy, the English.

When she reaches the town she crosses the river in a boat.

She walks through a gate in the town wall.

Her route goes along cobbled streets.

She passes tall houses with timber frames.

She climbes steep steps up the hill and crosses a moat into the castle.

Inside the castle she tells her plan to the king and his courtiers.

Later she has a suit of armour made in the town to wear in the battle.

She wins the battle against the English.

70

Going to market

Monsieur Lomax has a refrigerated van.

the farm   baker's shop   the market

the Post Office   a café   the town centre

Sri Lanka

Learning targets

On completion of this unit children should understand that:

1 ➤➤ an island is an area of land surrounded by water
2 ➤➤ food and items we use come from different places
3 ➤➤ different places have similarities and differences.

Before you start

Background knowledge

Sri Lanka is a tropical island off the south-east coast of India. The coast is fringed with sandy beaches. Inland there are high mountains and some rainforests. It has a long history of Buddhism. There is continuing conflict between the two peoples, Tamils and Sinhalese, with many displaced families without homes. English is taught in schools and is widely spoken. Sri Lanka produces most of the world's cinnamon, more tea than any other country and is rich in gemstones.

Teaching points

Places differ for a variety of reasons – weather, location, religion, and politics – but we can find similarities as well as differences. A study of Sri Lanka reveals its geographical similarities and differences as well as its links with the UK.

Geographical skills

- Aerial and plan views
- Use of artefacts

Vocabulary

island, ocean, goods, tourist, crops, tropical

Resources for Lesson 1

Potted plant, model of a house, objects to draw, OHP, paper, felt-tip pens, atlas, world map

Resources for Lesson 2

Copymaster 71 The town of Kandy, flashcards, blank maps, pencils

Resources for Lesson 3

Tea, coconut, coconut products, batik, rice, cinnamon, gemstones, masks, elephant ornaments from Sri Lanka; Copymaster 72 It comes from Sri Lanka, pencils, PE hoops

Resources for the activities

Local manufactured and farmed produce, outline map of Sri Lanka, tourist brochures, pencils, paper, Copymaster 72 It comes from Sri Lanka, blue paper

Assessment indicators

- Can the children identify islands on maps?
- Can they name items which come from Sri Lanka?
- Can they identify similarities and differences between places?

Teaching the lessons

Lesson 1   ① ③

Introduction   15 min

Have a collection of objects for children to look at as both horizontal and vertical views. Include a potted plant and a model of a house. Ask individual children to draw the item from above (its aerial or plan view). Use the blackboard or paper on an easel. Small items placed on an OHP give plan views projected on the wall and can create a 'What is it?' quiz. Introduce the idea of visiting an island called Sri Lanka by boat and by aeroplane and question the children on the different views you would see depending on how you arrived.

Sri Lanka is an island   40 min

Each group or pair should produce two pictures: 'Sri Lanka by boat' and 'Sri Lanka by air'. Both island pictures should show, sea, beaches, a river, trees, buildings, and mountains. The sea and river should be coloured blue and a simple key made. The 'Sri Lanka by Air' picture should match the 'by boat' picture except that features should be in plan view. The potted plant can give an idea of trees from above, and the model house can be drawn around to show a plan view of a building. Differentiate by giving less able children outlines of the islands to fill in.

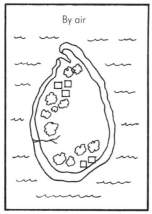

Two views of Sri Lanka

Summary
|10min|

With small groups, look at atlases and globes to point out islands (include Britain) and identify Sri Lanka in the Indian Ocean. Put an arrow on a wall map of the world to indicate Sri Lanka.

Lesson 2
(3)

Introduction
|10min|

Make two large flashcards, Kandy and the name of your town. Play a comparison game with the class. Ask questions such as 'Is it near here?', 'Does it have schools?', 'Do tourists visit?' and some odd ones like: 'Do people keep elephants?', 'Does it have a car factory?' (or your local industry). For each question, hold up the flashcards in turn and ask for the answer.

The town of Kandy
|30min|

Copymaster 71 **The town of Kandy** provides pictures of features of Kandy for children to colour and write captions for. Blank maps give an opportunity to add country, town and ocean labels. At the end of the work, children can assess whether features are similar or different to their local town. Reference books or tourist brochures would give a useful resource for the children to use.

Summary
|5min|

Make five more flashcards: homes, shops, schools, transport, jobs.

Use your town name and that of Kandy and hold each one up in turn to discover whether the children know if each place has the same features, even though the details of the features may differ.

Lesson 3
(2)(3)

Introduction
|5min|

Make a display of as many of the following items you can collect. Tea, coconut and its products, some batik, rice, cinnamon, gemstones, masks, elephant ornaments. The day before the activity make sure that every child has had the opportunity to look at the display and talk about it with you or each other.

It comes from Sri Lanka
|45min|

Copymaster 72 **It comes from Sri Lanka** provides a sentence about each of eight food or manufactured items from Sri Lanka. Below the items a Carroll diagram sorts them into local or tourist use. Differentiate by setting a task for children that uses both the display and the copymaster.

1 The children can choose one item, draw it, describe it and write down everything they know by looking at it.

2 They can make a poster advertising things for sale that a tourist may buy in Sri Lanka.

3 They can use the information on the Carroll diagram to make a Venn diagram with pictures or words.

Venn diagram of Sri Lankan produce

Summary
|10min|

With groups of children make a large Venn diagram on the floor with PE hoops and place the display items in the appropriate ring, as in the illustration above. You could create a second Venn diagram that shows 'sold in Sri Lanka' and 'exported'. Exported items are tea, coconut products, cinnamon, gemstones.

Extra activities

UK comparison

Make a similar lesson to Lesson 3 with goods from your local area. Include food from the nearest farming area, products from local factories and items that are particularly British, both farm and manufactured goods. Choose differentiated activities from Lesson 3.

Ceremonies with lanterns

On the full moon in May, to celebrate the birth and death of Buddha, Sri Lankans make 'vesak' lanterns from paper to light up the island. Children can design and make their own lanterns. A comparison with a religious ceremony held in this country could be incorporated into an assembly.

A drop in the ocean

To record and assess children's knowledge, give each child an outline, or let them draw their own shape of the island. They colour a ring of water and a ring of sandy beach around the shape. Inside the island they record their impressions of Sri Lanka, in answer to one or more enquiry questions, e.g. 'What is it like?', 'Where is it?', 'What would I see if I went there?'

171

71

The town of Kandy

Kandy

homes  transport

work schools

Special events

UK

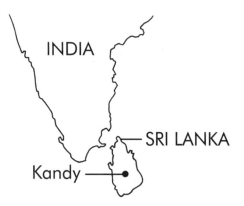

INDIA

SRI LANKA

Kandy

similar things	different things

It comes from Sri Lanka

Sri Lankans eat rice every day.

Coconut palms produce food
mats, and leaves for roofs.

Gems are coloured stones used
to make jewellery.

Batik is a way to print patterns
on cotton, using wax.

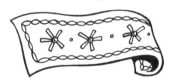

Tea is grown in the mountains.

Cinnamon is a spice made from
tree bark.

Masks are used in religious
ceremonies and dances.

Tourists buy elephants made
from wood from the forest.

A Carroll diagram

made in Sri Lanka   food grown in Sri Lanka

for local use

mainly for tourists
and other countries

UNIT 5 | Conservation in Sri Lanka

Learning targets

On completion of this unit children should understand that:

1 ➤➤ different plants and animals are found in different countries
2 ➤➤ endangered animals need protection
3 ➤➤ fragile environments need to be cared for.

Before you start

Background knowledge

Sri Lanka has a long tradition of conservation, from a history of conserving water in early times to managing nature reserves today.

Turtles: five of the world's eight species of turtle come to nest ashore on Sri Lanka's beaches. Although protected by law, they are still exploited for eggs and shells and disturbed by tourists.

Elephants: they still live wild in Sri Lanka's shrinking forests, and are also used by people for work, carrying heavy loads in awkward places. They are used in religious ceremonies, painted and decorated with bells and lights.

Cinnamon: the tree grows in the forest; its branches are cut and the bark is peeled off and smoked to produce cinnamon sticks. The tree is unharmed and grows more branches, rather like coppicing hazel or chestnut in the UK.

Teaching points

There needs to be a balance between what people take from the wild and whether it can be regenerated. A thematic study of the environments found in Sri Lanka shows how people need to manage those environments to sustain beautiful and rare wildlife.

Geographical terms

- Use secondary sources to obtain geographical information
- Use geographical terms

Vocabulary

environment, ocean, rainforest, protect, conservation, wildlife

Resources for Lesson 1

Turtle outlines, paper, pencils, felt-tip pens

Resources for Lesson 2

Copymaster 73 Elephants, elephant stories, pencils, felt-tip pens

Resources for Lesson 3

Cinnamon products, Copymaster 74 Cinnamon – a spicy tree, ingredients for chocolate drink, glue, card

Resources for the activities

Old newspapers, paper, pencils, felt-tip pens

Assessment indicators

- Can the children suggest a way to conserve an environment/species?
- Do they know that people affect conservation of animals and plants?

Teaching the lessons

Lesson 1 ① ②

Introduction [15 min]

▨ Brainstorm with the children the things they know about turtles. Fill in the gaps in their knowledge to cover the following points.

- Turtles live in tropical seas for 40–80 years.
- Females lay eggs in deep holes on sandy beaches.
- Baby turtles hatch at night and find their way to the sea.
- People collect eggs to eat (the main reason for possible extinction in ten years).
- People make jewellery from turtle shells.
- Tourists disturb nesting sites.

- Other dangers are: drowning in fishing nets, litter in the sea, destruction of coral reef feeding grounds, lights on shore attracting babies away from the sea.

Turtles [45 min]

▣ Children draw and cut out a large turtle. In the shell they write their message to encourage one method of conserving turtles. These turtles can be posters, handouts to locals or tourists or can be mounted on a wall to make a 'rockery' of baby turtles making their way to the sea.

Summary [5 min]

▨ Reinforce the conservation ideas by asking the children to read out their variety of messages to the rest of the class.

174

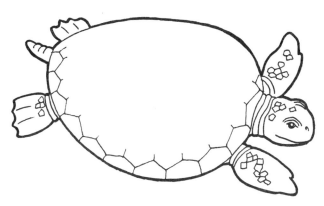

Turtle outline

Lesson 2

Introduction ⏱ 15 min

 A story about elephants such as 'The Blind Men and the Elephant' could stimulate children into researching facts about elephants. Talk to the class about the Sri Lankan elephants. Some live wild in the forest, but farmers are gradually cutting down the trees and the forest is becoming too small for them. Builders use elephants to carry heavy loads. Decorated elephants are used in religious ceremonies and processions. If you want to raise an issue, ask for the children's views on whether elephants should be tamed and used for work.

Elephants ⏱ 40 min

 Copymaster 73 Elephants assumes knowledge of coordinates. It uses simple coordinates as in an atlas or a road map. Children colour the squares listed to make an elephant shape. The three blank elephants are for children to add the habitats. One is wild in the forest, one is working and should carry a load, and the other is to be decorated for a procession. Differentiate by asking children to add captions to each elephant or to write their views on the problems each elephant encounters in its life.

Summary ⏱ 10 min

 Have a class discussion on the elephant situation in Sri Lanka and allow children to express their views and ideas.

Lesson 3

Introduction ⏱ 5 min

 Display as many cinnamon products as possible, e.g. ground cinnamon, sticks, herbal teas, spicy biscuits, and a branch of any tree or shrub with new shoots on it, or a large drawing of one.

Explain that when you cut the branches of some trees, new shoots grow to produce more branches.

There may be examples nearby where hedges are cut or roses are pruned. Continue to explain the process of producing cinnamon while children look at the pictures on **Copymaster 74 Cinnamon – a spicy tree**.

A spicy tree ⏱ 30 min

 Copymaster 74 can be coloured and cut up to make a simple container, glued onto a card base. Children can make models of cinnamon sticks from rolled Plasticine® or brown corrugated paper to stand in their containers.

This chocolate drink can be prepared by a group of children, heated up under supervision and tasted during or after this activity.

Frothy Chocolate Drink

Ingredients

100 grams grated plain chocolate

1 teaspoon honey	2 drops vanilla essence
1 tablespoon cornflour	4 tablespoons water
powdered cinnamon	1 pint milk

Method

Warm the chocolate milk, sugar and vanilla in a saucepan stirring all the time. Do not let it boil. Dissolve the cornflour in the water and add slowly to the saucepan, still stirring. Whisk until it bubbles, then sprinkle with cinnamon.

Summary ⏱ 5 min

 Taste the chocolate drink or some food flavoured with cinnamon.

Extra activities

The coral reef

The coral reef is easily damaged by boats and swimmers, and those who collect pieces for sale. Ask the children to design a beach sign to give a conservation message, such as 'Don't destroy the reef' or 'Don't buy pieces of coral to take home'. Older children may be interested in one holiday company's motto: 'Take only photos, and leave only footprints'.

Coconuts

The beaches are fringed with coconut palms. Men shin up the trees to cut coconuts, and slice the tops with a machete. They sell them to tourists on the beach for a cool drink. Children can draw speech bubbles to show the conservation between the Sri Lankan and a tourist about coconuts and what it is like on the beach.

Newspaper elephants

Children fill an outline of an elephant shape with cut up newspaper print. Different sizes of print give different degrees of greyness, which can be used to give tone. An Indian newspaper, available in city newsagents, would add an authentic touch.

Elephants

Colour these squares to make an elephant.

A4, A5, B4, C4, C5, ½ C6, D2, D3, D4, D5, D6, E4, E5, E6, F4, F5, F6, G2, G3, G4, G5, G6.
Put an eye in C5.

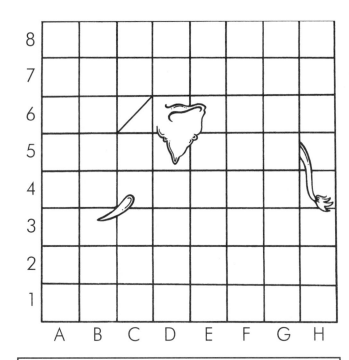

Here are three elephants.

The first lives wild in the forest.
The second carries heavy logs for building a house.
The third is painted and decorated with bells for a procession.

Colour each elephant and draw its environment.

Cinnamon – a spicy tree

The frame can be cut out to make a box for cinnamon sticks.

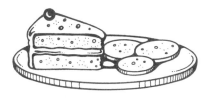

Cinnamon is used
in cooking.

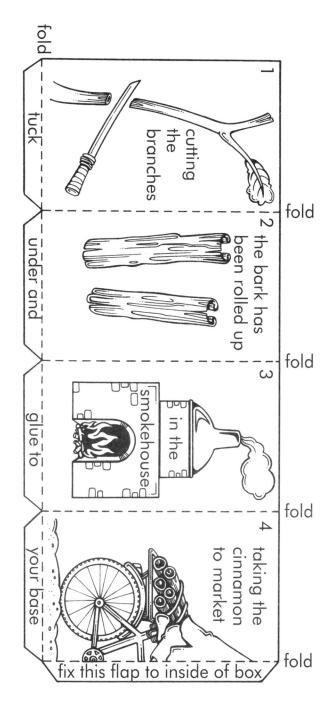

fold

tuck

1 cutting the branches

fold

2 the bark has been rolled up

under and

fold

3 in the smokehouse

glue to

fold

4 taking the cinnamon to market

your base

fix this flap to inside of box

fold

OUR WORLD

Focus

This section deals with the wider world and global awareness. Through activities where globes, world maps and atlases are in constant use for matching country shapes, for reference and locating places, the section aims to familiarise the child with the world. Through these lessons children will learn the names of the continents and major land masses and start to see the diversity that exists on our planet. The section progresses from looking at what the world is like, to how people adapt to living in different environments around the world.

Content

Unit 1: Maps and globes
Unit 2: In the news
Unit 3: Discover the world

Source material

Globes are available in different materials and as inflatables. There are political globes showing countries, physical globes showing relief and black and white globes for teacher and child use with marker pens. Inflatables are available from Cambridge Publishing Services Ltd, PO Box 62, Cambridge CB3 9NA. Other educational catalogues supplying them include NES Arnold and Hope Education.

World playmats are available from NES Arnold.

Infant atlases are available from Oxford University Press or Collins Keystart.

Children's resources for researching countries:
Thomas, Sue and Scoffham, Stephen *Blueprints: Infant Geography Resource Bank*, Stanley Thomas Publishers, 1994
Thomas, Sue and Scoffham, Stephen *Blueprints: Junior Geography Resource Bank*, Stanley Thornes Publishers, 1994
Wayland Books, 61 Western Road, Hove, East Sussex BN3 1JD for catalogue

Photosets from Action Aid, Hamlyn House, Archway, London N19 5PG

Holiday brochures
A collection of postcards and calendar photos
Displays of food and souvenirs from different countries

Brainstorm

This brainstorm covers the lessons in Section 11 and can be added to for a cross-curricular topic.

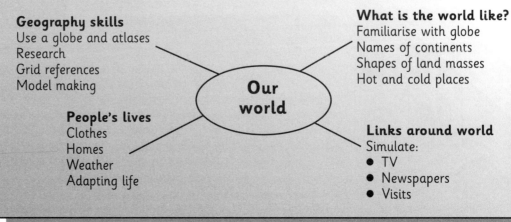

Geography skills
Use a globe and atlases
Research
Grid references
Model making

What is the world like?
Familiarise with globe
Names of continents
Shapes of land masses
Hot and cold places

Our world

People's lives
Clothes
Homes
Weather
Adapting life

Links around world
Simulate:
- TV
- Newspapers
- Visits

Teaching plan

This can be used as a medium-term plan and provides a scheme of work for a topic on 'Our world'.

Enquiry questions	Learning targets	Pupil activities
1 What is the world like?	The world is round and is made of land and sea. Different places have different names.	Use the globe to locate places: Unit 1 Lessons 1 and 2, Unit 3 Lessons 1 and 3; personal discovery research: Unit 3 Lessons 2 and 3.
2 How do we find out about the world?	World communication networks bring news as it happens. Newspapers and books give information about other places. People visit different parts of the world.	Simulation of TV news: Unit 2, all lessons; imaginary world trip: Unit 3 all lessons; individual research: Unit 2 Lessons 2 and 3, Unit 3, all lessons.
3 How do people live in different parts of the world?	People have to adapt to life in different places.	Choice of clothes to take on a trip: Unit 3 Lesson 1; life in a visited country: Unit 3 Lessons 2 and 3.

National Curriculum coverage

Unit 1 Maps and globes

National Curriculum links
- Global awareness.
- Use of maps and globes.

Unit 2 In the news

National Curriculum links
- Use of maps and globes.
- Global awareness.
- Use of IT for communication.

Unit 3 Discover the world

National Curriculum links
- Use of globes and maps.
- Global awareness.

Scotland Environment Studies coverage

The units cover the following contexts and content for Understanding People and Places:

- Using the globe as a representation of the world.
- Things we use and eat which come from distant places.
- Daily lives of some children elsewhere compared with their own.
- Different kinds of weather and simple weather recording.
- Major physical and natural features in the locality.

Maps and globes

Learning targets

On completion of this unit children should understand that:

1 ➤➤ land and sea cover the Earth's surface
2 ➤➤ continents and oceans have recognisable shapes
3 ➤➤ we use maps to find where places are.

Before you start

Background knowledge

Satellites send messages to the Earth to relay weather information, to help cartographers make maps and for live coverage of news and sports events on television. Using a globe enables us to see the shape and position of the main continents and the oceans which separate them.

The Earth's crust is a layer of rock 8–64 kilometres thick. Beneath the crust is a hot rock called magma on which the continents float. Land covers less than one third of the Earth's surface. The rest is covered by sea.
Continents: Europe, Asia, Africa, North America, South America, Oceania (Australasia), Antarctica.
Oceans: Pacific, Atlantic, Indian, Arctic.

Teaching points

Continents are great blocks of land which are surrounded by oceans. Looking at the world as if from space, children discover the shapes of land masses and discover their names from globes and atlases.

Geographical skills

- Use of globes and maps
- Global awareness
- Use of grid references

Vocabulary

globe, world, ocean, continent, country, map, grid

Resources for Lesson 1

Globe, Copymaster 75 World views, atlas, coloured pens and pencils

Resources for Lesson 2

World wall map, Copymaster 76 World jigsaw, pencils, felt-tip pens

Resources for Lesson 3

Atlas, world map with grid references, OHP acetates

Resources for the activities

Copymaster 76 World jigsaw, atlas, plastic world map, chinagraph pencil, toy spacecraft or aeroplanes, pencils

Assessment indicators

- Can the children recognise land shapes on the globe?
- Can they name some continents and oceans?
- Can they use an alpha-numeric grid?

Teaching the lessons

Lesson 1 ① ②

Introduction 10 min

Spin a globe. Stop it anywhere and talk with the group about what they can see. Point out sea, land and other features depending on the globe and children's ages. Children may ask about land which is coloured differently to show mountains, or rivers. Spin the globe and look at another view. Repeat this activity with small groups of children so that everyone can see and be included in the discussion.

World views 30 min

Where possible have a globe, a world map and some atlases available for the children to use. **Copymaster 75 World views** gives two views of the world from different sides of the globe. Children can colour the land and sea and make a key to show what their colours represent.

Differentiate by asking more able children to add the names of continents and oceans by using a globe or an atlas to find their names. Skilfull artists could add rivers and mountains.

Summary 5min

 Spin the globe and ask children to stop the globe and keep their finger on a spot. Is it land or sea? Ask more able children for the name of the continent, large country or ocean. Spin again for the next child.

Lesson 2 ②

Introduction 10min

 Use a world wall map to point out and label the large land masses and give each continent a name. Now take the labels off and hand them to children, asking them if they can put them back on the world map.

The land

Using **Copymaster 76 World jigsaw**, let the children have some time with a globe or a world map in an atlas to locate the continents you have labelled. Differentiate depending on the ability of the children.

1 Ask children to colour the land and sea with different colours.

2 Colour and label the continents.

3 Label the continents and add the major features which would be found in an atlas such as oceans, mountain ranges and rivers.

4 Mount the continents around a world map matching them with a line to world position.

Summary 10min

 Make up a game for children to point out the places they have found. Stand by the world map, spin the globe and say 'Ali took his spaceship around the world and landed in…' Let Ali point or fix a spaceship to the place he chooses.

Lesson 3 ③

Introduction 10min

 Draw a large grid on the board. Put ABCDE along the horizontal axis and 12345 along the vertical axis. Draw simple things in some of the squares. Demonstrate the use of grid references, giving the letter first and number second, e.g. 'Apple is in A5'.

Grid references 20min

 Give a pair of children an OHP acetate with a large grid drawn on it to fit over a world map in a classroom atlas. The acetate should already have the ABC123 labels along the axes, and the squares should be as large as possible, to fit over major continents.

Differentiate to suit the ability of the children.

1 Children can write a coordinate and the name of the continent it covers.

2 Children can make a route across the world naming large countries and continents with their grid references.

3 Give the children a list of places and oceans to find so they can record the grid reference.

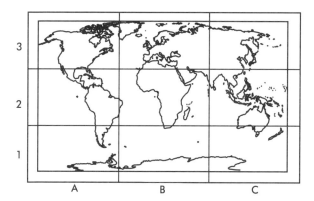

Grid references on acetate

Summary 5min

 Free use of atlas and acetate gives children an opportunity to try some for themselves or to make up a game with a friend.

Extra activities

World pelmanism

Make several copies of Copymaster 76 World jigsaw and make a set of cards to play pelmanism. The children turn over two cards. If they match, they keep the pair. If they do not match, they turn them back and the next player tries to match a pair.

Make a world map

Children can use Copymaster 76 to cut up the landmasses and make a world map, positioning each landmass in their world location. They may need an atlas for reference, but this could be used for assessment.

Playmat grids

Use a plastic world map as a playmat. Use a chinagraph pencil to draw a grid on it. Give children toy spacecraft or aeroplanes. Let them fly over the world and land in a square. They give the grid reference to get another turn. After three turns, another child tries the game.

Acetate grids

1 Use an acetate grid in a 'Where's Wally' book to give Wally's grid reference.

2 Use one in any detailed picture to locate certain people or items.

3 Use one on an island picture to make a 'Find the treasure' game.

World views

Here are two views of the world seen by a satellite.

Colour the sea blue.
Colour the land green or brown.

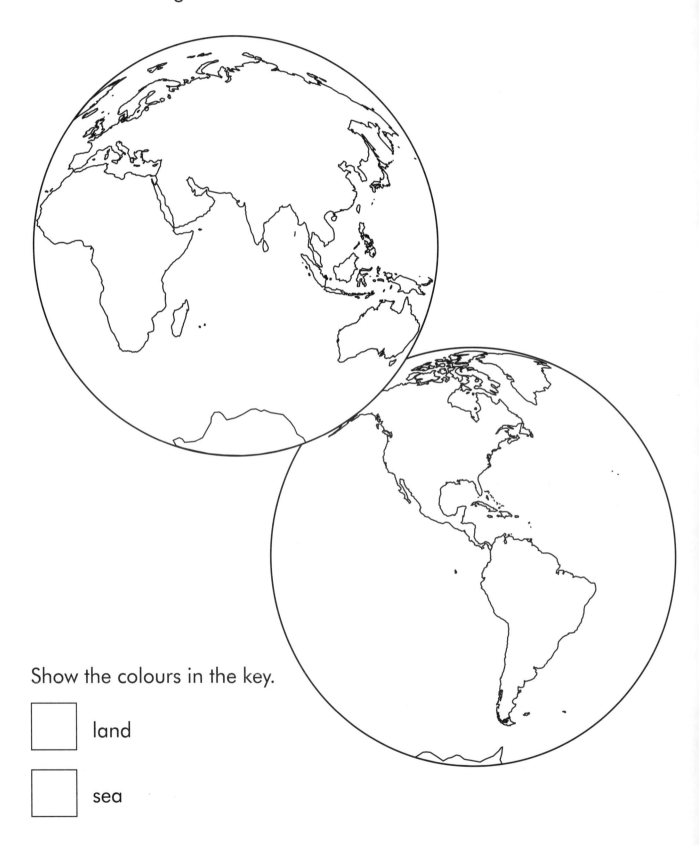

Show the colours in the key.

land

sea

76 | World jigsaw

Parts of the world are in each box.

Africa   North America   South America   Oceania   Europe   Asia

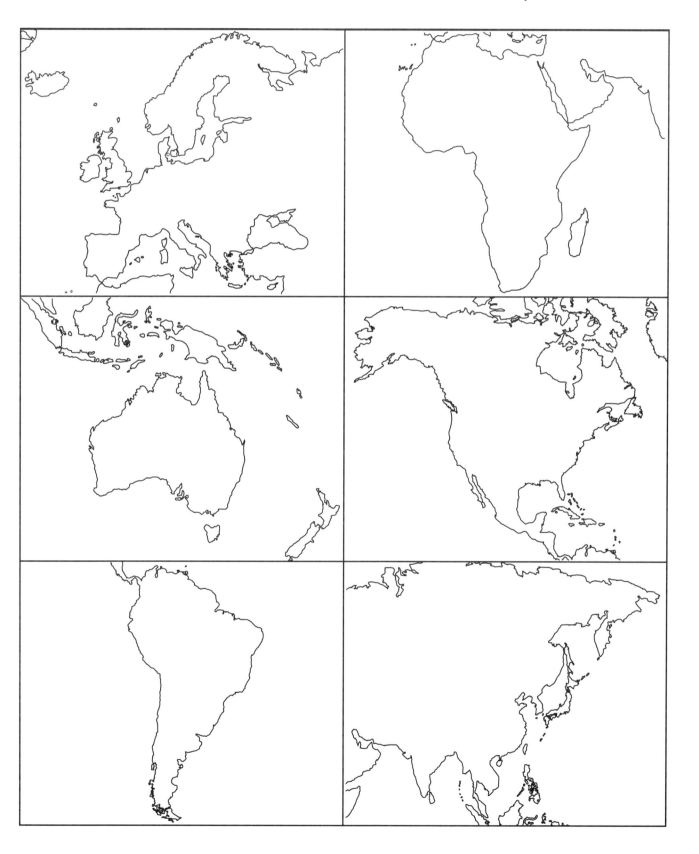

In the news

Learning targets

On completion of this unit children should understand that:

1 ➤➤ different things are happening all over the world
2 ➤➤ world communications use telephones, computers and satellites
3 ➤➤ television is a means of communication.

Before you start

Background knowledge

In January of 1998 ice storms hit Canada, causing electricity pylons to collapse and cutting off electricity supplies to thousands of homes. Newspapers showed pictures and live reports came from the scene as it became world news. Copymaster 78 deals with this event for children to make a news report about. You may like to substitute this copymaster for one you make up yourself on some topical news about people and places. Your sheet might cover expeditions, round the world races, natural disasters, special events or famous people. Children's news programmes often cover events of interest to children and could be a starting point. Collect newspaper photographs or video TV news footage as a stimulus to the work. Different groups of children could be covering different news items to produce a full news programme.

Teaching points

This unit looks at global communications by simulating live television news reports.
You may need to explain that 'Live' means 'it is happening at the moment we see it'.

Geographical skills

- Simulated use of IT
- Use of maps and globes
- Awareness of the wider world

Vocabulary

television, satellite, link, live, report, programme

Resources for Lesson 1

Copymaster 77 World links, cardboard box, A4 paper, modelling materials

Resources for Lesson 2

Copymaster 78 Live news, Copymaster 75 World views, paper, felt-tip pens, 'television' model

Resources for Lesson 3

Cassette recorder, paper, felt-tip pens, paint

Resources for the activities

Mobile telephone, fax machine, world map, string, video of children's news programme

Assessment indicators

- Can the children mark a country on a world map?
- Can they report a world news item?
- Do they know how live messages cross the world?

Teaching the lessons

Lesson 1 ③

Introduction 10min

Introduce the idea of a live news programme by showing a clip from a news item where the presenter says words that indicate it is live, e.g. 'We go over to … in Jamaica for his report'. If this is impossible, make one up yourself and retell it to the class with a newspaper photograph. Discuss how messages can be 'live' through telephone links, camera links, computer networks and satellites.

Communication models 40min

Each group will need a box large enough to take a sequence of A4 paper. **Copymaster 77 World links** shows a television and how it is linked to places across the world. Simple pictures are shown and groups can use them to simulate the design and making of the communication links. Each group makes a television set that they will use in Lesson 2 for their report. Each group could make a different communication model for a larger class display of a range of television links. Children should know that the television model will be used for slotting in their news programme and will need slits to fit a length of paper.

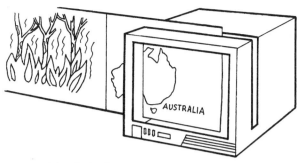

TV model with slits for paper

Summary `5 min`

Show a display of communication photos or pictures for the children to identify and name, such as telephone, computer, satellite dish, TV aerial, camera, newspaper, television, radio. Display them around a world map or globe. Talk about how these items bring us news from around the world.

Lesson 2

Introduction `10 min`

Explain that each group has become a news team in a different part of the world. Tell the children where they are, what event has happened by sharing **Copymaster 78 Live news** or newspaper photos with them, and ask them how it affects the people there. Stress that the news is so interesting or important that other countries want to get a report 'Live'. If groups are covering different news items, introduce each news item separately.

A news report `40 min`

Copymaster 78 offers children the format of a news report to follow. The task of creating the three parts of the news report, the map, the picture of the event, and the effect on the people can be shared between the group. Each group will produce three sheets of paper that can be joined together to slide through the TV set made in Lesson 1. A short commentary will be needed to accompany the news item, using vocabulary such as: 'live from …', 'straight from …', 'by satellite link from …', 'our reporter on the scene …', 'local people say …' The map maker can use maps from Copymaster 76. Finished sheets are joined together and pulled through the television model as each child makes their commentary.

Summary `10 min`

The class sit and watch as each group makes their live broadcast.

Lesson 3

Introduction `10 min`

Choose a news event or use the same one as in Lesson 2. Talk about the event with the children and encourage them to ask questions about it. Probe for

enquiry questions that ask 'Where?', 'How?', 'What was it like?', 'How did you feel?', 'What will happen now?' Write two or three of the questions on large speech bubbles and pin them on the wall.

Tape an interview `30 min`

Children work in pairs or in fours. They prepare a script, either written or practised and learned, that becomes a taped interview. Encourage the children to have an introduction which explains the event and introduces the reporter. Then the children can choose their questions, using the speech bubbles for guidance. Between them they plan the replies and practise the interview. Once they are ready, they can tape the interview, listening and changing it if they need to. Finally they paint a picture of the interviewer and the scene that will slot into the television model.

Summary `15 min`

Groups display their interviewer picture and then their scene in the television model while playing the taped interview to the class.

Extra activities

Using a telephone

Teach children how to use a telephone. Practise the sequence of events with a model or toy. Prepare a message that a child can remember. Use a mobile telephone or take groups to a telephone point to make a call to a prearranged person.

Send a fax

Prepare a piece of work about links with other places and about how long messages take to send. Send a fax to another school where you have a contact. Let the children see the fax being sent, and prearrange the arrival of a reply so that can be witnessed too. If you have no fax in your school, arrange this lesson at a local shop that sends faxes.

Newspaper cuttings

Ask children to collect newspaper cuttings or magazine articles with photographs of events around the world. Children can mount and label them, or use them to inspire paintings. These can be fixed around a world map and places matched and indicated by arrows or lengths of string.

Newsround

Video one of the BBC's ten-minute children's 'news programmes. Play it to your class. Discuss one of the world news items. Children can record their thoughts and views on pictures or written accounts presented in a TV screen frame.

World links

Different machines send news around the world:

- telephone
- fax
- computer
- satellite.

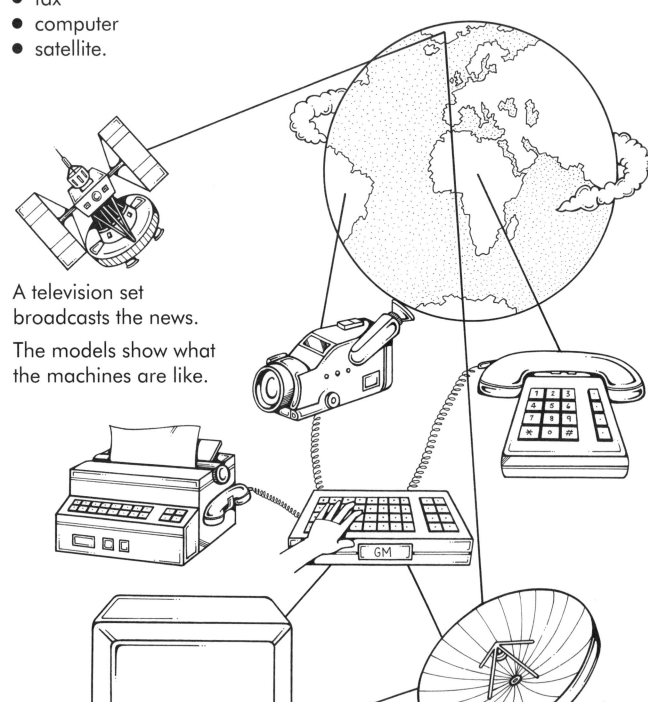

A television set broadcasts the news.

The models show what the machines are like.

Live news

This is _____

reporting live from _____

_____

_____

I can see _____

_____

_____

People are saying _____

_____

_____

_____

_____

_____

_____

Goodnight from _____

in _____

Discover the world

Learning targets

On completion of this unit children should understand that:

1 ➤➤ people live in contrasting places around the world

2 ➤➤ amazing natural features occur in the world

3 ➤➤ deserts are dry places with little or no rain.

Before you start

Background knowledge

The places and countries that you use for the third lesson in this unit will depend on your own knowledge and the non-fiction books available for use in your classroom. If resources are short, concentrate on just a few places and include hot and cold contrasting places. There are units in this book, with children's resources, covering Sri Lanka and Chinon in Section 10 (*see* pages158–77), and rainforests in Section 8 (*see* pages 130–33).

World facts and figures

Oceans in order of size: Pacific, Atlantic, Indian, Arctic.

Deserts in order of size: Sahara, Australian, Arabian, Gobi, Kalahari.

Longest rivers in order: Nile, Amazon, Mississippi.

Highest waterfall: Angel Falls, Venezuela.

Other waterfalls: Niagara Falls, USA/Canada; Victoria Falls, Zimbabwe.

Highest mountain: Everest.

Other mountains: Eiger, Annapurna, K2, Kilimanjaro.

Teaching points

In this unit the children become world travellers and drop into a range of countries with contrasting weather and features. The weather and type of land features make the world full of very different places. People have to adapt to different weather and terrain.

Making a passport is covered in Section 7 (*see* page 100)

Geographical skills

- Use of maps and globes
- Answering enquiry questions
- Using research skills

Vocabulary

world, travel, country, weather, different, adapt

Resources for Lesson 1

Globe, Copymaster 79 A balloon trip, flower arranger's basket, pencils, felt-tip pens

Resources for Lesson 2

Yellow paper, sand, balloon from Lesson 1, cactus, toy camel, Copymaster 80 Deserts, sugar paper; Heide, F.P. and Gilliland, J.H. *The Day of Ahmed's Secret*, Gollancz, 1991

Resources for Lesson 3

Card, resource books, 'balloon'

Resources for Activities

Cards, globe, atlas, world map playmat, coloured paper, string

Assessment indicators

- Can the children describe a place they have researched?
- Can they recognise ways in which places are different?
- Do they know how people adapt to a different climate?

Teaching the lessons

Lesson 1   ① ②

Introduction   15min

▓ Tell the children about people's attempts to fly hot air balloons around the world. Tell them they are going to pretend to fly around the world to look at different places. Brainstorm the types of places they may discover. Probe for deserts, mountains, jungles, the poles, oceans, as well as names of places they will have learnt in an earlier unit. For each one, ask 'What would you take if visiting that sort of place?' Point out some of the places the children mention on a globe.

A world trip $\boxed{30\,min}$

 With a group of children, make a hot air balloon using a globe as the balloon and a flower arranger's basket suspended below it.

Copymaster 79 A balloon trip requires the children to list the things they would take on a world trip to visit different types of locations. When they have completed the list, each child draws one of the items they would like to take on a separate piece of paper and puts it in the balloon's basket with their name on it.

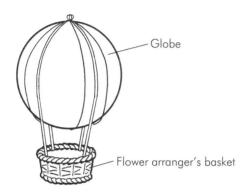

Globe

Flower arranger's basket

Hot air balloon

Summary $\boxed{10\,min}$

Take the children's pictures from the balloon's basket and tell the class what each child is taking. Ask the child why they decided to take that particular item.

Lesson 2 ① ③

Introduction $\boxed{15\,min}$

Bring the hot air balloon to rest on the floor on a piece of yellow paper, over which you have spread some sand. Ask the children what sort of place the balloon has landed in. You could add some other clues such as a cactus plant or a toy camel, available from model counters in toy shops. When you have established that it is a very hot and dry place, take the pictures from the basket and ask the children which items would be useful in a desert.

In the desert $\boxed{45\,min}$

 Children cut out the template of the lizard on **Copymaster 80 Deserts** and place it on the fold of a piece of green or brown sugar paper and cut it out. They decorate the lizard with eyes and scales before joining the two tabs together under the lizard's body. Making a fold in the legs stretches them out on either side. The other pictures and phrases on Copymaster 80 can be used in different ways. Differentiate the activities according to ability.

1 The template of the lizard can be enlarged for very young children.
2 Make a desert scene using the pictures on the sheet.
3 Write a short diary entry for the balloon of where you landed and what you saw there.
4 Make a model house from a box. Draw a desert background for it.

Summary $\boxed{10\,min}$

Find some deserts on the globe. Read a story about living in Cairo, such as *The Day of Ahmed's Secret* by Florence Parry Heide and Judith Heide Gilliland.

Lesson 3 ① ②

Introduction $\boxed{10\,min}$

Prepare a card to put in the balloon's basket. The front could have a picture of the globe or a picture of a person who is travelling in the balloon. Write some enquiry questions inside about the place where the balloon lands. Show the card to the children and tell them that they can use the set of resource books to help them choose a place to visit.

World discovery $\boxed{40\,min}$

 Small groups or pairs of children create a world discovery card. On the outside they put a map or globe picture with their chosen place marked and labelled 'We went to/landed in…' Give them time to browse through the resources and talk about what their place is like. Put large enquiry questions where the children can see them. Children record their discoveries inside the card.

Summary $\boxed{5\,min}$

Each group stands their card on a table below the hot air balloon and points out their place on the globe.

Extra activities ① ②

Where in the world is …?

Make some quiz cards for globe and atlas practice. Each one says 'Where in the world is …?' and a place to find. Children can mark the places on a playmat world map or a world map of their own. The cards can also be used for a class quiz at the end of the topic.

Documentary films

Use the television models from Unit 2 to present simulated documentary films about the places visited in this unit. In the same way as the news programmes, children make a television strip with a map, a picture of the place, and some of the interesting things found there. A commentary could be developed.

Animals around the world

Drawings of animals from different continents can be presented around the world map with lines or string joining them to the places where they are found. Colour code the mounting paper to distinguish between continents or whether the animal lives in a hot or cold place.

Country profile

Choose a country or continent. Give the children an outline of its shape. Ask them to use an atlas or world map to identify it. Inside the outline ask them to draw or write anything they know, think or can find out about it. Use a place that you have worked on before, or have pictures on the wall about or have available some other classroom resource.

A balloon trip

Pack your bag

Things for hot places:

Clothes for cold places:

To climb mountains:

To explore oceans:

To cross a desert:

To remember everything:

Deserts

Make a lizard.

cool houses

two ways to travel

clothes to keep cool

water is deep underground

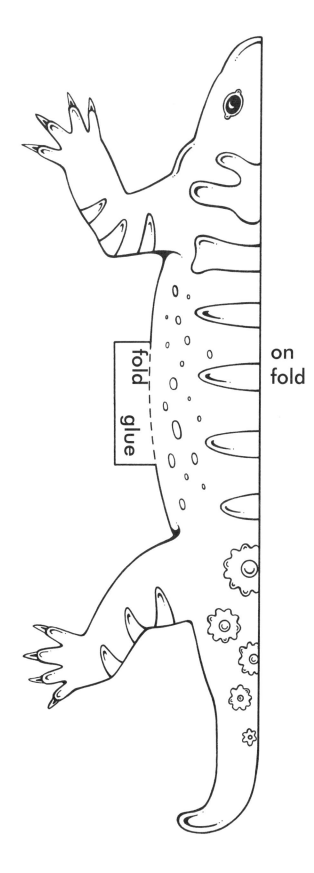

fold glue

on fold

play guitar with...
john lennon

Wise Publications
London/New York/Paris/Sydney/Copenhagen/Madrid

Guitar Tablature Explained

Guitar music can be notated three different ways: on a musical stave, in tablature, and in rhythm slashes

RHYTHM SLASHES are written above the stave. Strum chords in the rhythm indicated. Round noteheads indicate single notes.

THE MUSICAL STAVE shows pitches and rhythms and is divided by lines into bars. Pitches are named after the first seven letters of the alphabet.

TABLATURE graphically represents the guitar fingerboard. Each horizontal line represents a

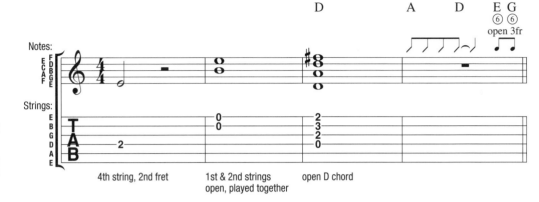

4th string, 2nd fret   1st & 2nd strings open, played together   open D chord

definitions for special guitar notation

SEMI-TONE BEND: Strike the note and bend up a semi-tone (1/2 step).

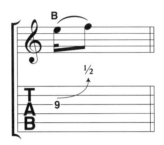

WHOLE-TONE BEND: Strike the note and bend up a whole-tone (whole step).

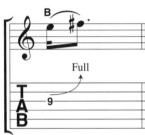

GRACE NOTE BEND: Strike the note and bend as indicated. Play the first note as quickly as possible.

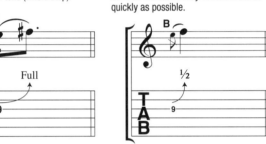

QUARTER-TONE BEND: Strike the note and bend up a 1/4 step.

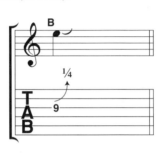

BEND & RELEASE: Strike the note and bend up as indicated, then release back to the original note.

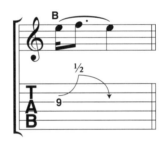

COMPOUND BEND & RELEASE: Strike the note and bend up and down in the rhythm indicated.

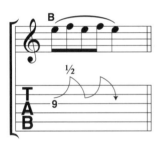

PRE-BEND: Bend the note as indicated, then strike it.

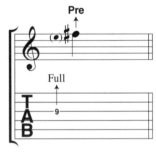

PRE-BEND & RELEASE: Bend the note as indicated. Strike it and release the note back to the original pitch.

UNISON BEND: Strike the two notes simultaneously and bend the lower note up to the pitch of the higher.

BEND & RESTRIKE: Strike the note and bend as indicated then restrike the string where the symbol occurs.

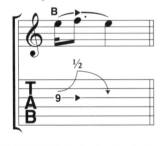

BEND, HOLD AND RELEASE: Same as bend and release but hold the bend for the duration of the tie.

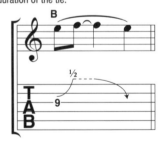

BEND AND TAP: Bend the note as indicated and tap the higher fret while still holding the bend.

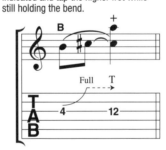

VIBRATO: The string is vibrated by rapidly bending and releasing the note with the fretting hand.

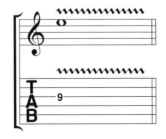

HAMMER-ON: Strike the first (lower) note with one finger, then sound the higher note (on the same string) with another finger by fretting it without picking.

PULL-OFF: Place both fingers on the notes to be sounded, Strike the first note and without picking, pull the finger off to sound the second (lower) note.

LEGATO SLIDE (GLISS): Strike the first note and then slide the same fret-hand finger up or down to the second note. The second note is not struck.

NOTE: The speed of any bend is indicated by the music notation and tempo.

SHIFT SLIDE (GLISS & RESTRIKE): Same as legato slide, except the second note is struck.

TRILL: Very rapidly alternate between the notes indicated by continuously hammering on and pulling off.

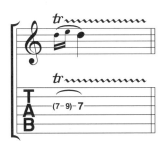

TAPPING: Hammer ("tap") the fret indicated with the pick-hand index or middle finger and pull off to the note fretted by the fret hand.

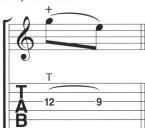

PICK SCRAPE: The edge of the pick is rubbed down (or up) the string, producing a scratchy sound.

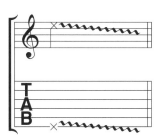

MUFFLED STRINGS: A percussive sound is produced by laying the fret hand across the string(s) without depressing, and striking them with the pick hand.

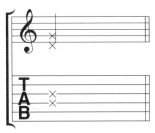

NATURAL HARMONIC: Strike the note while the fret-hand lightly touches the string directly over the fret indicated.

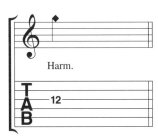

PINCH HARMONIC: The note is fretted normally and a harmonic is produced by adding the edge of the thumb or the tip of the index finger of the pick hand to the normal pick attack.

HARP HARMONIC: The note is fretted normally and a harmonic is produced by gently resting the pick hand's index finger directly above the indicated fret (in parentheses) while the pick hand's thumb or pick assists by plucking the appropriate string.

PALM MUTING: The note is partially muted by the pick hand lightly touching the string(s) just before the bridge.

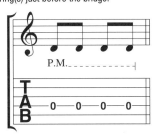

RAKE: Drag the pick across the strings indicated with a single motion.

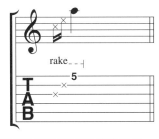

TREMOLO PICKING: The note is picked as rapidly and continuously as possible.

ARPEGGIATE: Play the notes of the chord indicated by quickly rolling them from bottom to top.

SWEEP PICKING: Rhythmic downstroke and/or upstroke motion across the strings.

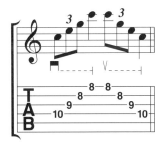

VIBRATO DIVE BAR AND RETURN: The pitch of the note or chord is dropped a specific number of steps (in rhythm) then returned to the original pitch.

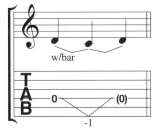

VIBRATO BAR SCOOP: Depress the bar just before striking the note, then quickly release the bar.

VIBRATO BAR DIP: Strike the note and then immediately drop a specific number of steps, then release back to the original pitch.

additional musical definitions

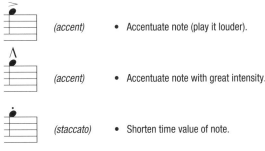

	(accent)	• Accentuate note (play it louder).
	(accent)	• Accentuate note with great intensity.
	(staccato)	• Shorten time value of note.
		• Downstroke
		• Upstroke

D.%. al Coda

D.C. al Fine

tacet

• Go back to the sign (%), then play until the bar marked *To Coda* ⊕ then skip to the section marked ⊕ *Coda*.

• Go back to the beginning of the song and play until the bar marked *Fine* (end).

• Instrument is silent (drops out).

• Repeat bars between signs.

• When a repeated section has different endings, play the first ending only the first time and the second ending only the second time.

1.   **2.**

NOTE: Tablature numbers in parentheses mean:

1. The note is sustained, but a new articulation (such as hammer on or slide) begins.
2. A note may be fretted but not necessarily played.

3

cold turkey

Words & Music by John Lennon

1. Tem - p'ra - ture's ris - ing,
(2.) bo - dy is ach - ing,
3. Thir - ty six hours,

fev - er is high,
goose pim - ple bone,
roll - ing in pain,

* Bend is flat (= ¹/₄ tone)

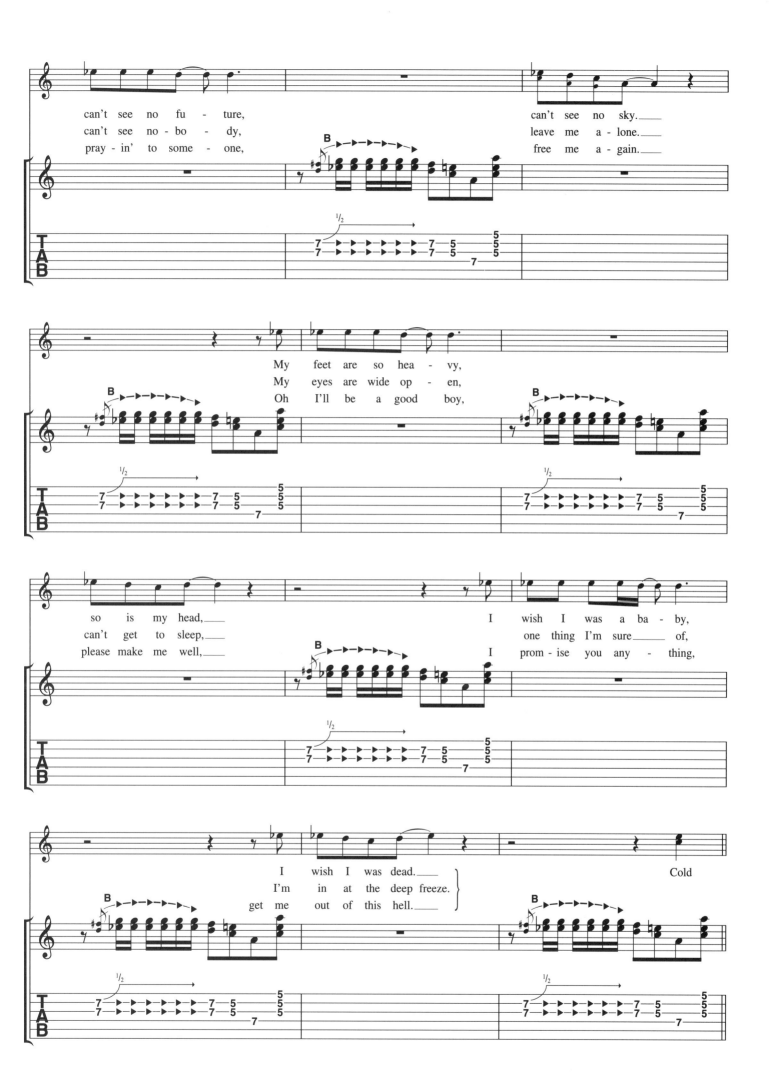

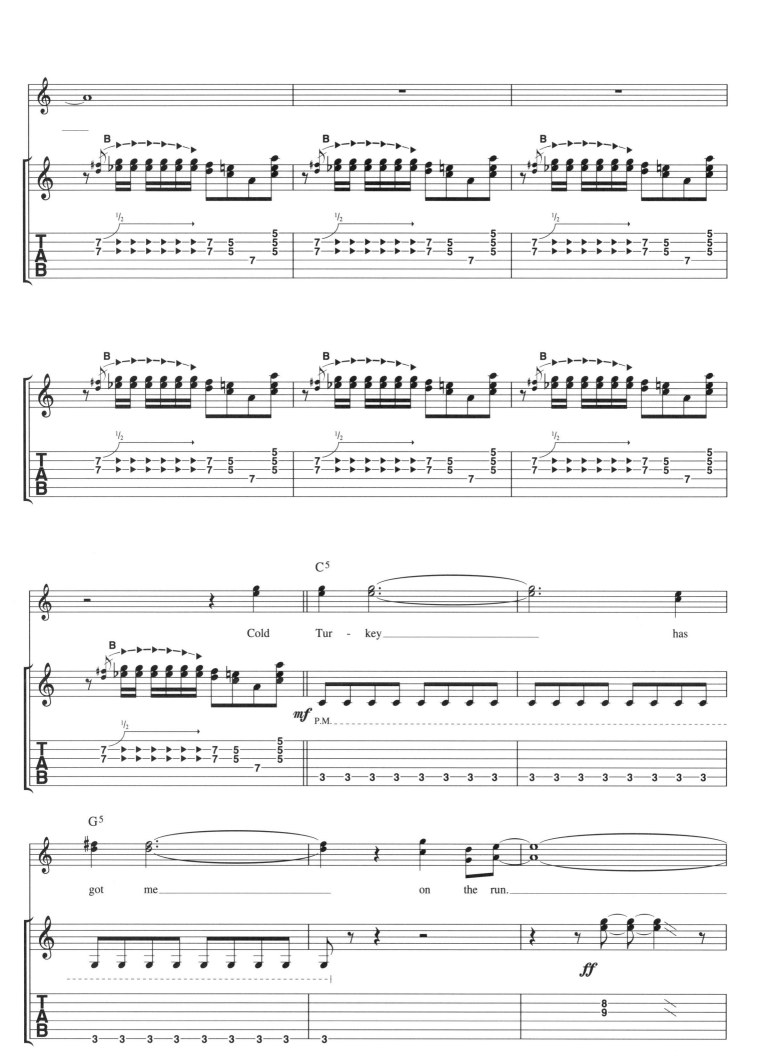

come together

Words & Music by John Lennon & Paul McCartney

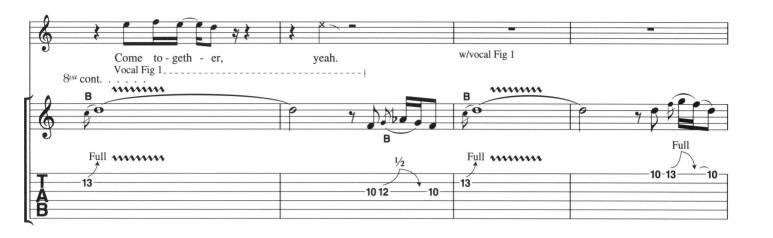

Come to-geth - er, yeah.
Vocal Fig 1

w/vocal Fig 1

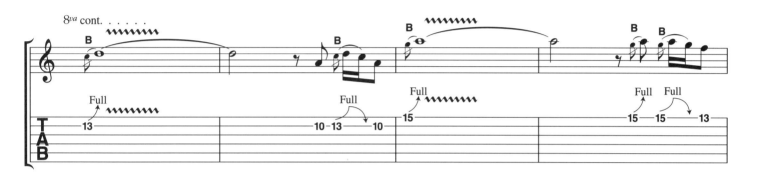

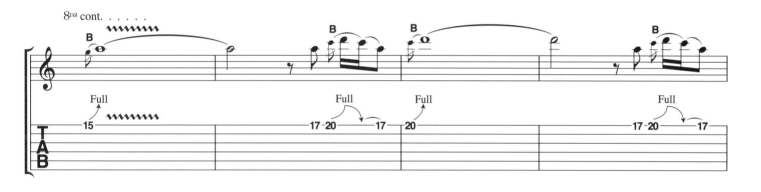

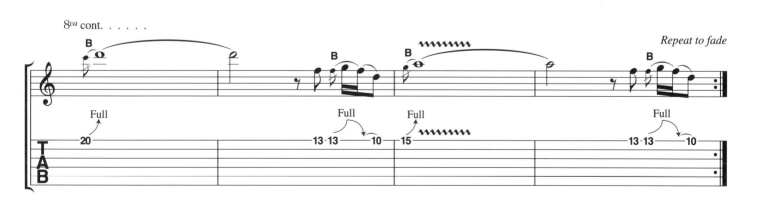

happy xmas (war is over)

Words & Music by John Lennon & Yoko Ono

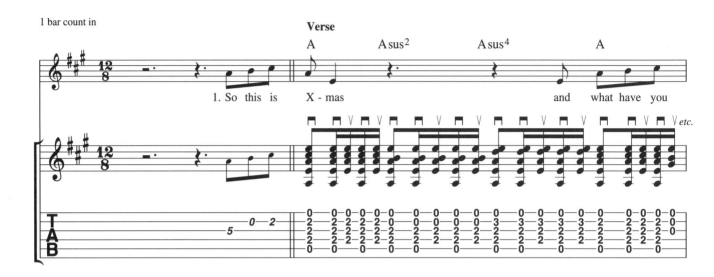

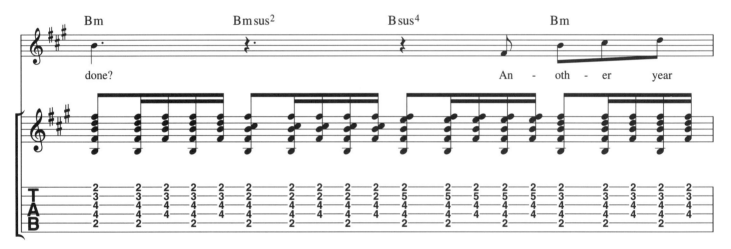

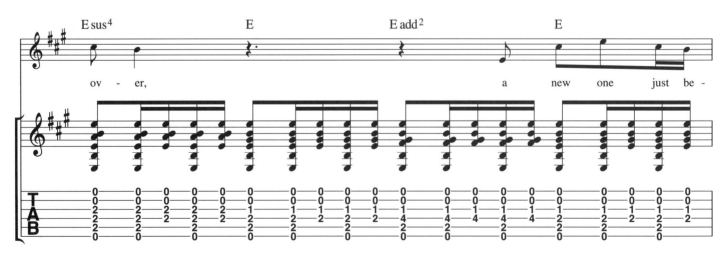

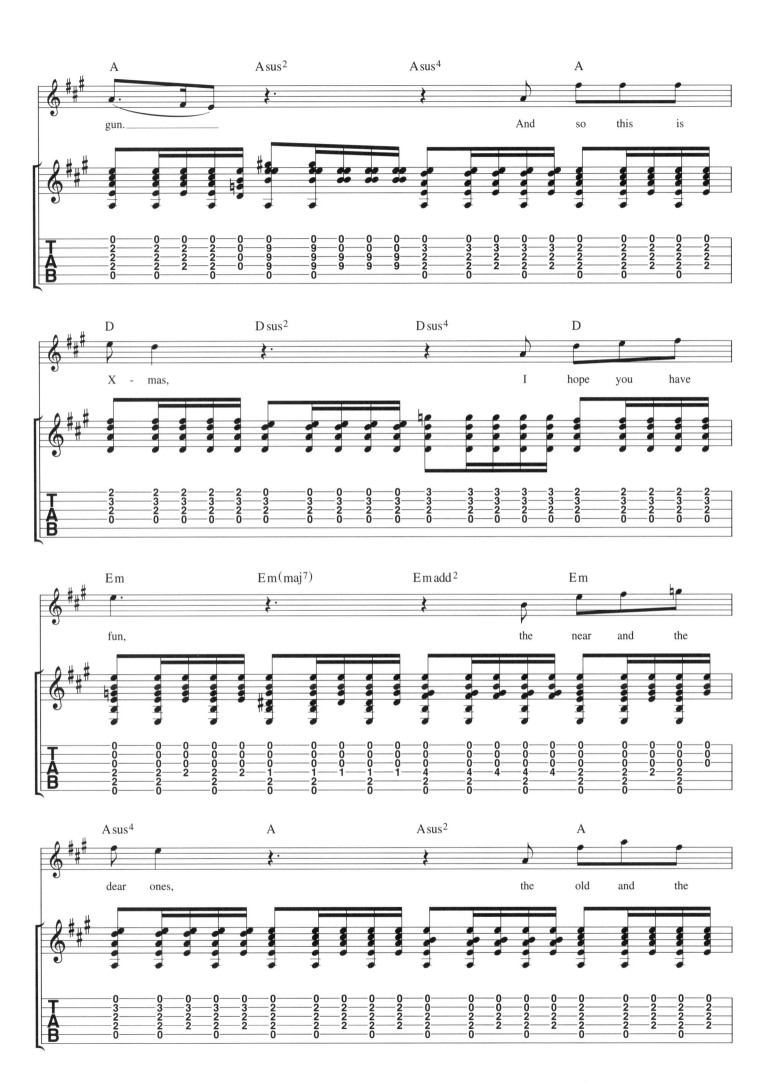

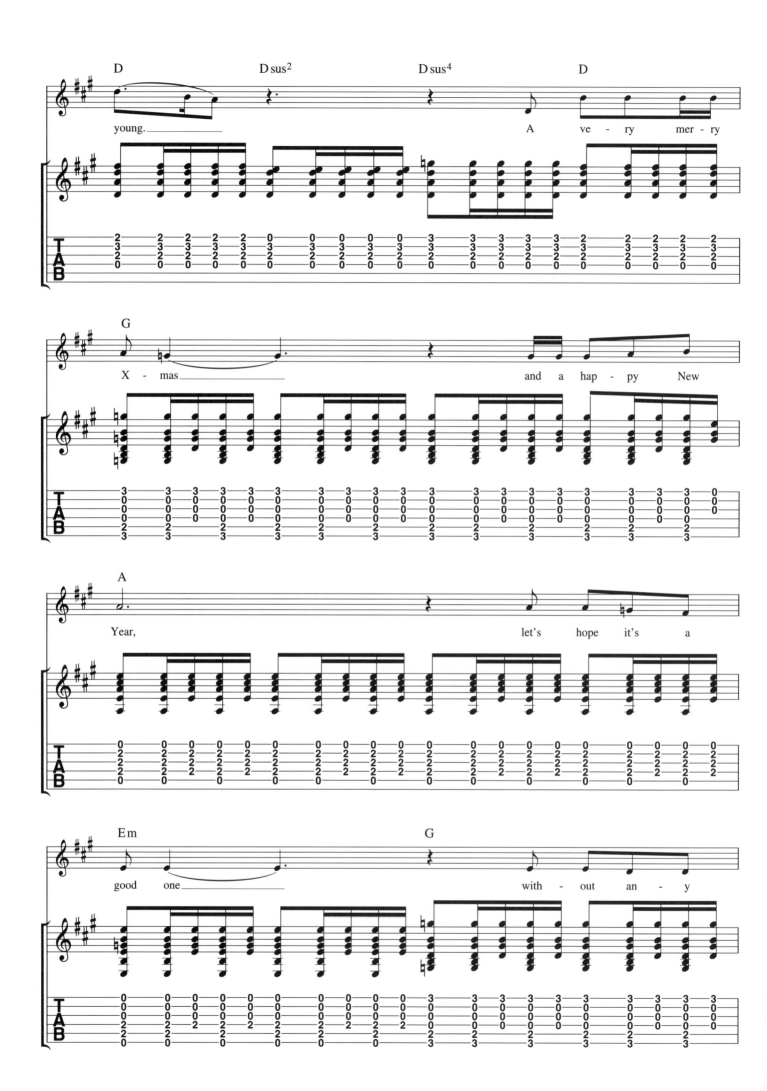

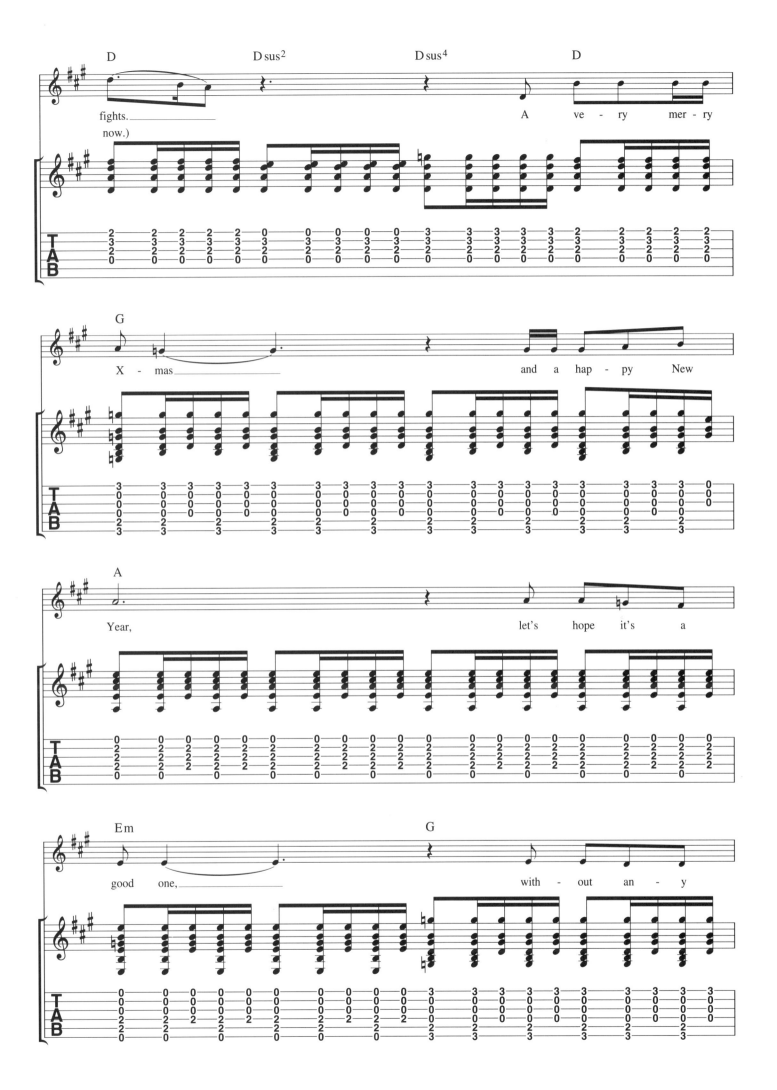

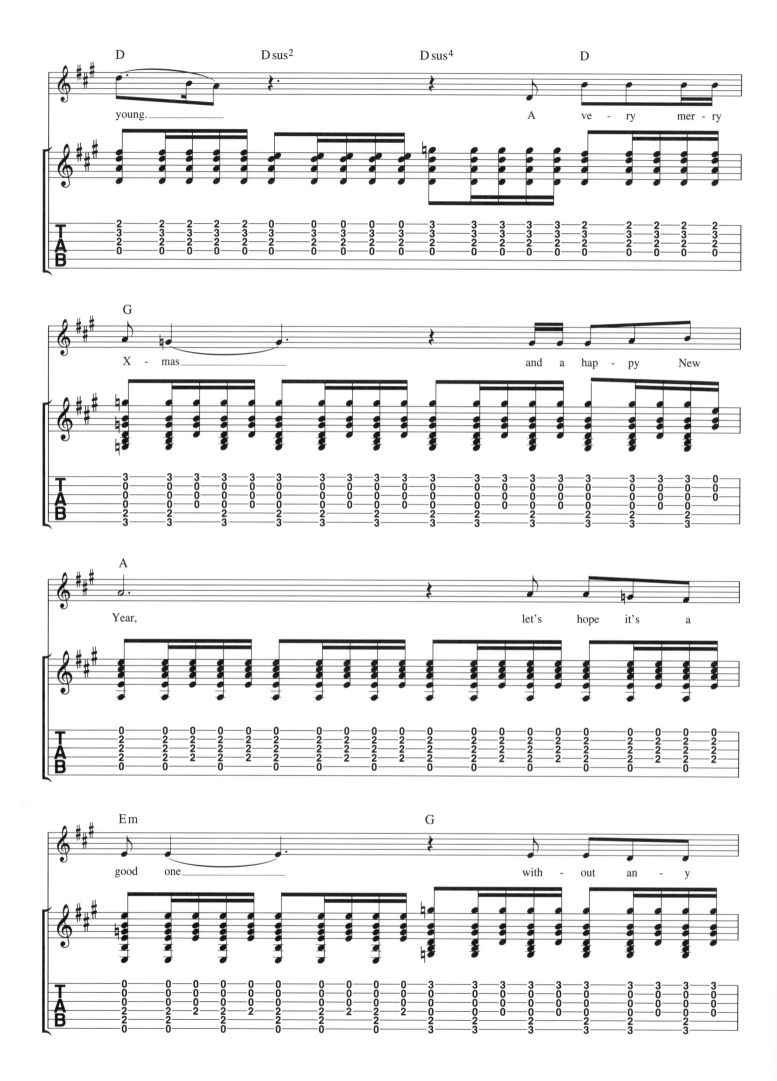

help!

Words & Music by John Lennon & Paul McCartney

© Copyright 1965 Northern Songs.
All Rights Reserved. International Copyright Secured.

young - er so much young - er than to - day,_____ I nev - er_____
when I_____ was young

C♯m

I nev - er need - ed an - y - bod - y's help in an - y way._____
need

F♯m   D   G   A

But now those days are gone_____ I'm
Now   these days are gone._____

A

not so self as - sured,_____ And now I find now I find I've

C♯m   F♯m

Chorus

Verse 2   And now my life has changed in oh, so many ways
My independence seems to vanish in the haze
But every now and then I feel so insecure
I know I just need you like I've never done before.

woman

Words & Music by John Lennon

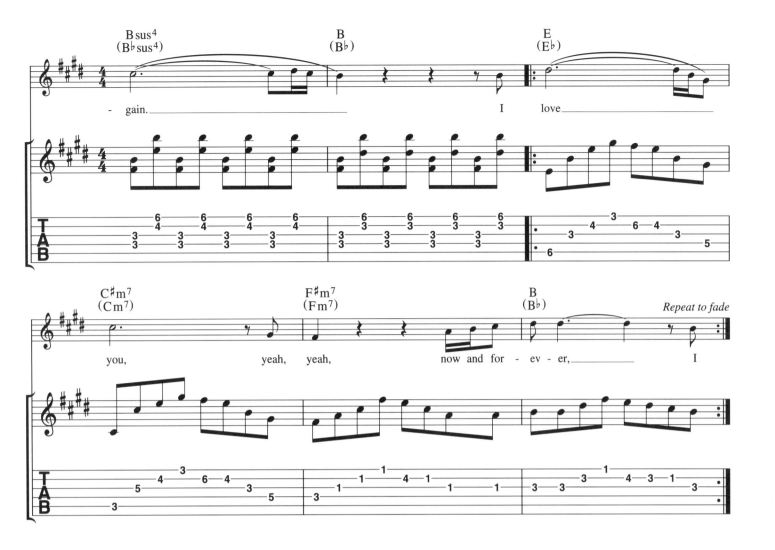

i want you (she's so heavy)

Words & Music by John Lennon & Paul McCartney

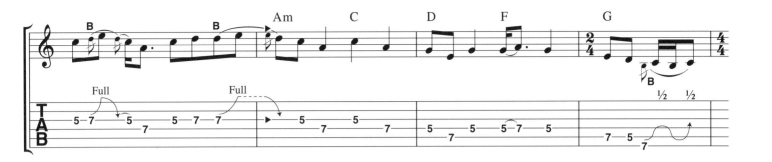

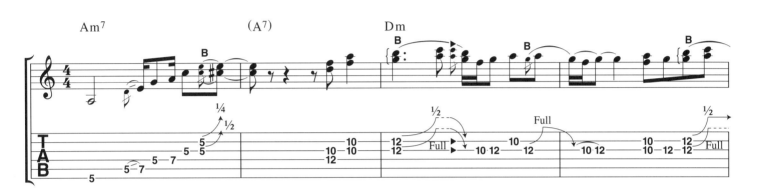

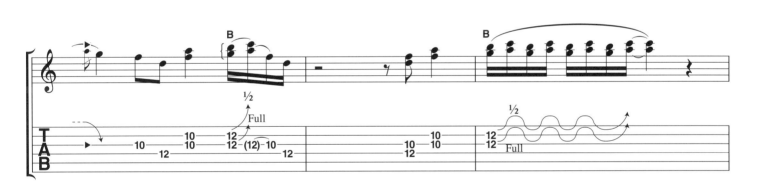

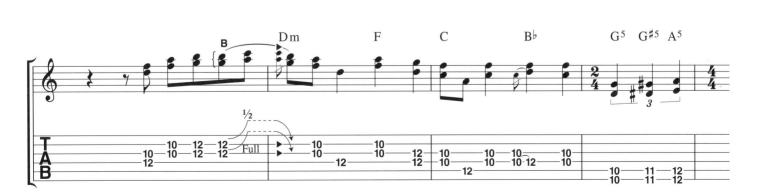